HONG KONG!
HONG KONG!

HONG KONG! HONG KONG!

Dick Wilson

UNWIN HYMAN
London   Sydney   Wellington

First published in Great Britain by the Trade Division of
Unwin Hyman Ltd, 1990.

Unwin Hyman Limited
15/17 Broadwick Street
London W1V 1FP

Allen & Unwin Australia Pty Ltd
8 Napier Street, North Sydney, NSW 2060, Australia

Allen & Unwin New Zealand Ltd
(in association with the Port Nicholson Press)
Compusales Building, 75 Ghuznee Street, Wellington, New Zealand

British Library Cataloguing in Publication Data

Wilson, Dick
    Hong Kong! Hong Kong!
1.Hong Kong
I.Title
951.2505

ISBN 0–04–440622–3

Typeset in 10 on 12 point Garamond
Printed in Hong Kong by Astros Printing Ltd

*Dedicated to the small team of underpaid
Cantonese, Shanghainese, Eurasians,
Welsh, English, Keralans, Americans and Portuguese
who helped in the early 1960s
on a slender budget to make the
Far Eastern Economic Review
a successful regional news magazine*

Contents

ix

Introduction

Hong Kong is a city as populous as Los Angeles or London south of the Thames, set in a land area almost half the size of Rhode Island or rather smaller than Surrey. It comprises Hong Kong Island, which occupies only 29 square miles, the bigger but less developed Lantau Island, 233 much smaller islands and the Kowloon peninsula, which has a land border with China. It is mountainous, but many of the hills have been flattened and dumped into the sea for reclamation building. On those still left you may see shanty hovels or luxury skyscrapers, but in the bustling streets you will mainly see well- off Chinese professionals, yuppies, office and industrial workers, because Hong Kong has joined the ranks of the prosperous newly industrialising economies.

The multi-coloured orchestra of neon signs on top of the central buildings advertises that this is a commercial city, but you can still find cultural tradition in this semi-Westernised mass – squads of shadow-boxers in a park, or the quivering peacock plumes of the Chinese opera. You will sometimes hear the thunder of horses' hoofs, for the Hongkonger loves a gamble and spends more on racing bets than the entire budget for the United Nations or the Israeli government. It is semi-tropical, and in the steamy humid summers there are typhoons which can disrupt shipping and flood even high-storey floors – and once drowned 10,000 people.

Hong Kong is a tiny piece of China which for 150 years has prospered as a British colony. A spoil of the Opium Wars, it was acquired in several bites between 1841 and 1898, during which time the Victorians lost their nerve. The result is a Hong Kong island and Kowloon peninsula which are ceded to the British Crown in perpetuity, and a much larger 'New Territories' hinterland which was only leased – for ninety-nine years. That lease will expire at midnight on 30 June 1997. But the ceded city and the leased land behind it have grown together so intimately that they cannot now be severed, so the whole of Hong Kong will become a part – an autonomous part – of China again in 1997.

This is no conventional story of a colony graduating to self-government. That destiny is barred, because China is for historical reasons defensively jealous about its national unity. Its protagonists in the civil war of 1927–49 are still at odds, maintaining costly armies to protect their respective parcels of China, one in the island of Taiwan and the other on the mainland. That is one reason why China remains, almost eighty years after overthrowing the effete and incompetent Manchu dynasty which had brought the country almost to ruin, one of the poorest countries in the world.

Han Suyin, whose novel *A Many Splendoured Thing* gave many Westerners their most vivid image of post-war Hong Kong, praised it for having achieved so much 'on borrowed time in a borrowed place' – a phrase which Richard Hughes used as the subtitle for his book on Hong Kong in 1968. Now the place is about to be returned to its owner, but time cannot be bandied about like that: once expended, it can never be recovered. One is left only with what one has achieved in the time. The time from 1841 to 1997 has been largely wasted by China, without sustained efforts towards progress of the kind Japan or Europe made at a comparable stage of their history: even the allegedly 'modern' doctrine of communism has left very little to show for itself in the hands of inexperienced and sometimes megalomaniac leaders.

Mao Zedong mocked Hong Kong in 1925 as 'that wasteland of an island'. Forty years later he made a wasteland of China in his Cultural Revolution. That is why so much of China's enterprise became concentrated in Hong Kong. Today Hongkongers have living standards twenty times better than China's. No wonder they are nervous about reverting to Chinese sovereignty. Yet China's best hope may lie in sustained life-enhancing injections of Hong Kong's economic experience.

This is the China to whose bosom Hongkongers must return, just when their city is about to become the first on the Asian mainland to enjoy European levels of income. To explain why and how Hong Kong became so prosperous, despite all its handicaps and lack of natural resources, is one of the aims of this book. We do not adequately appreciate just how well and productively the British administration system, rule of law and *laissez-faire* policy matched the innate entrepreneurial gifts of the Cantonese and Shanghainese who built the post-war Hong Kong economy.

Because of the clamour for passports and the vituperation over Hong-kongers' desire to emigrate before 1997, many outsiders suppose that the place must be doomed. Either all the middle class will leave or else the Communists will bully the Hongkongers and mishandle their delicately contrived economy, or both. But this is not foreordained. Hong Kong will survive, with losses that may well prove minor. A good 80 per cent of its population cannot afford to emigrate, even if quotas for them existed in other countries. China changes policies frequently and is likely to return to the liberal reform track before long. Its stake in Hong Kong's money spinning, which it cannot replicate itself, is bigger than most outsiders credit. There is a risk of China's totalitarian attitudes encroaching on the spirit of enterprise in Hong Kong, or of the leaders' plans to leave Hong Kong on a loose rein being nobbled by jealous rivals in Beijing or small-minded cadres on the ground. But these are smaller risks, when analysed, than some would paint them.

Meanwhile, commercial opportunities for service and profit continue to exist in Hong Kong. A shifting of gears, a drain of brains, a loss of competitiveness do not spell extinction, and the self-correcting factors – higher wages, expatriate recruitment, greater incentives for those staying behind – should not be underestimated.

This book seeks to identify the main factors in Hong Kong's success, both as a society and an economy. It starts, in Part I, with the people who created a brilliant city from barren rock – beginning with the Chinese, who form the dominating 98 per cent of the population. First came the hardworking and resourceful Cantonese, the original immigrants, followed after the war by Shanghainese entrepreneurs who brought wider horizons and that vital dash of financial ambition to Hong Kong. The roles which Hong Kong plays for Chinese people – as a political asylum, as a headquarters and communications centre for those who have gone to live abroad in Southeast Asia – are then sketched. In spite of being so small and so mixed, the Hong Kong Chinese have begun to acquire an identity of their own, for example, in carrying traditional Chinese social and political attitudes into a British legal and administrative framework. Neither democracy nor the morality of gambling in Hong Kong can be discussed exactly as they would be in London or New York.

In Part II we see that on top of this sturdy 98 per cent Chinese base there is a small minority of foreigners who lend the place an additional strength and variety: not only Britons and other Westerners involved in the colonial and commercial structure, but also Indians whose future under Chinese sovereignty is much in doubt. Hong Kong's status as a small European settlement with a flourishing economy allows it to play host to transient refugees – like Ho Chi Minh and Zhou Enlai in the past – and also to be a home for a small but influential community of Eurasians – the 'people in between' the two major constituent cultures. Hong Kong has achieved a reputation for neutrality in the Far East and may qualify as an important potential centre for the Pacific.

All these achievements are the work of individual human beings, and I therefore tell the Hong Kong story as far as possible through the careers of its famous men and women, its leaders and heroes. How did these people, Chinese and non-Chinese, create the economic miracle that Hong Kong is today? How did they overcome the virtual absence of natural resources? These questions are dealt with in Part III of this book before turning, in Part IV, to what is on everybody's mind today, namely, the future of Hong Kong after its returns to Chinese sovereignty in 1997. Will the 'brain drain' make it a hollow take-over for China? Will a Communist China, even though partly reformed, be able to cope with what is perhaps the purest example in the world of *laissez-faire* free enterprise capitalism? Each of the factors in Hong Kong's past success needs separately to be weighed up in order to evaluate its chances of survival after 1997. The result is a considered assessment of Hong Kong's future, a concerned but not defeatist view of its chances, which forms the conclusion of the book.

When I first saw Hong Kong in 1953, I felt as if I were stepping back into tranquil antiquity: everything moved slowly, and there was no sign of frenetic ambition. My prevailing impression was of little boats bobbing lazily up and down in the water. I went to work there in 1958 when the first buzz of concerted activity could be heard, and although I still found it provincial, philistine, rough and unpolished, it was impossible not to admire the people's determination to improve themselves and their lives. Now, when I go back on visits, I tingle with anticipated excitement even before the aeroplane touches down on that fragile finger of reclaimed runway that juts out into the sea. There is an electricity in the air, in which the radiance of the neon lights and the energy pulsing from the ubiquitous motors creating heat or cold, sound or light, merge with a collective will-power that steams off the torrents of individuals gushing along those humid streets. Nowhere else can you see such a concentration of people, especially young people, who have shaken off their past (save for sentimental inessentials) in order to apply their full intelligence and ingenuity to realising the dreams of modern man in their own society.

The tragedy is that this unique, though small-scale achievement by different quarters of mankind in harness may now be lost, dismantled and dispersed. Outsiders cannot do much to save it (only China and Hong Kong can do that), but the sympathy of outsiders might just make a difference, and that sympathy I seek to stretch with understanding.

Author's Note

Money

All sums of money or value are expressed in this book in US dollars unless otherwise stated.

Chinese names

Names of people and places in Hong Kong are spelt in the conventional way, which is usually on the Wade–Giles system. Names from the People's Republic of China, by contrast, are spelt in the pinyin system which is now standard there. The result is a little confusing, but there seems no practical alternative. All Chinese name put the surname first, except that a few Hongkongers prefer to follow the Western order, especially where they have a Western given name.

PART I

The Chinese Hong Kong

Chapter 1

The Cantonese Incumbents

The Cantonese *are* Hong Kong, if they do not quite *run* Hong Kong. About 70 per cent of Hongkongers are Cantonese and their native spoken language is the *lingua franca*. Before the war they effectively controlled the place, subject only to a thin red line of Britons at the top. This role was challenged in the 1950s by the Shanghai business élite who surged in to share the asylum of Hong Kong, but now the Cantonese are reasserting themselves.

The differences between the various kinds of Chinese who inhabit China are usually lost on a Westerner for whom that land is just another country like Britain or France. But China is so large that its 1,100 million people cannot be expected to behave identically, speak the same language or have the same customs. In a letter to the editor in a Hong Kong newspaper a few years ago, Benjamin Chan argued that it was better to talk of Chinese 'races' in the plural rather than of a single Chinese 'race'. There were good grounds, he went on, for contending that 'racially, we Cantonese are closer to the Vietnamese than we are to the Hopeh-nese' (in the province where Beijing stands).

The Cantonese, then, are those people who live mostly in semi-tropical Guangdong province but have sent out waves of emigrants in the past century or more, not only into Hong Kong but to Malaysia, Africa, America, Australia and Europe. Their written language, being ideographic (conveying meaning without sound), is shared by the rest of China, but their spoken language is quite distinct, and is hardly more intelligible to northern Chinese than, say, Portuguese is to Frenchmen. Guangdong has often been regarded by the central government in Beijing as somewhat rebellious – in this century it has produced more than its share of Chinese revolutionaries. But that has never led to any separatist movement: the Cantonese are proud to be Chinese even if, privately, they are just as proud of their Cantoneseness.

3

A Governor of Hong Kong used to call the Cantonese 'the Irishmen of China'–independent, charming, a trifle noisy. Xu Jiatun, China's 'ambassador' to Hong Kong in the 1980s, found them 'smart, keen and sensitive to things'. The childhood training and the ideology of the family which every Cantonese imbibes produces personalities which are disciplined and dutiful. The duty to parents is part of an attachment to the whole family tree, and there are towns on the communist side of the border whose present inhabitants enjoy factories, roads, bridges, schools and hospitals, all provided by the dutiful second or third generation making money in Hong Kong. Dongguan is one such town. Its sons and grandsons in Hong Kong are so numerous, their sense of obligation so strong, that there are seventeen different clan associations there for those recognising Dongguan as the original family home.

The Cantonese do not make a cult of the individual as Westerners do. Within the family and within the group even outside the family, egotism has no place in the Chinese tradition. The group is loved for the security and comfort that it offers. William Fung, who spent ten years at Princeton and the Harvard Business School, confesses to irritation at the Western habit of splitting the lunch bill. What he likes is the congenial custom which Chinese have of a business associate walking over, shaking your hand, asking after your health, and saying that he has paid for your lunch. That is the Chinese style of doing business, of mixing business with pleasure, of being in a circle where you all do things for each other. Next time Fung will pay *his* bill. Incidentally, Fung also hates it when waiters in America or Europe say dismissively, 'I'm not your waiter.' It's the same thing, it is an assertion of dissociation, of unconnectedness, of leaving you to fend for yourself individually.

Though fenced in by Confucian prohibitions in family life, the Cantonese is perfectly capable of asserting himself in a direction he chooses when dealing with the world outside his family. Dorothy Wong had minimal support from her family, her father being dead and her mother illiterate, yet she went on to become Hong Kong's first woman Rhodes Scholar at Oxford. 'The only encouragement I have,' she confessed, 'is from myself.'

Cantonese are no slouches. Dorothy Wong said about her own success, 'By working hard one can do anything. The limit is set by oneself.' Nobody shares the feeling of the British that it is shameful to work too hard, or without holidays, and that the smart thing is to show people that you do not care about work. The Cantonese, by contrast, enjoy all of life, including work. They do not hesitate to combine work and pleasure, or work and family life, in a way that would appear embarrassing in the English tradition.

But the Cantonese are not particularly good at collaborating with 'equals'. The cooperative movement was never successful in Guangdong, and the Cantonese were among the first to grow restive under Mao Zedong's People's Communes. Deng Xiaoping's agricultural policy of allowing families, or households, to carry out farming on their own lines under market principles has, by contrast, been highly successful in Guangdong.

Considerations of 'face' and deference to authority often puzzle Westerners in Hong Kong business situations. 'Traditionally, we are brought up never to challenge our parents, even if we think they are wrong,' says a Chinese business executive working for a British firm. 'The Chinese family structure values obedience, whereas in the Western culture you challenge and you are taught to be independent at a very young age, and, if you don't understand something, to speak up. A lot of my Western friends say, "How can I get my Chinese executives to speak up at meetings?" They are afraid they will say the wrong things or lose face, and if they are challenged on a point in front of everyone, they feel it makes them look bad – they would rather it was dealt with outside the meeting.' Asking a sharp question at a meeting makes your superiors think highly of you in the West, but among the Chinese it carries the implication that the superior has not instructed you fully, and if he turns out not to know the answer, he will lose face and blame you.

Another instance of the way in which these cultural differences affect business is the explanation given by Ronald Li about insider trading on the Stock Exchange. Li used to be one of the most colourful and successful Cantonese in town, and one of the richest – the undisputed king of the Stock Exchange until Black Friday of 1987, and founder of the notorious Volvo Club where the rich can be titillated by pretty girls of all kinds and nationalities on an hourly rate as measured by digital clocks. Until his prosecution for corrupt dealings, Li represented the flamboyance and rugged energy of Hong Kong. Asked about the problem of insider trading before that fall from grace, he explained that it was virtually impossible to stop in Hong Kong, because the Chinese culture of family loyalty made it difficult to prevent information spreading once a deal was being arranged. Family here means those many brothers and sisters, aunts and uncles, nephews and nieces, cousins, parents and children who may all be playing the market and expect to be apprised of what other family members know.

The Cantonese character, a Eurasian lawyer concludes, 'is to be most tolerant, up to a certain level, but then, more extreme afterwards'. More than other Chinese, the Cantonese bend with the wind and accommodate to the forces at work around them. Who else in China would have put up with European rule in their midst for 150 years? The Cantonese bend to pressure in order to survive and fight another day, but they can also be obstinate.

Some of this can be attributed to village origins. Cantonese lack the urbanity of the Shanghainese and Beijingese. They are often described as direct and plain speaking, quick to get to the point, purposeful. A Japanese woman said on first coming to Hong Kong that she became 'very agitated with the constant pushing and rushing on the streets, people are so much more polite in Japan . . . Perhaps Hong Kong people feel they have to be that much more aggressive to survive.' Jan Morris talks of the 'raw Chineseness' which she encounters in Hong Kong, so different from Singapore.

There is a village-like defensiveness, as if the Cantonese are on the look-out for attack. They resent the activities of other Chinese, such as the Shanghainese, and also of foreigners. They are also more credulous, more superstitious and more fatalistic than northern Chinese. Rumours are constantly flooding through Hong Kong, and with harmful effects. When Queen Elizabeth visited in the royal yacht Britannia, the story went round that there was no aircraft big enough to carry all the money that she would be taking home with her. When rumours spread about banks being in difficulty, or about the mainland Chinese planning retribution against various Hong Kong personalities or groups after 1997, the results can be most damaging.

The Cantonese reveal an unashamed attachment to money, another peasant trait. They tended to believe in the very early 1980s, for example, that China would not take Hong Kong because of the foreign exchange it earned from Hong Kong. Later, when the Chinese take-over was assured, many of them believed that China might still be persuaded to extend the lease to the British administration after 1997 for a very large rent. Respect for wealth and bending to the wind could perhaps jointly explain why Hongkongers have endured the Whitehall yoke for so long. Colonial subjects in other parts of the world might have spent their time belly-aching about foreign rule, 'but Hong Kong people just got down to making a lot of money, and in the end they became probably richer than the British themselves', as a leading politician puts it.

The business aptitude of the Cantonese is admired by all. Take the career of David Li, now chief executive of a leading bank and a candidate for the chief executive position after 1997. When he was an undergraduate at Cambridge, he made money from running a nightclub, used that profit to create a small bicycle business for his fellow students, and then invested those profits in antique maps which he was later able to sell in the USA for tenfold. He is not regarded as unusual in this. Gordon Wu, the developer, says that the Cantonese are 'capitalist by nature, it is in their genes'. Yet their entrepreneurial flair does not usually lead to the kind of extravagance which is seen among the Shanghainese. The old saying goes that northern Chinese will open their doors when they can offer callers a meal of rice, but close them when they only have *congee* (the far less satisfying rice-gruel). They like to show off their wealth but not their poverty, whereas Cantonese have the reverse instinct, preferring not to flaunt their good fortune.

A charming instance of the open esteem for wealth is the fact that Hong Kong's four television stations are named Gold, Diamond, Pearl and Jade. Two broadcast in Cantonese, two in English. Cantonese is a quite different spoken language from the *putonghua* or Mandarin which the government of China has been trying to make the standard national language in the People's Republic. The ideographic writing is the same everywhere, of course, but

Cantonese speak what appears to be an ancestor of Mandarin, involving two more tones than the northern language, and being so different from it that when Sir Sze-yuen Chung, Hong Kong's most active political leader in the 1980s, was received by Deng Xiaoping in Beijing, they needed an interpreter.

Cantonese is certainly more archaic than Mandarin. 'Tang dynasty poetry rhymes in Cantonese,' says Austin Coates, the author and former Hong Kong administrator, 'in the parts where it is meant to rhyme, that is, but not in any other Chinese language.' Hong Kong Cantonese differs slightly from what is spoken on the Communist side of the border, if only because of the many anglicisms that have been absorbed.

None of this alters the innocent amusement which we derive from each other's language. There are to be found in Hong Kong such establishments as Hang On Tailor, a name which literally means 'forever peaceful' but does not quite convey that thought in its latin-lettered form. Nearby are the Hop On Bicycle Company, the Lee Kee Boots Enterprise, and the Wo Clinic. There are even more jokes the other way but they cannot be explained in an English book.

Although there were so few people in Hong Kong when the British arrived, probably 5,000 or so on Hong Kong Island, it is not entirely without its own history. The last boy-emperor of the Sung dynasty lived briefly in Kowloon after his defeat by the Mongols in the thirteenth century. Prehistoric settlements have been found, most recently on Lamma Island (the small island lying south-west of Hong Kong Island, chiefly noted these days for its enormous power station). Archaeologists said they were some 4,000 years old, and a human bone was found which they believed to be Vietnamese!

The British were very supercilious about the people they found already living in the new colony. A Colonial Treasurer wrote crossly three years after the Union Jack had gone up, 'There was not one respectable Chinese inhabitant on the island . . . There is, in fact, a continual shifting of a Bedouin sort of population, whose migratory, predatory, gambling and dissolute habits utterly unfit them for continuous industry.' (The 'continuous industry' took just over a century to reach the point where the Colonial Treasurer's descendants were squealing about its competition.)

The real aristocrats of Hong Kong are those who can claim descent from the few farming and fishing families present before 1841. One of these is Allen Fong Yuk-ping, a film director, whose family has been in Hong Kong for 200 years, his great-great-grandfather coming to farm on Hong Kong Island. William Tang, an author who also designs clothes, can go better than that. His family home at Ping Shan in the New Territories is 800 years old. The ancestors of these two would have moved in the Hong Kong that was portrayed in James Clavell's novel and film *Taipan*.

There is a rather larger group of Hongkongers who can trace their family residence at least into the nineteenth century. David Li, the man who sold bicycles at Cambridge University, is one of them. His great-great-grandfather left China because he could not make a living from his small landholding there and came to trade in Kowloon just before Queen Victoria took it. In 1989, David Li, though Vice-Chairman of China's Basic Law Drafting Committee for Hong Kong, marched through the streets with Hong Kong's finance workers to mourn the Tiananmen Square dead. Just qualifying for the nineteenth century cachet is Sir Sze-yuen Chung, the man who needed an interpreter to talk to Deng Xiaoping in Beijing. His father came from another town in the Pearl River delta behind Hong Kong, Fatshan, at the very end of the century, an aspiring teenage merchant.

More Cantonese crossed into Hong Kong during the first half of the twentieth century. Perhaps the most famous was Lee Hysan, who was sent to Hong Kong's Queen's College for education. Hysan was the first Cantonese to become fluent in English, indeed one of his descendants has commented that he wrote better English than his family does today. He sent his first two sons, Richard and Harold, to Pembroke College, Oxford – and their children and grandchildren followed. The family founded a property business which is still a force in the market.

Stephen Cheong is an enthusiastic young politican and successful industrialist running a business with turnover of over $3 million. His grandfather, who had a small weaving business in Canton, moved to Hong Kong in 1936. The family lost everything in the Pacific War, and Stephen's father had to start again, working as an employee and saving up to form his own little firm in 1959 – which later diversified very profitably into denim.

The principal motivation of these immigrants from Guangdong province was the search for better trade or jobs. But as the Japanese invaders threatened southern China in the late 1930s, there was also a political motive. S. K. Chan, for example, fled from Canton in 1938 in order to escape Japanese rule, and stayed on to found a new company, Yangtzekiang, in 1949, which now has factories in many Asian countries and for a while operated a subsidiary just outside Liverpool.

During the Japanese War, as at other times of difficulty, many of the immigrants flowed back to the anonymity of Guangdong farmlands. But they began to return when the Union Jack was hoisted again in 1945, and they flooded into Hong Kong when a communist take-over of southern China became a serious prospect in 1948. During these post-war years refugees crowded in with whatever goods and valuables they could carry, especially gold. They brought gold in bars, in ingots, in rings, and even hidden about their bodies. A plainclothes policeman told Han Suyin, who was then a medical worker in a Hong Kong hospital, that he could tell if a woman carried gold in her vagina 'from the way she walks.'

8

The outstanding figure in this generation of arrivals must be Fung King Hey, who reached Hong Kong in 1950. He had been a moneychanger in Guangzhou. He had an exceptional memory but was not well educated: his English was never good. His business career has become a legend in Hong Kong. When he had saved a little from moneychanging, he topped it up with a loan and went into trading. He shipped fish to Taiwan, but they died of thirst on the voyage. He used the boat to carry back bananas for the Hong Kong market, but they all spoiled in a typhoon. He worked for 4 cents a day as a labourer in a Hong Kong shipyard, which he was later, in one of those satisfying turns of fate, to own himself. Eventually he settled into stockbroking and built up the biggest securities firm in Hong Kong with annual profits in the early 1980s of $30 million, enabling him to indulge his passion for European antiques.

The year 1949 brought hundreds of thousands of Cantonese into Hong Kong in the belief they could get a better living, or be spared political harassment. In the 1950s Cheng Yu-tung came from Shuntak to pursue his goldsmith's and jewellery business, but he went on to create with brilliant financial judgement the New World Hotel Property Group. At the end of the 1950s Chairman Mao Zedong implemented his grandiose Great Leap Forward and the People's Communes were launched in the farming areas: this was followed by two or three years of drought and famine in Guangdong. Tong Bing-woon was there when the Communists nationalised his father's herbalist enterprise and the family could hardly earn enough to eat. He crossed to Hong Kong in 1962, at the age of 17, and worked as a herbal salesman before following the familiar pattern of saving enough money to start his own shop, the Great Wall Herbalist's Shop, in 1980.

The illiterate old amah who cooked, washed and cleaned for me in my tiny Kowloon flat, in 1962, had grown-up children a hundred or so miles across the border, to whom she sent pathetic parcels of dried breadcrumbs during that famine. I had friends in for drinks one evening and she asked one of them to read her the letter she had received from home that morning. I went into the kitchen for ice and found her crying her heart out, while my friend stood grim-faced beside her – 'Her daughter has died of malnutrition.' Our party adjourned while we grappled with the kind of economics that could allow starvation so close at hand to plenty.

Then in the late 1960s came the Cultural Revolution, when many Chinese felt that life was being made so hopeless and cruel for them by the Red Guards that the risks of escaping to Hong Kong were worthwhile. Lau Chin-shek fled from his People's Commune in 1968, and arrived in Hong Kong as an illegal immigrant, a status which exposed him to much bullying and terrible working conditions. But he came through the experience to become a trade union leader, heading the Christian Industrial Committee in its campaign for greater safety and workers' compensation in Hong Kong's industries.

9

Aaron Liu Ming-chiang is a 1970s boy, reaching Hong Kong in 1973 in rather similar conditions. He still remembers his first taste of Coca Cola, his first stick of chewing gum. They called him Tai Luk Tsai, or 'mainland boy'. He sold cigarettes on the street, washed cars, pushed trolleys, and studied every night. Eventually he joined the staff of a multinational corporation.

Those are some of the ways in which Hong Kong came to be populated with the 4 million Cantonese inhabitants who live there today. There was always either a push in the form of natural disasters or man-made disturbance in Guangdong, or a pull in the form of the freer opportunities for commerce, for employment and for gracious living that existed in Hong Kong. Sir Sze-yuen Chung has already been cited in the context of the Cantonese language and his father's emigration to Hong Kong more than ninety years ago. He is now an elder statesman, whose career typifies the history of the Hong Kong Cantonese.

Born in Hong Kong in 1917, Chung was educated at St John's University in Shanghai and at Hong Kong University, and was working as a young engineer in the Kowloon docks when the Japanese invaded. He went to teach in the inland areas behind the Japanese lines but found there were no books available. Undaunted, he stole back to Hong Kong, hands and face blackened in the disguise of a fisherman, coolly landed at Aberdeen by junk, slipped home and packed up a suitcase of books and brought them back to the mainland past the noses of the Japanese guards. By the end of the war he was working on port, power, chemical and water projects and was offered vice-ministerial rank in Manchuria. But he preferred to go home to Hong Kong.

In 1946, he won a British Council scholarship for research in cold working of metals at Sheffield. There he developed a new theory for his M. Sc. and D. Sc. and his papers on it are still cited. The People's Republic invited Chung to work in China, but instead he went back to Hong Kong and eventually joined a company called Sonca, where he utilised his patent method of making flashlights with two different diameters by impact extrusion. At first, there were only a hundred workers but Chung built it up to be the world's biggest producer of flashlights, responsible for one in every ten made in the world – or 35 million annually. When he was approaching 50, and there was not much more innovation needed in the company, he went into unpaid public service, in the Federation of Hong Kong Industries, and then in the Legislative and Executive Councils, taking a lead on matters like metrification, technical education and export insurance, and now as Chairman of the two Polytechnics and the Provisional Health Authority. He is blunt, outspoken, practical and down to earth, and his integrity is doubted by no man.

The other model Cantonese leader in the post-war years was Sir Sik-nin Chau, whose uncle, Sir Shouson Chau, was the first Chinese to be appointed (in 1926) to the Executive Council, a Columbia graduate and a former Chinese diplomat who never let it be forgotten that he served under three emperors and five British monarchs. Sir Sik-nin Chau first pursued ear, nose and throat studies at Guy's Hospital and at Vienna, and later lectured on ophthalmology at Hong Kong University. He was said to have made a fortune buying up banknotes issued under the Japanese occupation and speculating on them, but after the war he became the strong man in Hong Kong's unofficial leadership, fighting for Hong Kong interests at international conferences and winning the trust of the Shanghai industrialists in order to present a united front against the West's protectionist attacks on Hong Kong. Bishop R. O. Hall, who acted as the 'conscience' of Hong Kong in the first two post-war decades, took a different view of him, writing home to say that the British had made a 'serious blunder' in allowing Dr S. N. Chau (as he then was) 'and his gang of Hong Kong property owners to dominate the Hong Kong government'. Chau was a very Hong Kong figure, blurry round the edge but steely inside.

Often lumped in with the Cantonese are the Chiuchow (or Teochiu) who hailed originally from around Shantou (Swatow) on the marches between Guangdong and Fujian provinces to the north of Hong Kong, and were never easy to identify. Having lived for generations alongside much larger Cantonese populations, they often passed as Cantonese. Possibly accounting for as much as 20 per cent of the Hong Kong population, they have traditionally dominated the rice, wood and oil trades. One of the wharf companies in Hong Kong used Shantou coolies rather than Cantonese because 'they could carry 200lb of rice', a retired executive explained.

One famous Chiuchow is Martin Lee, who has a Nehru-like charisma but may more aptly be compared with Abraham Lincoln, a brilliant legal mind and the darling of the liberal left in politics. Where the Chiuchows shine most is in business. The Great Eagle empire was built up by the Chiuchow Lo Ying-shek. Today, it is his three sons who are famous, the eldest running the family business, the second becoming a genius at corporate finance and controlling eight listed companies in property and hotels, while the third, Vincent Lo, also went it alone to create the Shui On property empire and enter politics.

Many of the Chiuchows migrated to Singapore and Thailand rather than Hong Kong, but some of those eventually settled in Hong Kong. A well-known Thai Chiuchow in Hong Kong is Wong Chong-po, a ruthless businessman who will 'step on you on the way up', as his competitors complain, but has built the Stelux watchmaking company into a world giant. Another Thai Chiuchow is Robin Chan, eldest son of the legendary Thai entrepreneur Chin Sophonpanich (the man behind the Bangkok Bank and the Kra Canal project). Chin had to leave Bangkok in a hurry when his political backers lost out in a *coup d'état*, so he came to Hong Kong (where else?) and afterwards left his son Robin there in charge of the family interests. Robin was actually born in the original home district of Chiuchow, because his father had sent his pregnant wife all the way back there from Bangkok precisely to enable the child to be genuine Chiuchow-born.

But the winner in the Chiuchow stable is Li Kashing, who is certainly one of the richest men in the world. He came from Chiuchow as a boy to study, and if the Japanese had not interrupted his career he might have become the proverbial poor scholar. Instead, since his father died soon after the Japanese invasion of Hong Kong, he had to leave school to support his mother and the rest of the family. Beginning as a plastic comb salesman in the late 1950s, he built up his own plastic flowers factory just when those products were about to shoot up in the world's demand, and went on from strength to strength in property, trade, hotels and utilities. He is a director of the Chiuchow Chamber of Commerce in Hong Kong and owns the Hilton Hotel.

There are even smaller minorities within the Cantonese community, including the Tanka boat people – 'people of the water', as they call themselves – who speak Cantonese but are looked down upon by the rest of the Cantonese. The Hoklo are also boat people, originally from Fujian, who speak a dialect not dissimilar from Chiuchow.

The Cantonese are thus the backbone of Hong Kong, and the main body of people who will bear the brunt of the change of sovereignty in 1997. In spite of the veneer of British colonialisation, they can express their Cantoneseness in a manner denied to their 60 million co-provincials across the border. But they were threatened with overshadowing by the *nouveaux arrivées* from their rival city, Shanghai.

Chapter 2

The Shanghai Gatecrashers

Until 1940 Shanghai was the greatest modern city of China and the focal centre of the Far East. It was Asia's New York as well as its Paris, an oriental stage for all the great cosmopolitan dramas of the day. When Shanghai began its decline, bombarded first by Japanese shells and then by communist sequestrations, Hong Kong was merely, in the words of one of its Governors of that day, 'a small village'.

The arrival of the cream of Shanghai society in hundreds and thousands in 1948–9 gave rise to mixed feelings in Hong Kong. To the foreigners it was a welcome spicing of the Cantonese pot, but the Cantonese themselves feared a new source of competition. Some Cantonese already knew about Shanghai. These were the so-called 'Shanghai Cantonese' families which had been so successful trading in Guangdong that they had established themselves also in Shanghai, rather in the way that a Liverpool business might set up in London. This tradition goes back to the nineteenth century when British traders going on to Shanghai used the Cantonese intermediaries they had come to know already in Guangzhou.

Baroness Dunn comes from such a 'Shanghai Cantonese' family. When her grandfather, one of the biggest tea merchants in China, moved from Guangzhou to Shanghai the family came to regard Shanghai as its home. Lydia was actually born in Hong Kong but started school in Shanghai, becoming bilingual in Shanghainese and Cantonese. She went on to study at Berkeley and then to join the Swire Group in Hong Kong, rising to be a member of Legco and Exco and one of the most successful politicians under the non-elected system. Her command of Shanghainese and her memories of the old Shanghai served her in good stead in dealing with international trade and industry. There are other examples of 'Shanghai Cantonese', for instance the Kwoks of the Wing On Group and the Mas of Sincere Co.

13

Most Cantonese, however, were suspicious and resentful of the Shanghai arrivals in the 1940s. No one would disagree that they had a lighter touch and greater sophistication than the Cantonese already in occupation. The Shanghainese, one of them unblushingly claimed, were 'more intelligent, efficient, flexible and generous than the Cantonese'.

After forty years of spicing, it is a problem to know which community has influenced the other more or contributed more to Hong Kong's success. The famous story of the English QC is a case in point. The lawyer was hired for an important Hong Kong case, put up at the best hotel, and was seen to drink a $1,000 bottle of superb, if a little travelled, claret every evening. A passer-by, wondering why a man of intelligence would throw his money away like that, had it explained by an 'old hand' that the lawyer's client would meet all his local bills and would lose face if anything but the best were provided or consumed. Was the client Cantonese or Shanghainese? It is a moot point, as is the ownership of the fabled lavatory seats embedded with gold coins, and similar vulgarities involving the yellow metal which so fascinates the Chinese.

One uses the label 'Shanghainese' rather loosely to denote those who speak (or whose ancestors spoke) the Wu dialect which is common to the Yangzi River delta around Shanghai. H. C. Ting, the founder of Kader Industries, Hong Kong's leading plasticware manufacturer, hailed from Wuxi, and Sir Run Run Shaw, Sir Yue-kong Pao and C. Y. Tung, of film-making and ship-owning fame, come from Ningpo, towns which are seventy-five or a hundred miles from Shanghai, but they still count, by Hong Kong criteria, as Shanghainese.

'Ever since I was a child,' Sir Yue-kong Pao, the richest and most famous of the Shanghainese Hongkongers, lamented, 'the Chinese had been fleeing the turbulence and harsh conditions of their homeland.' The international political circumstances of the twentieth century, one could add, left in practice only one place for a Chinese to aim for – Hong Kong.

Shanghai businessmen tested the Hong Kong water in the three years before the Japanese conquest. The textilemen were in the vanguard, with Rong Zong-jing, T. K. Ann and Cha Chi Ming. Godfrey Yeh transferred 'a few hundred' craftsmen from Shanghai to switch his construction business in 1939, and the I-feng Enamel Co. bought an enamel factory in Hong Kong. When the Japanese overcame the British defence forces and took Hong Kong in 1941, Ann and Cha fled inland by sedan chair and whatever other transport was available, to sit the war out behind enemy lines, but they both came back afterwards and remain today two of the heavyweights of Hong Kong industry.

When the Japanese were expelled in 1945, Shanghai's industrialists found that their problems were not over. The ruling Guomindang or Nationalist Party had grown to be bureaucratic, greedy, unprecedentedly corrupt, and quite incapable of managing an economy. The Generalissimo, Chiang Kai-shek's son, Chiang Ching-kuo, was put in charge of post-war Shanghai. He took the opportunity to grab assets indiscriminately for both party and personal use. Industrialists trying to restart after the war years found the dice still loaded against them, and looked again to Hong Kong.

The first textile magnates to cross in this second wave were Chen-che Lee and T. Y. Wong. Lee, frustrated in setting up a mill in Chongqing during the war, had ordered new spindles from the United States in 1945 but lacked an import licence. With the steamer already on the high seas on its way to Shanghai, he ordered the equipment to be offloaded in Hong Kong, and brought sixty skilled workmen down to set it up.

These were the well off. Most refugees had to make it the hard way, like George Kay, who had learned from his grandfather how to make clothes for the British residents in Shanghai so well that they nicknamed him 'Baron'. In 1948, when he was 16, Kay decided to desert the city and get to Hong Kong with, hidden inside his belt, four gold bars worth $200 to give him a start. He was destined, from his discreet premises on the first floor of Mody Road in Kowloon, to make suits for Ronald Reagan and dresses for Elizabeth Taylor. He still resists invitations from China to go back and teach young Shanghai novices the secrets of cutting and stitching. Who would have thought that Shanghai would ever beg for lessons from Hong Kong?

The refugee panic peaked in the months preceding the Red Army's capture of Shanghai in 1949. T. K. Ann and Cha Chi Ming returned for the second time to keep their textile enterprises going, Cha bringing a few technicians with him to start his China Dyeing Works. Many of today's public figures crossed the border as young children in those stormy times. The present Chief Justice, Sir Tiliang Yang, was sent on his own, his parents not following for another eight years – when they reached Hong Kong with only 50 cents each.

A famous trio were three great ship-owners, C. Y. Tung, T. Y. Chao and Y. K. Pao. All three arrived breathless in 1949. Tung came from Shanghai harbour on one of his own best ships, while Chao could only manage to bring such a battered old tub from his Shanghai fleet that he was described as arriving in Hong Kong 'with half a ship'. Pao was not thought of as a shipping man at all in those days. In Shanghai, he had been a banker. He arrived in Hong Kong speaking no Cantonese, with faltering English, accompanied by a wife and two children, and without a home to go to. 'Perhaps,' he reflected later, 'it was the spur I needed.'

Others were caught away from home, not to return to Shanghai for many decades, if at all, like Francis Tien whose family had sent him to Britain to study power station engineering with Vickers. On board the boat home to take up a job with the Shanghai Power Company, he received a wire from his family telling him to get off in Hong Kong. He was there when the regime in China changed, unaware of the extraordinarily successful career in trouser manufacturing to which chance was to lead him. There were many cases of Shanghai boys arriving, like Deacon Chiu in 1950, with only one suitcase and gradually building up a business empire – starting for him with a little cinema at Tsuenwan, then more cinemas all over the New Territories, followed by the Far East Bank, and then hotels and property, before he overreached himself and lost much of his fortune.

Some of the refugees, particularly those who had been obstructed by the Guomindang before 1949 and shared the widespread hope in China that the Communists, for all their dogmatism and antipathy to business, would at least clean up the country and restore some integrity in public life, actually went back to Shanghai after the communist victory, hoping to resume work on their home ground. Cha Chi Ming, perhaps the most travelled Shanghainese of his generation, went back in 1953 to see if the blandishments of Premier Zhou Enlai, who sought to persuade intellectuals and professionals to return to work in the 'New China', had any truth in them at all. He was back in Hong Kong in a very short time, a disappointed man. Even John Keswick, the experienced Jardine, Matheson *taipan* who knew the pre-war Shanghai – and Zhou Enlai – well, was tempted to go back, indulging a romantic fascination for China which his nephews who run the firm today resolutely resist. In the first year or two of the communist regime, there was a kind of truce in the class war, but in the early 1950s the fierce anti-bourgeois and anti-capitalist campaigns, known as the Three-Anti's and the Five-Anti's, forced some of those businessmen who had gone back from abroad to jump out of high windows or collapse in nervous breakdown if they could not negotiate an exit permit for Hong Kong.

By ingenuity and with good luck a small trickle of refugees from Shanghai continued to reach Hong Kong in the later 1950s. Bell Wong, one of the leaders of the international movement for Chinese democracy, was brought to Hong Kong in 1956 at the age of 7 to join his father who was already there. His parents could not support him, because his father was unemployed, so he went back again and only came out finally in 1960 at the age of 11. His mother had by then found work as a cleaner for an American diplomat, and when her employer went back to the United States, she and Bell accompanied him. He became an American citizen, worked as a waiter, married a Hong Kong girl and ran his own restaurant in Virginia before becoming vice-chairman of the Chinese Alliance for Democracy in New York. Another case was Francis Yuen who left Shanghai to be educated in Hong Kong in 1957, and stayed to become the Chief Executive of the Hong Kong Stock Exchange thirty years later.

When the Shanghainese had settled down after the initial uncertainties of domicile, they found that they numbered about 100,000 in Hong Kong, something like 4 per cent of the population. The odds seemed to be well stacked against them. They knew the language neither of the Cantonese majority nor of the English élite (although a lucky few of the Shanghainese with their American degrees spoke English even better than their Cantonese counterparts). They were ignorant of the laws and administrative procedures of this British colony. Eventually, they came to admire the fairness and openness, the relative lack of corruption in this equal-dealing system that was operated in Hong Kong, but to begin with they were baffled and uncertain how to proceed.

Most Shanghainese felt uncomfortable living amidst the Cantonese whom they regarded as uncouth provincials. They banded together in their own small communities, and by the 1950s the North Point district had already acquired its label 'Little Shanghai'. The Shanghainese were aware of discrimination against them in the shops and markets. 'If you had Shanghai servants', a senior British official remembered, 'they would have to pay twice as much as the Cantonese would in the market.' When the Shanghainese industrialists needed credit from the British and other foreign banks, they disliked the local custom of going through traditional *compradors*, who had been the convenient channel for Chinese seeking loans and who were invariably Cantonese. Indeed, when the Cantonese saw how the Shanghainese would walk boldly into bank offices and ask to see the manager and deal directly with him, they began to follow suit and the outdated institution of *comprador* began to fade away.

The lawless butchery of the Cultural Revolution in China in 1966–7 was the turning point for the Shanghainese. It finally squelched the dream of going back to Communist China, and the Shanghainese community began to spread roots and display more commitment to their new home territory. By this time, the pioneers were seeing their grown-up children, born, brought up and educated in Hong Kong, barely able to identify with Shanghai. There was business collaboration, for example, between Cantonese businessmen and the Shanghai Commercial Bank, the second biggest local bank, which had many Shanghainese directors, including T. K. Ann and Sir Run Run Shaw, but it also had J. S. Lee, a Cantonese and the son of Lee Hysan, on the board.

As the amalgam proceeded, the Shanghainese could claim much of the credit for the obvious improvement in all aspects of Hong Kong life. One of them conceded in the 1980s that the Cantonese had 'improved a lot' after forty years of Shanghai influence. 'We can no longer tell the difference,' she admitted. 'We can only name them all "Hongkongese". The "Hongkongese" are certainly the most efficient and brilliant people in Southeast Asia or the Far East.'

At first, the two communities were distinguishable by their speech. But the children of the refugees learned Cantonese in school, had to perfect it to socialise with their schoolmates, and were exposed to Cantonese every day on television and radio. There were no programmes in the Shanghainese language. They therefore became fluent in Cantonese, and came to know it better than Shanghainese – which they heard only from the older generation at home. When the grandchildren came on the scene, they usually went to English-medium schools, and often went on to university in America, Australia or Britain. Hence the aphorism of Cha Chi Ming, spoken in both sadness and pride, that: 'We speak Shanghainese, our children speak Cantonese, and their children speak English.'

It is not quite as cosy as the Shanghainese paint it. The Cantonese retain their general dislike of the Shanghainese. They find the big business ideas of the Shanghainese, leading either to astounding fortunes or ignominious collapse, embarrassing and uncomfortable. They particularly did not like it in the 1980s when China seemed to open its door more to Hong Kong's Shanghainese leaders than to the native Cantonese. It seemed that China trusted the Shanghainese more. China likes to deal with the powerful, and the Shanghainese have more economic weight than the Cantonese. Once approached, the Shanghainese had to respond. T. K. Ann was the first to visit China at the invitation of the Deng Xiaoping regime, hoping to find coexistence and reconciliation in the new political climate. The others were more suspicious, but in the end curiosity outweighed suspicion. Now some of these rich tycoons have taken houses in Shanghai, and the wife of one of them was until recently spending ten months of every year there – almost like the old days.

There is another factor which favours the Shanghainese in Hong Kong-China relations. Many of them graduated from St John's University in Shanghai, and were therefore contemporary fellow-alumni with such leading officials of the People's Republic as Lu Ping, Deputy Director of the Hong Kong Affairs Office in Beijing. These ties are even more important than they are in England. So some of the Shanghai industrialists in Hong Kong have been recruited to join high-level committees and conferences in China. 'You cannot refuse', T. K. Ann wanly explains. On the Basic Law Drafting Committee to settle Hong Kong's post-1997 'constitution', Ann and the others are leading lights, and again this has aroused a certain resentment among the Cantonese. Some talk darkly about a Shanghai mafia, now become reborn Chinese and invited 'home' to Shanghai – perhaps to get Shanghai back on its 1940s tracks to challenge Hong Kong in the twenty-first century, though that would be a thankless task!

Cantonese often complain that the Shanghainese shut themselves up in powerful clan or township associations and exclusive clubs, but that is no more than the Cantonese do themselves. Anything that does not directly profit your company or yourself does not usually appeal to the successful Cantonese and that is why the government had to take the initiative in forming the Federation of Hong Kong Industries, to which the Shanghainese gave most support - as they did to the Chinese Manufacturers' Association and the Chinese General Chamber of Commerce in Hong Kong.

The Shanghainese flair for organisation is particularly valuable in the field of higher education. They helped to start the New Asia College and patronised the Chung Chi College, and these two eventually coalesced with a third college to form the Chinese University of Hong Kong. Two of Hong Kong's three university vice-chancellors are Shanghainese, and the third was educated at Nanjing University in the greater Shanghai cultural belt.

The British are in no doubt that the Shanghai intrusion was a good thing. 'They thoroughly woke the place up,' Austin Coates recalled. 'Suddenly there were wonderful restaurants, nightclubs and cabarets.' The British author Richard Mason made the heroine of that famous Hong Kong novel, *The World of Suzie Wong*, a Shanghai girl.

By the 1970s, when the Shanghainese had been in Hong Kong for twenty-five years, they were being systematically cultivated by the government. By then they had also achieved their first headship of department in the civil service, in the person of Peter Tsao, a quick-witted, down-to-earth, fast-talking bureaucrat who neither courted nor won general popularity.

The economic impact of the Shanghainese industrialists was decisive. The government conceded in the 1970s that Hong Kong had gained a 'ten to fifteen years' start in industrialisation' over other Asian countries because of the 'injection of Shanghai experience and capital'. Shanghai people think big. They will make \$1 million of capital do \$10 million worth of business, quite the opposite to the Cantonese.

The doyen of the Shanghai textilemen was the autocratic P. Y. Tang (1898–1971). Born to a textile family in Wuxi, outside Shanghai, he graduated from MIT and then had twenty-five years industrial experience around Shanghai before moving to Hong Kong. He diverted equipment a year before the communist occupation, bought sites for it in Hong Kong and then transferred hand-picked workers from his mills only days before the Red Army marched in. His South Sea Textile Manufacturing Co. was one of the earliest to begin production (in 1948) and eventually became one of the largest in Hong Kong, pioneering the American market. He was succeeded by his popular son Jack Tang who was born in Shanghai in 1927 and educated at MIT and Harvard.

The other two giants in the Shanghai textile circle are C. C. Lee of the South China Textile Plant and T. Y. Wong of Hong Kong Spinners, whose father was the acknowledged 'King Cotton' of pre-war Shanghai. When the old man died in Hong Kong in 1956 his coffin was temporarily lodged at a Hong Kong cemetery, meaning that the family hoped to bury him eventually in China and that he had not felt settled in Hong Kong.

The Shanghainese are not the only spice in the pot. There are other Chinese 'nationalities', groups and subgroups to be found, the most numerous being the Fujianese, hailing from the coastal province of China immediately north of Guangdong. There was much emigration from the coastal areas of Fujian, to Malaysia, as well as Hong Kong, in the nineteenth and twentieth centuries. The early arrivals in Hong Kong were described by the Governor of that day as 'a very peculiar race, being far more commercial, migratory and maritime in their habits' than the Cantonese or Shanghainese. They retained their distinctiveness and their language in Hong Kong. They are now demonstrating their business prowess and their capability in other realms of life. Michael Sze Cho-cheung, Director of Trade and a high-flyer in the Hong Kong civil service, came from Fujian at the age of 4.

Then there are the Hakka, wanderers like the Jews or gypsies of Europe, who originated in Shandong province but left after persecution in the third century BC, to begin millennial roamings in search of an alternative home. They arrived in the New Territories about 300 years ago, occupying the more difficult hilly land to the east, and leaving the already settled Cantonese on the more fertile ground of the western plains.

Over those two centuries there has been some specialisation of jobs; the Cantonese monopolise the oyster fisheries in the New Territories, for instance, while the making of bean curd and stone quarrying are exclusive to the Hakka. To farm the mountains is difficult and so the Hakka are industrious and pushful. Many of the New Territories leaders now are Hakkas rather than Cantonese (both Deng Xiaoping and Singapore's Lee Kuan Yew, to name two famous Chinese leaders outside Hong Kong, are of Hakka descent).

The other provincial communities are very small. A Shandong group formed when the British started to recruit policemen from that province – because they looked fiercer than the Cantonese. Leung Chun-ying, the Bristol-trained surveyor who was secretary of the Basic Law Drafting Committee in recent years, is the son of such a policeman. Allen Lee, the politician and industrialist, is also of Shandong origin.

So Hong Kong has ingested the cream of the Shanghai entrepreneurial class and used it in the ensuing decades to vault over its northern rival, and become what it had never been before, the wealthiest, most advanced and most sophisticated Chinese city. The smaller but telling minorities from Fujian and Shandong, etc. all contributed. Virtually all the refugees from Shanghai and the other cities and provinces to the north of Guangdong were white-collar professionals or middle class. By contrast, most of the people who crossed with their few possessions on their backs from Guangdong province itself came from farming families.

Having made all these distinctions between the various Chinese communities living in Hong Kong, one has to concede that the visiting Westerner would not normally be able to tell them apart. The younger generation of non-Cantonese has had to learn Cantonese speech and uses it as a *lingua franca*, having probably forgotten much of its original mother tongue brought from other provinces. In that sense Hong Kong becomes more Cantonese day by day. Nevertheless, without the general stimulus of élite immigration from other provinces, and especially without the business skills of the relatively few Shanghainese, Hong Kong would never have achieved such heights. Now this potent population mix has the challenge of exchanging the British for new masters in Beijing.

Chapter 3

Asylum and Stairway

Not every Chinese came to Hong Kong to look for gold. The British colony was the main place of asylum for Chinese escaping from the oppression of their rulers. A leader of the Taiping rebellion against Manchu rule in China in the mid-nineteenth century, Hung Jen-kan, went to Hong Kong to be baptised, and collaborated with European missionaries there – returning to the mainland to become the Taipings' chief military adviser. Another Taiping fled to Hong Kong later to help Dr James Legge translate Chinese classics.

When the Taiping rebels were threatening the city of Guangzhou, Legge in Hong Kong described how many of the 'families of means' of Guangzhou 'flocked to this colony; houses were in demand; rents rose; . . . and new commercial Chinese firms were founded'. The rebellion was crushed and its leaders executed, although there is evidence that a son of Hung Hsiu-chuan, the Taiping 'emperor', was born clandestinely in Hong Kong after the failure of the rebellion. The story handed down is that the boy was taken beyond the revenge of the Manchu emperor to Borneo, where his descendants still live to make the claim.

That was in the 1850s. In the remaining decades of the empire, ministers who fell from the court's favour sometimes took sanctuary in Hong Kong, notably Kang Yuwei who had tried unsuccessfully to press reforms on the Manchu court. He first visited Hong Kong in 1879, and was astonished by 'the elegance of the buildings . . . the cleanliness of the streets, the efficiency of the police'. Recognising the good organisation and administration of the Europeans' colony, 'I realised that we must not look on them as barbarians, as our older and more conservative people have done.'

Kang visited again three years later while travelling from Guangzhou to Beijing, and after his ultimate failure to make reforms stick in 1898, he was brought from Tianjin under British protection to become a refugee in Hong Kong. (In those early days the distinction between Hong Kong and

China was not so rigidly drawn, and some Chinese dignitaries, including Prime Minister Liang Hsiyi, actually had houses in the colony.) Sir Robert Hotung, the Eurasian leader, put Kang up at his house and paid his fares to lobby foreign governments on behalf of the Chinese reform movement (a foretaste of 1989).

The drama intensified at the end of the century with Sun Yat Sen, who simultaneously gratified and embarrassed the British by using Hong Kong as a base for Chinese revolution. Without Hong Kong, it is doubtful if Sun's nationalist republican movement would have toppled the Dragon Throne.

At the beginning of the 1880s, the young Sun Yat Sen returned to his Guangdong village after a brief exposure to the West as the guest of his brother in Hawaii. He found the old rural rituals and observances absurd, and one night, in disgust, he deliberately desecrated the wooden statue of the village god. He was indignantly expelled, took refuge in Hong Kong where he started school again and was baptised by an American missionary. Later, he started medical school in Guangzhou. Then, 'I learned that an English medical school with a wider programme than that of the Guangzhou school has been opened in Hong Kong. Thereupon, attracted by the thought that I should have a wider field for my revolutionary propaganda, I went to Hong Kong to continue my education.' He enrolled at the Hong Kong College of Medicine at the age of 21.

Revolution appealed more to him, however, than anatomy. In 1895, Sun assembled 3,000 triad members in Hong Kong to sail to Guangzhou on ferry boats, their pistols packed in drums labelled 'cement'. His plot was leaked and the mercenaries quarrelled over the weapons. Sun had to flee from China, disguised as a woman in a curtained sedan chair. Two of his close colleagues were beheaded, another was beaten to death with 600 strokes of a 'military stick', while a fourth was hacked to pieces in 'the death of a thousand cuts'. Sun's life now changed. Henceforth he was a hunted criminal, forbidden to return to Chinese soil, with a price of 10,000 taels on his head.

Sun's old medical school teacher in Hong Kong, Dr Cantley, advised him to consult an English lawyer who had helped save other Chinese from being turned over to the Imperial Police for torture and execution. 'Beijing's arm, though weaker,' the lawyer warned, 'is still a long one, and in whichever part of the world you go you must expect to hear of the Tsungli Yamen (Foreign Office).' Cantley helped Sun to disguise himself for an escape to Japan.

When Sun applied again for residence in 1897, the Colonial Secretary replied that the Hong Kong government had no intention of 'allowing the British Colony of Hong Kong to be used as an asylum for persons engaged in plots and dangerous conspiracies against a friendly neighbouring empire'. He would be arrested if he tried to land. All that changed, of course, when Sun became President of the Republic of China in 1912.

After Sun's death in 1925, his left-wing widow, Soong Ching-ling, lived in Hong Kong 'with a single maid in a secluded apartment building about half-way up the peak'. In February 1940, before the Japanese conquest of Hong Kong, she was joined by her two sisters, Mei-ling (wife of Generalissimo Chiang Kai-shek) and Ai-ling (wife of the Chinese Finance Minister). For a few days the three Soong sisters, as they used to be known, sank their political differences, forgot their public roles and enjoyed themselves. One night the three dined at the Hong Kong Hotel and all heads turned to see them. 'I'll believe two of them are there,' a newspaperman protested, 'but I won't believe that's Madame Sun. She would never never be with the other two – and in this outpost of Empire!' Ai-ling arrived again in 1946 with her husband, H. H. Kung, the former Guomindang Finance Minister, to take up residence in Sassoon Road in Pokfulam.

The famous brother of the Soong sisters, T. V. Soong, once Prime Minister under Chiang Kai-shek, fled from his last post as Governor of Guangdong in January 1949. At Kai Tak Airport, in double-breasted business suit and grey homburg, a cane in his hand, he asked for a British police guard, being under threat not only from the Communists, but also from his enemies in the Guomindang who claimed to have documented vast embezzlements by him. Another Guomindang minister, the former Foreign Minister, Eugene Chen, retired to a 'well-guarded residence in Kowloon'. Hong Kong was becoming a residential suburb for China's 'Shadow Cabinet'.

Another beneficiary of Hong Kong's neutrality was Wang Ching-wei, the leftist rival to Chiang Kai-shek for the leadership of the Guomindang. He fled to Hong Kong in 1928 after the collapse of his anti-Chiang government. He proceeded to France and then came back via Hong Kong, but when he left China yet again for Germany the Hong Kong authorities would not allow him off the ship. It was always a dilemma for Hong Kong. Humanitarian considerations dictated giving asylum, and it was also good for business, but the colony was too small and vulnerable to become involved in active subversion against the Chinese government of the day. If a rebel actually became a wanted man, the best thing was for him to leave quickly for some remoter, safer destination. In 1989, in the furore over the Tiananmen Square massacres and the fate of the student organisers, precisely the same arguments were heard.

A key backer of Chiang Kai-shek was Du Yuesheng, sour and unwholesome boss of the infamous Green Gang, the most powerful of the Shanghai secret societies. In the 1920s, Du had arranged for mass executions of the Shanghai Communists in order to deliver the city to Chiang, but when the Japanese guns began to bark in Shanghai, in 1937, he slipped aboard a French ship and sailed to Hong Kong accompanied only by his valet/masseur. From a palatial suite in the Peninsular Hotel, he sent for the newest of his four wives and evidently hoped to sit the war out in safety, although he made short visits to Wuhan to keep in touch with his government friends – and, on one occasion, be interviewed by W. H. Auden and Christopher Isherwood. He later acquired his own house, with a high wall all around it. The fall of Hong Kong found him inland at Chongqing, and from there he returned to his native Shanghai on the Japanese surrender. Four years later, as the avengers of the Communists he had butchered twenty years earlier approached Shanghai in triumph, Du stole away yet again on a boat to Hong Kong. This time Du took an apartment on Kennedy Road. He had begun to fall out with his patron, Chiang Kai-shek, refusing to follow the Generalissimo to Taiwan. His prestige and power faded, and the final posthumous insult was that after his death, in 1951, under British rules he could not be buried in Hong Kong (that required an eight-year residence), so his coffin had to be shipped to Taiwan. He was in any case penniless by then, having four wives and ten children to maintain and mounting doctors' bills to meet.

Among the many other Guomindang figures who took refuge in Hong Kong, two of the most reputable were Tsai Yuan-pei – probably the greatest educator of his generation and Chancellor of Beijing University in the early years of the republic – who retired to Hong Kong for his last years, and General Li Yinwo, who was the first Chinese to gain a doctorate of pharmacy at Lyons University and knew Zhou Enlai in France (they once spent an entire day arguing about communism). After the communist victory in 1949 General Li preferred to settle in Hong Kong rather than live under either of China's alternative regimes in Taiwan or the mainland.

His son, Martin Lee, the liberal Hong Kong politician, recalls:

> Zhou Enlai sent an emissary every year to my father asking him to go back. And my father said no, he did not like communism, because it does not recognise the family as a unit, and my father is a classical Chinese scholar. To him the family is the core of society. And he did not want to go to Taiwan because he thinks the government is too corrupt. So he brought us here. Later on he told us that if the Communists had taken Hong Kong, he and my mother would have taken the family and jumped into the harbour.

The old man changed houses in Hong Kong every year in the hope of throwing Zhou Enlai's emissary off the scent.

Such examples – and there are many more – underline the unusual importance of Hong Kong's role as an asylum. Simply because this tiny piece of territory had a different jurisdiction, the lives and future contributions of key actors on the public stage were saved. China would have been much the poorer without Hong Kong.

Whichever party had the upper hand in China, the other needed refuge. The most famous communist refugee was Zhou Enlai himself. Routed after his uprising at Nanchang in 1927, and pursued by Chinese reactionaries down to the coast, Zhou apparently rented a boat with his last cash and took it, penniless and in tatters and periodically unconscious with fever, to the safety of Hong Kong. There he got leftist help, and held court at the Queens Hotel with He Long, Ye Ting, and Nie Rongzhen, all communist leaders who were to hold high office in the People's Republic. His secret stay was probably no longer than two or three weeks, enough to set him up for another military campaign, another revolution. If such a place had not existed, where the arm of the local anti-communist forces could not reach, Zhou might well have fallen – to sickness, to enemy search, or to the many dangers that attach to a man at the end of his tether without friends or money. Without Zhou, its future Premier, the People's Republic might have joined the ranks of lost causes.

The British authorities were probably not aware of Zhou Enlai's presence in 1927, but if they had been, they would certainly have deported him to the mainland, as they did many other Communists in the 1920s and 1930s. Zhou and his party were able to slip back in their own time to rejoin the fight, but Tao Chu, the Cantonese Communist leader, also in Hong Kong in 1927, was not so lucky. He was arrested and returned to Guomindang custody. Worst of all was the fate of Cai Hosen, Mao's closest friend from childhood, who was handed over by the British Hong Kong Police to Guangzhou where the Guomindang 'spread out his limbs, nailed him to the wall, beat him to death in cold blood and cut his chest and stomach to pieces'.

Rather luckier was a man from whom chance snatched the communist crown, Chang Kuotao. Rebuffed by fellow Communists in his bid to take over the party leadership from Mao Zedong in 1937, Chang saw his fortunes wane and by the time he sought refuge in Hong Kong, in 1949, he was sick and impoverished. Mao sent Chang's wife with some funds to help him, and Chang later emigrated to Canada.

The Guangdong provincial communist leaders were always of special potential importance to Hong Kong. The most feared in 1949 was the man who combined the posts of governor and military commander of Guangdong and mayor of Guangzhou, Ye Jianying. He had a brother, Jaoying, who had lived in Hong Kong and run a trading business there before. When the People's Republic was founded, the brother returned to Guangzhou, leaving some of his children behind in Hong Kong. Ye Jianying is said to have built houses in Hong Kong and to have joined his brother in a new trading company there even after 1949, and there were stories that the two brothers used to go to Hong Kong to enjoy themselves in the early years of the People's Republic. It was also widely believed that Ye Jianying owned a bakery on Castle Peak Road in the New Territories, making cheap bread for the locals, and the place was burned down by anti-Communists in the Cultural Revolution disturbances of 1967. His son Ye Xuanping governed Guangdon in the 1980s and supervised its open-door policy towards Hong Kong.

In the 1940s, some Communists were able to establish a legitimate presence in Hong Kong. During the war with Japan, in which the Communists were official legal partners with the Guomindang in resisting Japanese aggression, Liao Chengzhi was the Red eyes and ears in Hong Kong, and in 1948, as the possibility of a Communist victory in the civil war became clear, the famous duo of Qiao Guanhua and Kung Peng established the Hong Kong branch of the Xinhua News Agency, which would serve as the unofficial embassy of the Chinese Communists. Their son is one of its senior officials today.

There are still some in the Beijing leadership, after more than forty years of the People's Republic, who have a Hong Kong page or two in their *curriculum vitae*. Chen Yun, regarded as the leader of the octogenarian conservatives in the party, was chosen in 1935 to carry the news of the changes in party policy and leadership made during the early months of the Long March, to Moscow. His route took him via Hong Kong. More interesting is the case of Premier Li Peng, whose name is now excoriated in Hong Kong as the man who told the army to shoot at the students on Tiananmen Square. When he lost his father at the age of 3 at the hands of the Guomindang, his mother took him to Hong Kong where she worked in the underground communist movement. It seems that the young Li may have spent much of the 1930s in Hong Kong before returning to the mainland for education – through the generosity of Zhou Enlai, who eventually adopted him.

It is not clear what contribution, if any, these fleeting impressions of British colonial life may have made on the future leaders of China. Sun Yat Sen was the only one to have referred openly to the superiority of Hong Kong's system of administration. Most of all he praised its orderliness. His own family in China had to have firearms to protect itself, surrounded by corruption and filth. Yet Hong Kong boasted fine streets and parks. He wondered 'why Englishmen could do such a thing on this barren rock within 70 or 80 years?'

Speaking once to Hong Kong University students, at the invitation of Sir Robert Hotung, Sun described how painful it had been for him to go back to his native village and see what a mess the elders were making in running it, and it was the same with the higher levels of administration right up to the imperial government in Beijing. How was it the British were able to govern Hong Kong so much better? 'We must carry this example of good government to every part of China,' he said.

There were thus two ways in which Hong Kong contributed, simply by keeping its doors reasonably open to the reform movement across the border. First, it made possible the physical survival of those at the losing end of the current battle, and secondly it offered to both sides a living model of another style of government. The numbers were never very high. Political refugees were always outnumbered by the 'economic' refugees whose goals were more mundane. But Hong Kong helped many people with talent and ambition who were not able to develop and demonstrate those talents in China. Some gifted Chinese used Hong Kong as a stairway to a cosmopolitan world to which they could give their best, instead of languishing unappreciated in a homeland which did not accept equal dealing with foreign countries, even in cultural matters.

Han Suyin, the Eurasian novelist and doctor, did not use Hong Kong directly in this way. She stayed in Hong Kong on her way back to China from Europe, rather than the other way around. Her few days in 1938, after sailing from Marseilles with her husband, did not make much impression. But after the war, when she finished her English medical training and was ready to return to China, she hesitated. China was, after all, in the final throes of a vicious civil war. So she flew to Hong Kong and waited there to find out at a prudent distance what the new China was going to be like. 'Even if I could not live in the New China that the revolution would bring forth . . . I could at least stand on the threshold.' She spent three years observing China from the sidelines and wrote *A Many Splendoured Thing*, which made her famous, and which William Holden and Jennifer Jones brought to life on the screen. Afterwards she went to live in Malaysia, and then in other parts of the world. She never came back to live in China, but then she was, after all, only half Chinese.

Han Suyin is a writer. There were other Chinese – artists, musicians, thinkers, professionals, scientists – who were frustrated in China and came to Hong Kong to develop their skills and tastes in freedom, often to find an arena for them in the West. For them Hong Kong was a stairway to individual fulfilment, just as for other Chinese this anachronistic European colony was an asylum from the violence of political change or merely a place where the monetary grass was greener. It is a role likely to shrivel when China resumes sovereignty in 1997.

Chapter 4

Capital of the Overseas Chinese

First starved or repressed in China, then alien and cold-shouldered in Southeast Asia, the overseas Chinese have made full use of Hong Kong – looked up to it, enjoyed its freedom and affluence, drawn on its safe transit facilities. Those who knew only the furtive lives of minority Chinese in Southeast Asia or the inhuman poverty of the Chinese mainland could be astonished by Hong Kong. 'Never in my life,' exclaimed a Malaysian Chinese visiting for the first time in 1975, 'had I seen so many Chinese living together in such a peaceful and prosperous place.' Hong Kong has been a safety net for those Chinese whom China cannot support or tolerate, and also a staging point on the way to safer or more affluent lands. Albert Yee, a fourth generation Chinese American and recently professor of psychology in Hong Kong, wrote a book '*A People Misruled: Hong Kong and the Chinese Stepping Stone Syndrome*' about China's need to find a stepping stone to Western culture, and how Hong Kong played that role, in both geo-political and psychological terms. 'The Chinese made increasing use of Hong Kong as a . . . springboard to opportunities abroad and increased awareness of the world.' More poetically, the writer Ai Qing called Hong Kong 'the bridge that reaches towards the Four Seas and the Five Continents'.

Hong Kong is like the cottage on the edge of the Chinese estate, the place where Chinese can begin their adjustment to extra-mural living beyond the Confucian pale. It also serves those who, having shaken China's dust from their feet, need a place from which they can communicate with their family at home and make business arrangements for them free from Chinese government interference. Until 1912, emigration was a crime in China, so Hong Kong was a halfway house for those coming back as well as those trying to get out.

The overseas Chinese are almost like another nation. Numbering at least 25 million today – another Canada – they have been likened to an overseas 'province' of China, and that indeed is how the Chinese state in some ways regards them, allocating seats to them on legislative and advisory bodies in both Beijing and Taipei. If they *were* an entity, whether 'province' or 'subnation', their capital would surely be Hong Kong. The Jews were able to remain a nation in spite of being distributed among scores of states, but the Chinese lack the religious and ritualistic basis for such a feat. Theirs is more like the Anglo-Saxon diaspora. But the Chinese went to their destinations as underdogs, not as conquerors.

Most of the overseas Chinese are in the states of Southeast Asia – Singapore, Malaysia, Thailand, Indonesia and the Philippines. There they live as small minorities in an alien ground, surrounded and outnumbered by people of a different race, a different culture, and different religions. Small wonder that they feel insecure, even the lucky few who made their fortunes from the rich resources of those countries. The first generation usually went to work on mines and estates, often on contract to European owners who found local labour unreliable and lacking the work habit. Many of their children and grandchildren became entrepreneurs, profiting from boundless opportunities to exploit natural resources in which the indigenous people lacked interest.

Another pattern was for new emigrants to go to Southeast Asia to gain wealth over the backs of their compatriots already there. Aw Boon Haw was a Fujianese who emigrated to Burma and invented a patent medicine which he called Tiger Balm, an ointment possessing numerous restorative properties. From there he went to Singapore to forge a newspaper empire, partly as a means of promoting his Tiger Balm, but also to sustain Chinese culture in a place where it was neglected. Aw became a noted philanthropist, and since he had no sons, his daughter Sally Aw Sian inherited his newspaper group on his death. She still runs it – from Hong Kong, where her flagship is the *Hong Kong Standard*.

The Aw Boon Haw fortune begins and thrives in Southeast Asia, but in the end the heirs find Hong Kong is a trouble-free headquarters. To make the direct comparison with Singapore, most overseas Chinese find Hong Kong more congenial, if only because it is almost fully a Chinese society. The Chinese in Hong Kong are 98 per cent of the population, whereas in Singapore they are only three quarters. Besides, Singapore is a small island in a Malay sea, and both Malay and Western cultural modes have rubbed off on the Chinese there. Hong Kong has no other social context than Chinese, and is therefore more comfortable for most Chinese. On top of that, British colonialism in Hong Kong had no policy of discrimination against the Chinese of the kind that made life difficult from time to time in the Southeast Asian states. For practical purposes, European colonial rule which observed a basic respect for China and its government was better than colonial states further off to whom Chinese immigrants were a nuisance, or independent states in Southeast Asia where Chinese lacked the protection of a rule of law.

So the overseas Chinese used Hong Kong as a family and business headquarters, to keep every option open if the political, social or economic climate in Southeast Asia deteriorated. It was a place in which to educate your children, letting them keep their fundamental grasp of the Chinese tradition and yet acquire the cosmopolitan touch that modern business life in Southeast Asia demanded. Incidentally, if you could arrange for your children to be born in Hong Kong, they would, in pre-war days at least, become British citizens and could return freely to a country like the Philippines (where Chinese nationals were restricted) to take over their fathers' businesses quite legally. And at the other end of the life cycle, with the waiting coffins in the Hong Kong mortuaries bearing witness to the desire of many overseas Chinese to be buried in the ground from which they were born, Hong Kong served the needs of the dead as well as the unborn.

A new variation on this came in the 1970s with Hong Kong's rapid growth as a financial and business services centre for the region. Overseas Chinese family corporations which had succeeded in Southeast Asia began to use Hong Kong as an investment and financial base, while keeping their substantive operations where they were. In 1921, two brothers, Chia Ek Chor and Chia Seow Wooy, sailed from Shantou in northern Guangdong to sell seeds to Thai farmers. They found the prospects inviting, stayed in Thailand and built up a profitable business there which extended after the war to feed mills and big processing plant. By 1974, it had become a comprehensive agribusiness enterprise, and in that year the company, called Charoen Pokphand, came to Hong Kong, to open a feed mill and later to develop numerous enterprises in China itself.

By then the wheel had turned full circle. The young men who had originally taken Chinese technology to Thailand were now selling even better Western technology to their compatriots in South China. The official headquarters of this extraordinary food empire, the international nerve centre and main administration, are now lodged in Hong Kong. With annual turnover exceeding $80 million, the question being asked by investors and bankers is whether family control can now be converted smoothly into professional management leadership.

Another case is that of Liem Sioe Liong, a Fujianese who sailed to Java in the 1930s to join his brother there, and who also launched successful businesses in both agriculture and manufacturing. He had the luck to befriend a young officer called Suharto who later became President of Indonesia, and that enabled Liem to take his companies to the top of the Indonesian economy. When the need arose to have an investment arm outside Indonesia, with its perennial foreign exchange difficulties and pettifogging bureaucracy, Hong Kong was the choice. But instead of merely setting up a branch, Liem created the First Pacific Group, a finance and trading empire covering the Pacific rim, which went on in the 1980s to be an investment holding company with global vision run by a group of professional Asian managers (from the Philippines, Japan, Hong Kong, etc.) fully trained in American financial management.

And the process continues. In 1989, when Formosa Plastic, a giant of its kind, looked for a long-term base for worldwide sales and servicing outside Taiwan, it chose Hong Kong. This was partly because of the imminent prospects for Taiwan–China trade. 'We hope the closer it gets to 1997, the better Chinese and Taiwan people can work together,' said Han Shiao-min, a company executive. Hong Kong, with its low taxes and minimal government regulations, is a very attractive place in which to set up a company or family business. The profits of Hong Kong's many banks bear witness to the overseas Chinese enthusiasm for depositing money there. Not only money, but valuable possessions are also considered more secure in this 'safe house' of the region.

More mundanely, Hong Kong shopkeepers and commercial agents profited immensely from the orders which the early overseas Chinese placed with them, for Chinese as well as Western or Japanese goods. Chinese in small towns in Borneo or in the Thai interior had few means of procuring the articles they wanted except through the Hong Kong network. There was always somebody coming from or going to Hong Kong, and there was always somebody in Hong Kong who knew where and how to get a thing.

Profit was also made from the piety of the overseas Chinese in sending money to their parents, wives, brothers and sisters and children in China. It was understood that the emigrant would send money back to help the impoverished family remaining behind, and these remittances were sent entirely through Hong Kong, if only because Chinese banks did not have enough branches, or any branches at all, in the Southeast Asian states, and were not much trusted. True, some remittances were paid through the Bank of China and other communist banks in Hong Kong, but most of those probably went first through the Hongkong Bank, which was in the happy position of being well represented in Southeast Asia, familiar with the Chinese financial system and yet free from the eccentricities of Chinese financial administration. The funds were naturally welcomed, both by the families and by the Chinese government, which was made a free gift of the foreign exchange value in return for paying the beneficiaries in Chinese currency. Even the communist administration made no bones about benefiting from these remittances, which it called the 'fruit of the labour of the overseas Chinese', pretending not to know that most of the money came from the exploitation of Southeast Asian nationalities by highly bourgeois Chinese moneylenders, businessmen, bankers, traders, etc.

Overseas Chinese remittances via Hong Kong now reach at least $500–600 million a year. In the 1960s, China introduced the idea of sending fertilisers and food for Chinese families, as well as actual cash. That was during the famine years in China. But the cash remittances continued year after year, testimony to the sense of family duty among the Chinese abroad – and a valuable addition to China's foreign exchange income as well as to Hong Kong's banking business.

Having passed through Hong Kong on their way to another country, the overseas Chinese sometimes returned to spend the money they had made. When Kwok Gook Lock had earned enough from the Australian gold rush in 1890, he sailed back to Hong Kong, hoping to find a republican China that would be better to live in than the imperial one he had left. He was a little too early, so he opened a vegetable shop in Hong Kong's Queens Road and went on in later years to start insurance and textile businesses. In 1934, he launched the Wing On Bank.

That kind of reinvestment of overseas savings in Hong Kong was not uncommon. During the first three post-war decades many Chinese business-men went on putting money into Southeast Asian countries because they believed it would be safer and easier to get a quick return from them. Southeast Asia was full of countries with rich resources but short of enter-prise. That was the period when China was going through the final throes of civil war, followed by communist rule, and when Hong Kong was felt to be not entirely safe, considering its proximity to China and the numerous scares it experienced over immigration control, Guomindang-initiated riots, the Cultural Revolution, etc. But from about 1976 onwards the flow reversed. With Deng Xiaoping's open door policy and the extraordinary blossoming of the Hong Kong economy in the 1980s it became attractive to overseas Chinese to make more use of the Hong Kong market, to invest their money there and share in the big profits being made.

The overseas Chinese also came back in order to enjoy the experience of living once again in a Chinese atmosphere. I was introduced, in 1961, to a young 'Welshman' whose Cantonese parents ran a restaurant near Cardiff. Having arrived at London University, this young man decided to learn Chinese and then come out to Hong Kong to discover his roots. Was he Chinese, as his parents and his physical appearance told him, or British, as his upbringing indicated? Eventually he settled in Hong Kong, married a Cantonese girl, and found a career there. To him Hong Kong provided the overlapping of the two cultures to which he was heir.

'For a Chinese,' one of Hong Kong's Shanghainese industrialists observed, 'Hong Kong is the best place to live. The next best is Taiwan. Being an overseas Chinese in Southeast Asia is no comparison.' The Communists are strictly speaking at fault in creating this situation whereby China is so disliked by the overseas Chinese as a place to live in. Yet their representatives can be matter of fact about it. 'Quite a few overseas Chinese . . .,' Qiao Zonghuai, a senior Xinhua official in Hong Kong told me, 'do not like the system either on the mainland or in Taiwan, but they do like a community such as Hong Kong where the Chinese are in a majority.'

Overseas Chinese from almost every host country are to be found in Hong Kong. From Latin America there is Louis Chan, the *naif* painter born in Panama who settled in Hong Kong in 1907. The late Percy Chen and Donald Yap, two distinguished lawyers, along with Selwyn Alleyne and Hilton Cheong-leen, represent the Caribbean branch of this remarkable clan. The Jamaica born Yap became President of the Law Society. But the most renowned West Indian Chinese in Hong Kong was Percy Chen, the son of the first Foreign Minister of the Chinese republic, Eugene Chen, who was himself partly black – or what his American contemporaries called 'high yellow'. Percy Chen was born in Trinidad. He trained in law in Britain, helped his father in China in the 1920s, and eventually settled down to practise law in Hong Kong, pleading cases in court on behalf of the People's Republic, and founding the Marco Polo Club where selected foreign correspondents and businessmen were able to meet pro-Beijing left-wingers at a time when that was not easy.

Chen was a resourceful man, considerably Anglicised (he went to prep school in St John's Wood and never spoke much Chinese), and his wartime exploits were remarkable. A British Army officer, captured by the Japanese and held as a prisoner of war in Hong Kong, escaped only to run into armed bandits. He despaired of his life, but 'then along came an amazing chap,' he remembered, 'a half-Jamaican, half-Chinese, and told us to take no notice of them and to follow him'. Percy Chen led these British escapees to a Red Army base, whence they were able to make the overland trip to India and freedom. Only in the 1980s did this English officer discover who his helper had been and thank him. The Hong Kong Chinese, with their customary intolerance, referred to Chen privately as that 'nigger-black-man'.

A very recent trend is for American-born or American-raised and educated Chinese to come to live and work in Hong Kong. 'As a Chinese–American,' said Steve Chu, a financial specialist, 'there are certainly some advantages to being at least substantially Chinese in a Chinese society, as opposed to being Chinese in a western society, as far as acceptability is concerned and access.' A public relations executive, born in China but brought up in the United States and now living in Hong Kong, said: 'Middle management opportunities especially are a lot greater here. You can get back a lot of what you put into things here quickly . . . This is where the future lies, it is the place to be.'

From Australia came early returnees like Kwok Gook Lock of Wing On fame, and also the Ma's of the Sincere Department Store; the Louie's of Kowloon Motor Bus; Tse Tsang Tai, one of the original investors in the *South China Morning Post*; and Harry Ching, the outstanding post-war editor of the *Morning Post* who had been born in Australia. From Europe there were cases like Loy Chung, born in Wales of Cantonese immigrant parents, who came to Hong Kong after having worked in Leeds for many years and acquired a Yorkshire accent. He became a senior manager of the Ramada Inns in Hong Kong.

From Japan came Paul Sun, born in Japan and successful in business. On a trip to Hong Kong in 1986, he liked it so much he decided to stay. He bought a hotel which was then under construction for $128 million, which he borrowed from a bank, and has since become a man whom the property market has to watch.

The reverse flow to Hong Kong is biggest of all from Southeast Asia, where the overseas Chinese feel so unloved and insulated. In the white domains of Europe, North America and Australia, an immigrant Chinese may feel unassimilated and culturally starved, but at least his hosts do not systematically resent his business success and express their fear in violent hatred. Southeast Asia is an Aladdin's cave of economic opportunity for the Chinese, but it is not a comfortable climate to live in or for the next generation to be brought up in. Education is not well provided in Southeast Asia, and overseas Chinese preferred to put their children in schools, colleges or universities in Singapore or Hong Kong, where standards are high and there is a Chinese base, or else in the Anglo-Saxon institutions of Australia, the US, Canada or Britain.

The largest number of Southeast Asian Chinese in Hong Kong is from Indonesia. Some Indonesian Chinese came to Hong Kong for education or for some other purpose, liked it and stayed, like Dr Rudi Khoo Kian-kang, who arrived in 1948 and never went back. He joined the government medical service and rose to be deputy director.

There is a well-travelled indirect route back to Hong Kong via the Chinese motherland. Alex Gouw took this path, and became a Hong Kong millionaire at about the third try, going from trading in hair for wigs to film-making and then into property. The Indonesian Chinese students were urged by Premier Zhou Enlai, when he visited Indonesia for the Bandung conference in 1955, to come to China and take up education there. More effective than such blandishments of the communist leaders was the strong hostility which the nationalist Indonesian government exhibited towards the Chinese residents of their new republic, leading to a Sino-Indonesian treaty which was signed during the Bandung conference and put into effect in 1960, regulating the status of the Indonesian Chinese in a much more restrictive manner than before. From then on large numbers of Indonesian Chinese were shipped back to China. In the end, about 300,000 overseas Chinese from Southeast Asia, mainly Indonesia, returned to China during the early communist years.

Most of them had come from South China stock and they expected to be able to settle in Guangdong or Fujian province. But they found conditions even less easy than in their host countries of Southeast Asia. The standard of living was lower, government controls were more oppressive, and political movements constantly changed direction and required time and energy in ways which were usually unproductive. Even the local people did not entirely welcome their arrival. Many of them therefore left China for Hong Kong and settled down there instead. A sudden demand was noticed in Hong Kong for Cantonese language primers for Mandarin- or Hokkien-speakers. This is how many of Hong Kong's Fujianese or Hokkien people first entered the Hong Kong scene.

Some left China to revisit their families in Indonesia or the Philippines, but found that their citizenship was now problematic and that they would not be allowed back into Indonesia at all. Turning their back on China, spurned by the country in which their family now lived, they fell on Hong Kong as the only harbour in a storm-tossed world, a temporary haven to begin with, but one which slowly became permanent. Isolated and vulnerable, this tragic subcommunity created an emergent subculture in Hong Kong. Speaking *bahasa*, the familiar Indonesian language, preferring Nanyang food, and nostalgic for the tropical way of life, they seemed out of tune with Hong Kong, although their children are beginning to make the adjustment.

Hong Kong officials and businessmen still wonder whether it is pure accident that so many of the rogues and villains who have stampeded through the Hong Kong scene, leaving monumental debts and corporate chaos behind them, hail from Singapore or Malaysia. First, there was Amos Dawe, the postal clerk who married a Thai princess and made a huge fortune in the 1970s which he quickly lost. Dawe, involved in complicated transactions in many countries including Singapore, was extradited from the USA, and gaoled in Hong Kong for several years.

In the mid-1980s, a colleague of Dawe's took over the headlines. Chang Ming Thien started life in Penang but eventually constructed a business empire which ran to Thailand, Taiwan, Singapore and Hong Kong. He was something of a linguist, speaking Malay, English and three Chinese languages. One of his ventures in Hong Kong, with Thai and Indonesian Chinese associates, was the Overseas Trust Bank, for overseas Chinese depositors. His son Patrick directed it. Meanwhile, another of his sons, Eric, was sent to prison in Singapore for complicity in a plot to kill his father's mistress. This was only the first hint of a power struggle within the family for control of the business empire which burst into the open after Chang died in 1982. The contests in the courts revealed several unsavoury episodes and 'disgraceful criminal acts' in the family's conduct of the business, which collapsed under the strain. By then it had become the third largest private bank in Hong Kong and the centrepiece of a complex secretive coalition of business interests ranging right across Southeast Asia.

That was nothing compared with the story of George Tan's nefarious Carrian Company. The name was an anglicisation of a Chinese phrase meaning 'good and peaceful' but the violent ripples which it spread over the Hong Kong pond were anything but that. George Tan was an engaging, charismatic personality. Born in Fujian in 1933, he trained in Britain as an engineer and followed that profession, along with business interests, in Singapore in the 1960s. Then, in the 1970s he transferred to Hong Kong as project manager on a building site. Three years later he was declared a bankrupt in Singapore, and was not discharged until 1980, although he became a company shareholder and director in Hong Kong in the interim. He never went back to Singapore.

His meteoric rise in Hong Kong began in 1975 when he persuaded the many members of his family to pool their savings and raise $2 million for him to go into business. It was typical of his style that rumours swept the market that he had been entrusted with funds emanating from the two most powerful men in the region, Presidents Marcos of the Philippines and Suharto of Indonesia.

So Carrian was born. Ten years after arriving in Hong Kong, Tan was employing 50,000 people and making $150 million profit a year. He bought one of the most prized buildings in Hong Kong's Central district, in 1980, for an enormous sum, and in the following year he took over Laker Airways. But in 1982, after two dazzling years, Carrian faltered and revealed cash problems. It needed a $60 million infusion of capital. The Hongkong Bank led the rescue package. But the total debts proved to be more than $1.2 billion, and evidence of systematic fraud began to surface. A banker who had been a key figure in Carrian's obtaining credit from a Malaysian bank was strangled with his bathrobe belt in a Hong Kong hotel bathroom. One of Carrian's legal advisers, an Englishman, committed suicide in his own swimming pool. The case became the grisliest in Hong Kong memory, dragging on and on, with little possibility of it all being satisfactorily unravelled.

George Tan's flamboyance and breezy enjoyment of his brief spell of fame and power was renowned. He kept six Rolls-Royces in his drive, and more than forty diamond-encrusted gold watches in his drawer. He carried wads of HK$1,000 notes in his back pocket, and when he threw parties for his own staff, the bill could reach $300,000.

To his credit, he was a workaholic more than a socialite. He was not one for the round of business parties and official receptions. He worked an eighteen-hour day, saying by way of explanation that it was, after all, 'a twenty-four hour world'. For travelling he had Singapore, Tonga and Paraguay passports, although his own taste and his business problems abroad kept him at home in Hong Kong. Europeans loved his swagger, his self-confidence, his ease with money. 'He had a magic about him,' a British banker confessed. 'He was the most articulate Hong Kong Chinese I have ever met.' Tan's philosophy was that, 'If you laugh together, you can make money together.' He certainly made many Hong Kong businessmen and bankers laugh with him, but they paid for it afterwards with tears.

There were honest Malaysian and Singaporean Chinese who returned to Hong Kong, such as K. C. Yeo who was sent to attend Hong Kong University but stayed on afterwards, marrying Sir Robert Hotung's daughter, Florence, and rising in the Hong Kong civil service. From Thailand came Vincent Lo's father in the 1930s and C. P. Wong, the creator of the Stelux watch empire in Hong Kong. When the Burmese government nationalised Xu Simin's company in the 1960s, he returned to China, only to find himself caught up in the Cultural Revolution. Not until 1976 could he get out again, to Hong Kong – of course! There he became a valuable publicist for China, and yet a critic of its human rights record.

The roll-call of overseas Chinese returnees would not be complete without Vietnam, which for its own well-known reasons has disgorged many thousands of unwanted Chinese into Hong Kong. One of them is Louisa Tung, whose history illustrates the newest phase of the overseas Chinese story, that of the globalisation of individuals. Louisa Tung works for an American bank in Hong Kong. She was born in China, raised in Vietnam, and educated in London. Her favourite authors are E. M. Forster and Virginia Woolf. She was educated in a Catholic school but considers herself Buddhist. She speaks six languages – Vietnamese, French, English and three Chinese languages. Of such polycultural stuff are the overseas Chinese increasingly made.

Hong Kong society is thus multilayered, like a good French stew. Each new layer flavours what has gone before, and vice versa. It is a mutually stimulating and mutually beneficial arrangement, with the additional advantage that the choice of Hong Kong by so many overseas Chinese as a base, information and banking centre and family headquarters, gives China itself a further interest in the territory. Hong Kong has become an indispensable place from which China can maintain contact with overseas Chinese everywhere, and keep tapping their capital (and patriotism). Hong Kong's utility to China is both intrinsic, for reasons only to do with the Hong Kong population, and also external in this sense of assisting China to meet its need to know what the overseas Chinese are doing and thinking, and if possible to influence them in directions beneficial to China.

Unfortunately, the same logic works the other way. When Lee Wing Tat toured the United States in August 1989 to lobby Hong Kong students and Hong Kong emigrants there in the cause of mainland freedom, he recognised that Hong Kong itself can recruit the overseas Chinese as potential allies *against* China, especially in contributing funds and personnel in the international campaign for a democratic Hong Kong with genuine autonomy from China. Until Tiananmen Square, Hongkongers had undervalued this particular significance of the overseas Chinese. Now the overseas Chinese have their affiliations competed for by both China and Hong Kong.

If the 25 million overseas Chinese were ever organised to act like a body, in the Zionist mould, they would have enough bargaining power to exert a strong influence on Chinese government policy – on trade and economic policies, for example, or civil liberties issues. But they are neither united nor regimented, knowing that such activities would create a violent backlash among their Southeast Asian hosts apprehensive about possible organised control of their affairs by China through the newly confident overseas Chinese. The most that these timorously circumspect ex-peasants will do is to shift their investments and the site of their children's education further away from China towards the West, as they have already begun to do. Even that is sometimes arranged by, in or through Hong Kong. All the more cause for Beijing to desire the continued existence of Hong Kong and access to its network of overseas Chinese contacts.

Chapter 5

Hong Kong's Gathering Identity

It would be something of a miracle if all these 6 million Chinese, of different provenances and vintages, and stamped by varying degrees of subjection to alien cultures, were to cohere in a harmonious fellowship simply because they shared the same few square miles of British colonial territory, the same cramped worm's-eye view of the Union Jack. Until 1949, when an ideological gulf first yawned between the Chinese residents of Hong Kong and their original motherland, and intercourse became for the first time narrowly restricted, nobody talked of 'belonging' to Hong Kong – except, perhaps, a few wealthy property owners and the small Eurasian community which had nowhere else to go. If you had asked the average resident of Hong Kong before 1949, he would most likely have said that he belonged 'to China'.

But since 1949 it has been a very different story, with a steady increase in the proportion of the Hong Kong born. In 1965, Singapore became a republic, something that aroused no little envy in a society which considered itself to be in a similar situation, though twice as sharp. Bishop Ronald Hall talked about Singapore to a middle school that year. He urged his young audience to become philoptolists, a word of which they had never heard, but which he defined for them as people who love their city, 'the great international city-state of Hong Kong' which by the end of the century would be 'the most influential and significant city in all Southeast Asia'. Two years later the Cultural Revolution effectively closed the China option in the psychology of most people in Hong Kong. After almost a decade of pointless violence and damaging anarchy on the mainland, these commuters from China to the West were ready to be welded into a single corporate being of Hong Kong – especially the Shanghainese, who had avoided final commitment until then. After 1967, 'Shanghai was in Hong Kong to stay'.

The next milestone was the Sino-British agreement of 1984 for Hong Kong's reversion. A couple of years before the agreement, over 60 per cent of Hong

Kong residents said they were Chinese. Only one-third called themselves Hongkongers, and a quarter admitted to roots in Britain. Afterwards, in 1988, almost 80 per cent agreed to having a strong sense of belonging to Hong Kong. Now that Hong Kong's future was something to be negotiated with China, Hong Kong identity acquired for the first time a political value.

The moving, often painful family reunions which Hongkongers experienced with mainland relatives under the open door policy in the 1980s after forty years apart considerably sharpened their self-image. One Hong Kong journalist arrived for the first time at his family's Guangdong village and tracked down his cousin and uncle. The latter was sick, the younger man feeding chickens. Shabby and poverty-stricken, they had no visible connection with the former scholar-gentry family from which they had all sprung in the 1940s. After many hours of listening, and drinking in how his brothers and sisters were faring in several continents as high-earning modern professionals under the wing of First Uncle who had fled to Hong Kong in 1948, the cousin gazed at his visitor through tearful eyes, and blurted out: 'I wish First Uncle had taken me as well.'

The separate identity of Hong Kong gains strength from such experiences. The difficulty is, where to pitch it? It is surely more than a municipal identity, yet falls short of a national one. Another problem is to put a content to it. Of what precisely does this Hong Kong identity consist? It is clearly a mixture of Chinese and British or Western ingredients, and one can try to list these, even if quantification is difficult. What is Chinese in the Hong Kong personality? Biology must come first. The people are physically Chinese, and what is more, they betray typical Chinese racial attitudes. When an African delegation arrived, and the government asked a senior member of Legco to entertain them, he is said to have refused, with the remark: 'You may have to, but I do not.' A manager in a Hong Kong construction firm observed, 'We find it impossible to mix Hong Kong workers and workers from other parts of Asia.' At the same time, there is the subconscious pull of the European physical type which leads, in Hong Kong as in Japan and China itself, to the cult of Caucasian features, and the prominence of Eurasian pop singers and models. Interestingly, the question of Chinese race has suddenly acquired significance in the run-up to 1997, given the ambiguities of Chinese nationality laws. An Englishman with a Chinese wife recently tried to register their son in his Chinese name, but was told that only 'persons of Chinese race' could bear Chinese names on their Hong Kong birth certificates. The Englishman complained that his son was apparently declared to be 'some kind of genetic misfit who has slipped down a crack between two single "races" '. He demanded to know the criteria for being of Chinese race, but of course got no satisfaction.

Confucian social attitudes are another legacy which almost every Chinese in Hong Kong has acquired in some degree or other. The protection of self-respect in social situations – 'face' – is frequently observed, for example in students who hate to answer questions in tutorials. The traditional family structure is now somewhat fragmented. As early as 1970, an opinion survey by university sociologists showed that if a young man's parents told him not to take up a job that had been offered him, one-third would disobey and take the job, almost 60 per cent would argue and try to convince the parents of their own viewpoint but would accept their final decision, and only 6 per cent said they would obey their parents without question and turn the job down. Young individuals are forging more freedom for themselves, particularly women, whose status is much better than before. So there is now a middle-aged 'sandwich generation' which treats its own parents in the old way, neither contradicting them nor arguing with them, but allows its own children to enjoy their freedom, thus 'losing out' at both ends.

One could go on listing features of the Chinese personality which are present in Hong Kong, but there would be an equally long list of ways in which Hong Kong society differs from that in China. Lau Siu-kai of the Chinese University in Hong Kong lists these differences as follows: (1) there is in Hong Kong more social and interpersonal trust, personal freedom, civil liberty and social and political tolerance; (2) there is more tolerance of social conflict, less fatalism and less egalitarianism; (3) economics are distinguished from politics and are accepted as being non-egalitarian, the capitalist system being fully endorsed; (4) Hongkongers expect fair treatment from government and are less frightened by it; and (5) law is respected and distinguished from politics.

The written ideographic language is something that is shared by Hong Kong and China, but the spoken language divides and perplexes Hong Kong. An early post-war debate concerned the desire to elevate the Cantonese language to a higher status *vis-à-vis* English in Hong Kong. There was a language movement of some strength among Hong Kong intellectuals in the early 1970s. Dr Denny Huang, the chief organiser of the campaign, took 330,000 signatures to No. 10 Downing Street on one occasion. Now that British rule has had a term set to it, Cantonese is beginning to infiltrate into corners of public life previously dominated by English. Shareholders of public companies are able to win votes for instant English–Cantonese translation at company meetings. About 120 government schools now teach in Chinese instead of English.

But this is partly because of the falling away of standards of English teaching. A Hong Kong University professor has described the English spoken in Hong Kong as 'the worst English in the world', and Shell was shocked to discover that its recruits in Beijing spoke better English than those in Hong Kong. The university revealed that it might have to switch to Cantonese after more than a century of the English medium, and wanted to add a compulsory fourth year to the undergraduate course to allow for extra English language tuition. Banks and commercial companies are sponsoring radio and TV English language programmes. They are openly backed by the communist corporations, which acknowledge that standards of English need to be improved if Hong Kong is to maintain its position as an international financial and commercial centre.

Meanwhile, there is a third candidate for the ear of Hong Kong in the shape of Mandarin or *putonghua*, the *lingua franca* in the People's Republic but not native to the vast majority of Hongkongers. It was taught for a time as a subsidiary subject in government schools, but with no demand and a shortage of teachers it was dropped. Only at the beginning of the 1980s was it reinstated, and now Mandarin has become more acceptable. In earlier decades Hongkongers used to recoil on hearing it, whereas today they at least try to understand it. Recent surveys at the Chinese University find sixth formers positive and favourable towards Mandarin. One teacher there predicts the arrival of a polyglottic situation in 1997, with Mandarin used for politics and administrative affairs, English for business, and Cantonese for the family and intimate relations. It is a mighty burden for young language learners to bear and a heavy price to pay for identity.

Patriotism is contagious in any language and it is certainly part of the Chinese personality in Hong Kong. A recent poll had almost 80 per cent of a sample of Hongkongers proud to be Chinese, while more than 60 per cent were convinced that Chinese culture was the best on earth. The events of the 1980s, especially the agreement for Hong Kong to revert to China, have made Hongkongers susceptible to nationalist appeals by China. When the Hong Kong government unwisely cornered itself into a position of inviting Hongkongers to express an opinion about their future and their future ties with China, David Tang, whose family pedigree in Hong Kong yields to none, remarked, 'We are all Chinese and it would be a loss of face, as well as unpatriotic, for us to express a bias against the motherland in favour of foreign colonial rule' – whatever the weighty practical advantages of that foreign rule.

The knowledge that Hong Kong would return to China brought out feelings of patriotism from surprising quarters. Regence Lam, the fashion designer trained at St Martin's School and the Royal College of Art, was moved to explore Chinese culture. 'I am beginning to feel a sense of belonging,' he remarked. 'I don't really have any roots, but now that we see more of the mainland Chinese I feel a need to identify.'

The easy way out for Hongkongers itching to express solidarity with China, without going so far as to say that they would like to follow the People's Republic system, is to embrace a Chinese cause that has little relevance to Hong Kong and can do no damage. Japan is a perfect target for this vicarious patriotism. In the early 1970s Hongkongers demonstrated against the Japanese claim to the Senkaku or Tiaoyutai Islands considered by Chinese to be part of China. It was a 'safe' kind of demonstration, in the sense that Britain had no view, China and Taiwan both welcomed it, and Japan could not stop it. Next came demands for war reparation payments, and demonstrations against the revision of Japanese textbooks to downplay Japan's responsibility in the war against China. At this point, in the early 1980s, Japanese department stores in Hong Kong were damaged, posters were carried saying 'Attack the Japanese', and as many as 10,000 Hongkongers demonstrated in Victoria Park.

There was worse to come. In 1989 the Zueguang (Blood and Light) Dare-to-Die Squad threatened to kill Japanese individuals in Hong Kong in revenge for the atrocities of the war forty-five years earlier. The Japanese consul and business leaders had to take security measures. These various campaigns built on Hong Kong's own bitter memories of the war. One senior Hong Kong Chinese in the government has never invited a Japanese to his house, and never gone to any Japanese reception, in all these forty-five years, because his anger over Japanese aggression and atrocities has never subsided. To feel anti-Japanese is a vivid yet cost-free advertisement that you are Chinese, a Hong Kong Chinese maybe, but Chinese all the same.

Another strand in this identification with China concerns research and scholarship. When the Chinese University of Hong Kong was founded in 1963, it housed Hong Kong's first Institute of Chinese Studies, including a section for contemporary studies and relations with Southeast Asia. The Chinese University caters for intellectuals who feel that their real roots are in China, and that more Chinese thought and tradition needs to be tapped. for Hong Kong's nourishment. Some see it as a candidate to be the world's centre of Chinese learning precisely because, taking full advantage of Hong Kong's unique role, it disregards the ideological divisions which so distract both mainland and Taiwan institutions.

Hong Kong became from roughly 1950 to 1980 the main centre for China-watching, since China normally excluded foreign newsmen or scholars. Like 'solemn gulls on Victoria's Peak', as *The Daily Telegraph* called them, a dozen or two sinologists or specialist writers studied all the available evidence from or about China in order to provide a verdict or analysis, as space-watchers did of the moon. Even the Leningrad Academy of Social Sciences subscribed to the US Consulate-General's *Survey of the Mainland Press*, better informed than anything in the Soviet Union. Father Ladany of *China News Analysis* was the first to subscribe in Hong Kong to mainland magazines and newspapers, central as well as provincial. After 1959 they were stopped, except for *People's Daily* and *Red Flag* which never revealed anything bad, so Ladany joined the BBC and its American counterpart in monitoring Chinese radio broadcasts (the Chinese priest who sent him papers after the ban was jailed).

China-watching was mostly for non-Chinese but many local Chinese were employed as translators, and Zhang Guotao and Carson Chang helped to produce, with American funding, a useful anti-communist magazine in the early post-war years. After that the British became more careful so that the universities hid their contemporary sinology under such labels as 'Centre for Asian Studies'. Father Ladany swears there was once a Taiwan man gathering information on China in the same room as a People's Republic representative researching on Taiwan. In the 1980s, China-watching became split between Hong Kong and a more welcoming Beijing.

Now that Hongkongers have lived through the Tiananmen Square massacre of 1989, their identification with China has been badly shaken. On reflection, however, it might be more true to say that, while their identification with the Chinese government and ruling party has come unstuck, their fellow feeling for the students and intellectuals, and for the younger generation which will determine the future of China, has intensified.

Yet Hongkongers remain surprisingly ignorant about China in factual terms. When the British first began in the early 1980s, to negotiate with Beijing about Hong Kong's future, only one Hongkonger that I know of took the trouble to go and work in China for a year in order to find out what made the prospective new masters tick. 'When I first went to live in China in 1983,' said David Tang, 'I could not understand its people's attitude or thinking, even though we were both Chinese. I felt a complete foreigner. Yet after only a year, I appreciated their point of view and, whether I agreed with them or not, I at least understood them.' David Tang was the exception, and most Hongkongers' image of China is formed either as tourists, as newspaper readers imbibing sensational accounts of Chinese events, or as children learning from parents or grandparents the horror stories of an earlier era.

Hong Kong's Chineseness is not a cut and dried affair. As Dr L. Z. Yuan once declared, the Hong Kong Chinese are 'the most modernised Chinese community in the world', but that did not, he insisted, mean 'Westernised'. The rich Chinese cultural heritage would not be swept away by the Westernising or modernising process. Hong Kong Chinese did, however, enjoy the freedom to choose and discard, adopt and adapt, those Western life-styles and ways of thinking which could comfortably and usefully be grafted on to the Chinese tradition. What, specifically, have Hongkongers selected from the Western supermarket? Maria Tam, one of Hong Kong's most capable politicians, says, 'I am emotionally Chinese, but rationally British.' To have a Chinese heart but a British brain comes very near to the much earlier slogan of mixing Chinese culture with Western science. The two halves of life do not divide so neatly, of course. But the aspiration is widely shared. In political terms, it is what Lydia Dunn calls 'the magic mix of British administration and Chinese entrepreneurial energy and flair', which together create Hong Kong's 'unique society'.

What most distinguishes the Chinese political system from the Western is the lack of any concept of the individual in the Western sense, which necessarily means that there is no concept of the equality of individuals – and thus no rule of law. The Chinese tradition is hierarchical and centres on authority, not freedom. Dr Michael Bond of the Psychology Department at the Chinese University of Hong Kong attributes this difference largely to contrasting methods of bringing up children.

Western parents liberate children to be able to think for themselves and to be ready for self-management, self-protection and self-assertion. This kind of childhood enables the adult to deal with conflict in an open and candid way, without excessively damaging his or her relationships. Westerners are not frightened of conflict.

Chinese children, on the other hand, have their values heavily dinned into them from an early age, so that they flinch from conflict. Chinese culture does not provide a means of resolving conflicts between equals, and Chinese caught in that position usually seek first to establish which one is boss (and the boss is always allowed to win). Among other things, this means that it does not come easily to the Chinese to run a parliament or to accept the concept of loyal opposition. You cannot be both loyal and an opponent in Chinese culture.

But it is precisely this family solidarity which has enabled Hong Kong to survive its post-war experience. When your nephew arrives from China with no job and no money, wants a bed in your hallway, and offers to act as your nightwatchman, if you would just pay him a few dollars while he gets on his feet, then you accommodate him. This is how many Hong Kong successes, corporate and personal, have begun.

Dr Lau Siu-kai of the Chinese University of Hong Kong believes that modernisation is producing what he calls utilitarianistic familism, meaning that Hongkongers still place their family interest above those of society at large, or of the state or other individuals, but those family interests are now increasingly complex and sophisticated precisely because the family members are interacting in many different ways with society or the state or other individuals – in factories, in trade, in education, in taxation, etc. In other words, the family bundle of interests begins to rise to the point where it overlaps more and more with those larger entities of state and government. Family loyalties no longer challenge the state so directly – and yet the individual remains unliberated.

The Westernisation that seems to make some Chinese so easy for foreigners to get on with is not usually achieved at the expense of these basic Chinese characteristics. 'Westernisation is like a suit of clothes for most Chinese,' says

Dr Bond, 'that expands your range of contact, of access, of opportunity.' But underneath there remains an inner being which is not affected, embracing family ties and duties, sexual propriety, moderation and a kind of social restraint.

Vincent Lo, chairman of the Shui On group, and one of Hong Kong's outstanding younger millionaires, is not untypical. His father 'would not let an opportunity go by without teaching us something about business, or . . . how to behave ourselves. We were constantly lectured . . . We were all hoping he would stay away from the house, because every time he walked into the room we all trembled.' Vincent Lo knows what is meant by 'large family': he is aware of 600 individuals who are members of his. When he himself joined the family firm, he did not enjoy it, because: 'It is very much a traditional Chinese family business where father makes all the decisions.' Eventually, he resolved to leave and get a job in another company but his mother talked him out of it, saying that he ought not to work for others. She convinced her husband to lend their son $1,200 to start his own business. Now Lo runs a multimillion-dollar construction empire, earning more than his father ever did.

Businessmen are practical and quite capable of being specific about biculturalism. T. K. Ann, the intellectual among the Shanghai industrialists, said, 'There are three untold laws in Hong Kong. Firstly, bank notes can buy gold. Secondly, the Inland Revenue never comes to search your house, they just write to you. And thirdly, the police don't come at midnight without a warrant.' When the final history of China's modernisation is written, we may be surprised to find that Perry Mason was as influential as Henry Kissinger, in the sense that his courtroom dramas from American television, which are relayed over Hong Kong stations to millions of viewers in Guangdong province, captivate their audiences by the sheer lack of arbitrariness, the openness and absence of political predetermination, that attend the Western legal process. In Hong Kong, said Ann proudly, 'We have a common law system. There is judgment by argument.'

This is in the context, as a Chinese newspaper columnist put it, that Hong Kong is 'the only Chinese society that . . . lived through an ideal never realised at any other time in the history of Chinese societies – a time when no man had to live in fear of the midnight knock on the door'.

The appreciation by the Hong Kong Chinese of their civil liberties and rule of law under the colonial yoke needs no further demonstration. But the enjoyment of a rule of law is not necessarily carried over into individualistic behaviour as such, and the Chinese borrow less of that than Westerners expect. To borrow those clothes would mean losing the benefits as well as the drawbacks of the large family system which pampers the Chinese individual from cradle to grave.

In one area of life this particular tension has caused grave problems, and that is over nationality. In pre-war and early post-war years, the British actively encouraged ethnic Chinese who took British nationality to think and act as British nationals and not as Chinese. This ethnic dissociation was reinforced by the fact that British nationality made it easier to get into certain professions. The trauma of having to renounce one's nationality for another, very different one has been severely aggravated by Britain's new reverse policy of telling such British nationals of Chinese ethnic descent that they no longer have the full status of British nationals, can never settle in Britain, and should make their peace with Chinese citizenship once again (see Chapter 20 below).

Hong Kong has to be considered, for all these reasons, as a bicultural society. An important turning point was 1949. Before then, the middle class used to send its children to good universities in China, like St John's University in Shanghai. The communist victory changed that and nobody wanted to risk their children – or their children's future acceptance in the international capitalist world – by sending them to communist institutions. One might have expected the Taiwan universities to step into the breach. But the Guomindang was so politically aggressive, applying such merciless pressure on 'neutral' Chinese to declare their anti-communism, that Hong Kong parents were equally repelled, and so the big waves of Hong Kong students flowed for the first time into the neutral West, to North America, Australia and Britain. The result was to turn off some of the Chinese taps, and turn on many new Western ones, tilting the balance of the Hong Kong personality towards the West.

'I am a product of the belief in a bicultural society,' said Jean May Wong, a ballet dancer. 'I like Chinese dance as well as classical ballet. I was in a unique situation because I could understand both. It is the same with Chinese and Western paintings. It is unique in Hong Kong, which is really a melting pot where East meets West.'

A few years ago the American correspondent Stanley Karnow found Hong Kong 'turning into a bicultural community with a singular yet somewhat undefinable identity of its own'. In the 1960s, he went on, Westerners and Chinese had lived apart with little socialising. A British lawyer arriving in Hong Kong at the end of the 1950s as a young clerk was told by his boss that marrying an Asian woman would ruin his career. Today, half the senior partners in that firm have Chinese wives. Chinese are no longer ashamed when their women have affairs with Americans. 'Hong Kong's prosperity,' Karnow concluded, 'has put the attractions of Westernisation within the reach of the colony's rising Chinese middle class.' Jan Morris noticed how the new younger generation of Chinese have 'achieved some synthesis of their own, freed from their own conventions, but by no means subservient to ours'.

There are plenty of critics to say that trying to be good at two cultures means finishing second rate in each. Listen to Tsim Tak-lung, about his life in Hong Kong after returning from seven years in Britain:

> The sense of aesthetics I've acquired . . . is foreign, not Chinese. The music I listen to and the movies I see are foreign, not Chinese. And I am painfully aware of the fact that in the world that we live in, the centres of change are London, Paris and New York. They set trends in fashion, art, music and most other forms of human activity. We get everything second-hand . . . Cultural imperialism bothers me. I believe there is a lot of resentment against this sort of thing amongst educated Chinese. I can see there are a lot of advantages to being Westernised, but not at the expense of one's dignity.

A social activist in his thirties, Fung Ho-lup, reproached Hong Kong teenagers for having 'no positive social values. They have no respect for any authority, but won't take sides in any social debates. They just don't care for anyone or anything. It is very hard to change such attitudes which are a bad mixture of Western individualism and the Chinese tradition of not bothering about anyone else's problems.' A former Vice-Chancellor of Hong Kong University complained about the 'ugly Hongkongian', thick-skinned and shallow-rooted: 'Both Eastern and Western cultures tend to be shallow here, and thus we take on the worst aspects of the West while retaining the least desirable aspects of the East – litter in public places, jumping queues, using bad language, pushing and jostling, are all part of daily life now.'

The easy way out is for a young Hongkonger to say that he is not a Westerner but doesn't want anything to do with the Chinese mainland either, so he projects himself purely as a Hongkonger. It is a unique amalgam, but the identity has to be worn with circumspection. As Lydia Dunn often repeats, 'we are not masters of our own destiny and never can be'. Hongkongers must therefore put up with such irritations as not having an easy answer for immigration forms. Hong Kong is not a political entity. 'I am neither British nor Chinese', a typical Hongkonger expostulates when asked to state his nationality. Such things are the more irritating in the knowledge of Hong Kong's economic success. Karnow concluded that Hong Kong had 'turned colonialism upside down'. Instead of oppressing the natives, Hong Kong's British imperial masters preside over the maintenance of law and order so that the 'natives' can make lots of money.

So Hong Kong finds part of its identity in opposing British rule, at least in principle. 'Any Chinese,' said a teacher in 1982, 'who admits that our prosperity is due to the British rule is belittling his own race.' There was a profound sense of alienation on this account in the late 1960s, when students made it clear that they felt no sense of belonging to Hong Kong because it was all for the benefit of the UK. 'Colonialism', a local journalist wrote of Hongkongers in 1988, 'has taken away their sense of being Chinese. They need to build up their identity as Chinese.' Along with the acceptance of the constructive parts of Western rule, like civil liberty, there is still a revulsion against authority with a white face. Now the Commissioner of Police is a local Chinese, but the *Yellowthread Street* TV series shows how ingrained is the myth of the moral authority and physical drive of the young white-face chasing the Chinese villains, whom Chinese passers-by do not wish to antagonise by helping the police.

Hong Kong must become Chinese in the long run, but whether that 'Chinese' will encompass 'Cantonese' or not depends on the future development of China itself, and whether the decentralizing process will go so far as to allow a degree of Cantonese autonomy within which Hong Kong would happily nest. That was the burden of the language movement in the early 1970s, which under the circumstances was a cover for a 'nationalist' movement. To lobby for the Cantonese language inevitably took its standard bearers into the realms of Cantonese nationalism, and even revived echoes of an independent Cantonese republic.

But Hong Kong, which is a British spelling, will become after 1997 Xiang-gang (the Mandarin version) rather than Heung Gong (the Cantonese pronunciation). Is it possible, perhaps, that Hong Kong may relate to China rather as the Welsh do to England? That is the attractive analogy proposed by Lynn Pan. But Hong Kong is smaller than Wales, China is bigger than England, and the Hongkongers have very recently left China whereas the Welsh marches with England go back many centuries. The day when many Hong Kong Chinese are installed in positions of state and professional leadership in Beijing, in the way that the Welsh shine so brightly in England (or in Hong Kong for that matter), is the day that all our predictions about China can safely be dropped into Hong Kong harbour.

Somehow or another, China will fill the gaps in Hong Kong's identity. 'When China takes over,' Eddie Lau, the fashion designer predicted, 'we will have an identity to match with our skills. China will need designers to reach out to the world, and they will find them here.' But that was before Tiananmen Square. The students who were killed there in 1989 carried to their graves the early hopes of 6 million Hongkongers to have a rational and civilised role in modernising China – so that it could become once again a country of which even the bicultural hybrids could be proud.

Hong Kong has forged a vulnerable, blended and fast-changing identity, as a largely modernised, slightly Westernised Chinese community. It can light the way that stretches ahead of China, but knows that China's dinosaurian doubts could derail both the reconnaissance car and the main convoy.

Chapter 6

Colonial Chinese Politics

Post-war Hong Kong was transformed by the relentless waves of new refugees arriving. Most places assimilating refugees can treat them as a more or less welcome minority. Hong Kong was unique in being taken over by a refugee majority ignorant of its new host territory and lacking any roots in it. The population of 600,000 at the time of the Japanese surrender was ten years later distended to 2,500,000, and it has doubled again since then. Only three in five of the people you see on the street today were actually born in Hong Kong.

Many of the refugees thought of Hong Kong as only a temporary shelter from which they could go on to a new life beyond the edges of the Chinese world. The Shanghainese parents of the ballet dancer Jean May Wong fled to Hong Kong in 1949 intending to settle in Brazil, for example, and the more pessimistic Shanghai textile industrialists set up mills in places like Argentina and Taiwan, just in case Hong Kong also fell to the Communists. Hong Kong is a port of call, not necessarily the final destination. Its Chinese residents therefore keep elsewhere a good part of whatever wealth they can accumulate – and may eventually follow it. The place is subject to a permanent flight of capital. It was normal to keep a third or even two-thirds of your money in Zurich, New York, London or Sydney, and to put the rest into Hong Kong bank deposits (equally split, as a further precaution, between the communist and foreign banks).

Some refugees did indeed keep going. Jacky Chan, the *kung fu* film star, born in Hong Kong of immigrants so poor that they almost sold him at birth (for $26!), was whisked off to Australia at the age of 6 because his father got a job there as a cook. Others intended to go back to China once the bad time, the political oppressor, the spectre of famine, or whatever else they had fled from, was gone. The grandfather of the senior civil servant Donald

Tsang went back to Canton and worked on the railways when his Wellington Street furniture shop went bust in the 1930s.

This is the other face of the refugee syndrome, and it can be equally destabilising. When things are bad on the mainland, people crowd into Hong Kong for temporary relief, employment and food. When things are bad in Hong Kong, or in the great big international capitalist system of which it is a part, they trudge back to the farmlands of Guangdong where they can at least wrest an agricultural living. In the 1840s, the entire Chinese community left in a body for the mainland, in protest against the Governor's passing a law to register them and charge a fee for it. In the 1890s, half the population abandoned Hong Kong because of an outbreak of bubonic plague. There was an exodus in the First World War and another (including Donald Tsang's grandfather) in the great depression of the 1930s. The most recent recurrence came in 1941 when the Japanese army conquered Hong Kong and half its people thought it prudent to pack their bags and go to ground in the interior of China.

The feeling of not being sure whether you are waiting for the next train to somewhere else, or will be staying put for the rest of your life, is an edgy one. This essential transience is the reason why Sir Alexander Grantham, the second post-war Governor, when chided by British liberals for not strapping Hongkongers into the express train for democracy, explained that they had 'voted with their feet' for the status quo in Hong Kong as a deliverance from whatever else prevailed in China. They formed, in the words of Dr Lau Siu-kai, professor of sociology at the Chinese University of Hong Kong, a self-selected group who 'voluntarily subscribe to colonial rule'. They must be presumed to have come to Hong Kong to take advantage of its administrative and commercial system and opportunities. Far from clamouring for political independence from a colonial overlord who had unjustly conquered them, they sought the help of the British colonial administration to save their skins and livelihoods.

'Colonial rule,' wrote Dr Joseph Cheng in his *Political Modernisation in Hong Kong*, 'was an affront to national pride, but when compared with the rampant warlordism, chaos, corruption and the abuse of power in China in the first half of this century it was quite acceptable.'

So the railway station analogy found appeal. The Financial Secretary in the 1950s noted that Hong Kong indeed resembled a railway station, where the people in charge should look after the small core of permanent staff but did not have to shower benefits on passengers merely passing through. Professor Stuart Kirby of Hong Kong University elaborated the image by saying that demanding self-government for Hong Kong was like asking for the self-government of a railway station. People wishing political reforms on Hong Kong should stop to think what it might be like to live in a place where almost every other person was born somewhere else. 'We are all refugees', said Ronald Li, 'whether we came here fleeing the tyranny of the Qing dynasty of the last century, or the revolution of 1949, or the . . . Cultural Revolution. We all have only one thing in common, we are fed up with politics.'

The politics they got was a semi-Victorian plumed-hat British colonialism with no election nonsense. But at least it came with the rule of law, and for that alone most Chinese were very ready to swallow their pride. On their side, the refugees brought with them the Chinese political tradition. They had never experienced the development of representative government and they were socially trained to defer to authority. That predetermined a set of attitudes towards British political ideas which took Hong Kong along a road quite different from that of other British colonies. A third significant factor in their political behaviour once inside Hong Kong was an indifference to ideology.

'Never mind about capitalism or communism, I never speak about that,' said Henry Fok, a wealthy Hong Kong property developer who is very popular with Chinese officials. 'The fact is that the way of doing things in Hong Kong is much superior to that in China, and the Chinese who come here agree. China is so bureaucratic, they try to do everything in the same way. Even the lunch menus in the hotels are the same . . .' Hong Kong's lukewarmness for dogma goes back to the fact that China had no tradition of religious strife or exclusivity. The Chinese saw religions as overlapping in a population basically agnostic. Communist bankers in Hong Kong have always attended their friends' church weddings, Catholic businessmen drink Deng's health at receptions. Pragmatism prevails.

The religious affiliations in Hong Kong today involve a tiny fraction of the population. Much more important, in the popular mind, is simple superstition. Lucky numbers, lucky words, lucky names have a serious appeal even to the most intelligent and sophisticated people. A police superintendent's office boasts a *kwantai* shrine. Many buildings omit the thirteenth floor. Fortune-tellers and soothsayers earn good livings.

Take two famous examples of this, one pre-war and one post-war. Sooth-sayers told the millionaire Eu Tongsan in the 1930s that his life would be prolonged if he built three enormously extravagant follies, and so Euston, Eucliffe and Sirmio, Hong Kong's outstanding pieces of architectural frivolity, were constructed. Fifty years later George Tan of Carrian, whose murky company affairs occupied so much court time, would always ensure that the numbers involved in his business deals were lucky. Carrian's authorised capital, for example, was HK$998 million, and when Tan bought Gammon House (his big deal) it was also for HK$998 million. He would use different coloured pens and desks facing different ways at different times of day, following geomantic principles, and he had his fortune told every day of his life. If you live and work in a society so respectful of the occult, you get things done more effectively by swimming with the stream, so it is no surprise that Sir David Akers Jones, who has spent more years dealing with the New Territories than any other colonial officer, regularly consulted a leading almanac authority.

The laws of geomancy – *feng shui* in the Cantonese – are taken most earnestly. Why refuse to alter the plan or layout of a building if it might bring bad luck on the heads of those who will work or live there? Banks and offices frequently rearrange their furniture and mirrors, the angle of their escalators and the surfaces of their architecture, to improve their luck. When the Hongkong Bank put up its futuristic new building, its chosen geomancer, Lung King Chuen, resited the escalators and interior plants in order to counter the negative influences which he detected from the diagonal bracing. He also decided the day and hour of the opening.

The Bank of China had similar problems for its new headquarters, which local *feng shui* specialists said had too many sharp edges and triangles. I. M. Pei, the American Chinese architect, confessed to friends that he had never realised how seriously this kind of thing was taken in Hong Kong. In his native North China no one had ever heard of *feng shui*. And the problem has spread to England, where Knight Frank and Rutley prevailed on its Hong Kong associates to send basic instructions about *feng shui* after an Eaton Place property was rejected by a Hong Kong Chinese client on geomantic grounds.

The political spin-off of such pragmatism and scepticism is ideological neutrality. Successful entrepreneurs like Henry Fok will attribute their good fortune not to the concept of capitalism but to the specific rules and regulations of the British colonial administration. Others see no contradiction in wining and dining with communist officials. And this echoes the British instinct for tolerance in matters of ideology.

The one doctrinal dispute which strongly divides Chinese is more a conflict of factions and personal allegiances than of beliefs, namely that between communism and the Nationalist Party or Guomindang. The British always tried to avoid taking sides in this, while maintaining a correct working relationship with whichever party held power across the border. The two antagonistic parties are not allowed to operate as such in Hong Kong, but in practice they have branches, offices and followers under different names.

The Guomindang used to be stronger in the early post-war years and was at the centre of the ugly riots of 1956. Guomindang supporters stuck portraits of Chiang Kai-shek on buildings on their 'national' day. Housing officials stopped them, saying that the glue would be difficult to remove from the government buildings in question, and that provoked a night of terror in the course of which a Swiss diplomat was killed. Yet the Guomindang has its uses for the Hong Kong government: in 1967, when the Communists were rioting, the government had the Guomindang provide protection for bus and tram drivers in order to crush a transport strike.

The Guomindang can still get a good muster of flags flying for its national day. And it still has control of one single locality in Hong Kong, called Rennie's Mill, where refugees wanting to go to Taiwan repair. But there is little new recruitment to the party and it is ready to evacuate in 1997.

The Communists have been more discreet, but obviously have a much greater capacity to affect events. Recently, they have had the task of 'selling' to Hongkongers the Communist Chinese sovereignty over Hong Kong, to which they must submit in 1997. In the course of this persuasion, some interesting irreverence towards Marxist ideology was revealed. Xu Jiatun, China's 'ambassador' to Hong Kong in the 1980s, declared that the changes which were needed in Hong Kong related to colonialism, not capitalism. There would be no class struggle or revolution.

'We unequivocally and unmistakeably declare our intention to maintain the capitalist system in Hong Kong,' he told the Society of Accountants in 1985. 'We must insist on it in the context of building the Chinese socialist system. Capitalism is a hard reality in many parts of the world; its historical vitality has yet to be exhausted . . . We still have a great deal to learn from the advanced scientific technology in capitalism and its administrative experience.' He hastened to add that faith in communism was not shaken by this. 'Rather it is only a recognition that the productive forces of capitalism are still quite alive and have contributions to make to human civilisation.' In 1988, Xu explained that capitalism was hardly born during Marx's lifetime. 'We used to believe that capitalism would soon die out. Now it seems that there is still room for development.'

In 1989, he argued that the 'anti-feudal ideological, cultural, political and economic achievements of capitalism' were of great practical significance for countries like China still haunted by residual feudalism. Modern capitalism had tidied up its act, responding to the labour movement and the growth of socialism. It had legislated against monopoly, introduced social welfare and adopted income distribution policies. 'Without the cultural inheritance of capitalism, there would be no socialism.' These remarks illuminate the lowly role which ideology plays in Chinese politics, helping Hong Kong to observe a beneficial neutrality. Xu lost favour in 1990 when he took 'unauthorised leave' in the USA, but his views are shared by many technocrats in China.

The Chinese tradition formulates for Hong Kong an ideal relationship between government and people, similar to that 'between parents and children, or between a shepherd and his flock', in the words of an official report of 1966 on local administration. This traditional concept does not contemplate the people's direct participation in either the organisation or the processes of government.

Politics do not have to be dictated by tradition, of course, but strong traditions affect the way people implement new systems, and may even sabotage such reforms. In a note of reservation to their 1966 report, Paul Tsui, the foremost post-war Hong Kong Chinese civil servant, with two English colleagues, spelled the problem out in detail:

> In most western democracies election from amongst candidates nominated by political parties by majority vote is the accepted way of selecting representatives of the people. Fear of loss of face by failure at the polls does not normally deter a candidate from standing for election, and the general acceptance by the public of the elective principle is a natural corrective of abuse of the system. In Hong Kong the position is entirely different, and it is doubtful whether popular representation at the present time will be successful in bringing forward the best qualified and most widely accepted citizens to participate in local administration. There is indeed a definite risk that a system based on popular representation as determined by ballot box elections could quickly become controlled by unscrupulous or corrupt power seekers.

At a more personal level, democracy can feel to a Chinese community like taking a pharmaceutical drug too strong for the human system and causing painful side-effects. This is how one young British-trained politician described it to me in 1989:

> People like myself and leaders of the democratic lobby may not view public debates and arguments in strong language as drastic. We still end up as friends, drinking and eating together. But 99 per cent of the population, who do not know who is who, or what we stand for, or what we are arguing about – and this 99 per cent includes the big businessmen, entrepreneurs and professionals – are being constantly bombarded with a sense of uncertainty and uneasiness. It only reminds people, who have had bitter experience of political conflict in China in the past, of what they actually went through.

A Hong Kong Chinese stockbroker compares Westminster democracy for Hong Kong with 'a class of ignorant boys teaching the schoolmaster mathematics'. He argues that the average man in the street, interviewed for an opinion poll or asked to give his vote on some issue, does not have the experience of running public life and has never had the responsibility for it. 'He will shrug his shoulders, what the hell, he's nothing to lose. But if you ask the people who have got properties here, who have got business here, who are responsible, 99 per cent would rather see the political system remain unchanged, with no free elections.' One may discount such a view to the extent that it is a 'big business' view. Big business certainly does not want to see its control of the important aspects of government policy handed over to left-leaning demagogues. But underneath this lurks a distinctive 'Confucian' view of life in which the people really do behave like sheep and a conscientious government really does look after them.

Chinese who are aware of how the West runs its affairs rationalise this by arguing that, where it matters, Hong Kong *is* free. Paul Cheng Ming-fun says: 'I have yet to find another place where one can have so much simple "freedom". Freedom to express one's opinion, freedom to come and go as one pleases, freedom to create wealth in a favourable tax environment so long as one is willing to work hard.' The basic right of self-determination is as well respected in Hong Kong as in some 'democratic' countries. A psychologist at the Chinese University of Hong Kong, nine years educated in the USA, believes that, 'the right to vote *per se* is less important than having the right people willing to serve in the government'. And Leung Shu-ki, a town-planner who spent ten years in Britain, states his preference: 'an elected government is a politically attractive idea, but a good-functioning government is more important'.

Even the younger generation, where one would expect some fading of these values, is cautious about moving towards electoral democracy. A series of opinion surveys in 1988 concluded that a strong majority of young people wished the government to treat the people like a father, wished political reform to be gradual, believed that the present political system was the best Hong Kong could hope for in practice, trusted the government and believed it to be good, and confessed finally that 'any kind of government would be all right if it gives me a minimum standard of living'. About a quarter of the young people polled would confine voting for the Legislative Council to intellectuals, and a third said that only intellectuals and professionals should vote for the Chief Executive after 1997. As a matter of principle, one youngster in three felt that the votes of intellectuals should have more weight than others.

These are not the attitudes that make for healthy Western-style democracy. This is why policies which might seem self-evident to British officials sometimes rebound from Chinese public opinion. There are constant complaints, for example, that the government is 'too soft' on criminals. The Chinese like to see miscreants severely punished, even executed, as a warning and deterrent to others. The government has still not abolished the death penalty (although in practice it always commutes the sentence) out of sensitivity to local opinion, which would be alarmed if murderers could never hang. Until the 1980s some perpetrators of lesser crimes were still flogged with a rattan cane as a punishment. The British, on their side, complain that local Chinese will not come forward as witnesses in court. Local social values rest on the notion that justice should be summary and unflinching, and not involve the innocent in causing loss of face to a criminal, which might later be avenged by himself or his family.

The Westminster model, it is frequently argued in Hong Kong, has not been successful outside the Anglo-Saxon countries. 'Will you please name me one country in Asia,' asks a businessman, 'which has democracy that works?' The textile magnate Cha Chi Ming testifies from his own personal experience running cotton mills in West Africa how democracy is premature in Africa and, he believes, in Hong Kong and China as well. Even England, he adds, allowed democracy to go too far, harming the people's interests by encouraging governments to spend more than they received, thus threatening national bankruptcy.

The other 'Confucian' states of East Asia all lagged behind in the practice of democracy. With one-party government in China and Taiwan; one-party monopoly of government in Japan and Singapore; autocratic government, with strong military overtones, in Korea. how could Hong Kong hope to be an exception?

It is true that Hong Kong's young have begun to take some Western political ideals on board. The later 1970s provide a watershed for this because of educational changes. The university used to be little more than a playground for the children of the gentry. But in the late 1960s, they began to be outnumbered by the first phalanxes of students whose parents were poor and outside the élite of their day. These young people soaked up the heady potions of idealistic democracy, and propagated them in their adult life after graduating. That was the origin of a new tension which is steadily altering the course of Hong Kong politics.

The gap between the old politics and the new is bridged in the person of Martin Lee, about whom almost every Hongkonger has strong but ambivalent feelings. He is admired as a calm, determined, courteous but obstinate critic of the government. When Legco is in session, it is televised, and everyone can see the duel of wits between the legislator Martin Lee and the various heads of department whom he engages (the exchanges are also seen by millions of communist Chinese viewers over the border who never dare to question their rulers in public). But those same admirers in Hong Kong would not like to see Martin Lee actually running the government. The prospect makes them uneasy. He is honest and incorrupt, but would he be able to conduct a government where secrecy, horse-trading and behind-the-curtains deals are part of the stock in trade?

There is still corruption in spite of the cleaning up, which has been more thorough than in other East Asian societies. This is an area of public life where Chinese family ideals come into direct conflict with British methods of justice. Insider trading on the Stock Exchange is hard to combat, as we have seen, because families are involved more than individuals. An opinion poll a few years ago showed that two out of every three Hongkongers would approve someone in a position of power using that power or status to benefit his relatives or friends.

In the 1970s, the government tried to restrain corruption, but it had to yield to local opinion in agreeing that the acceptance of entertainment would not be a crime, even if it were offered and accepted for corrupt reasons.

Businessmen and the rural *kaifong* leaders joined in insisting that anything else would interfere unreasonably with the normal conduct of business life. Because of the Confucian legacy, Chinese feel troubled if they cannot express their gratitude to those, including officials, who do something for them. It used only to be a commonplace in Hong Kong to make a payment to the fire brigade when it puts out a fire in your house. Where should the line be drawn?

Richard Medlycott, a young officer of the Hongkong Bank, approved credit for a jewellery company. The company gave him a gold watch to express its gratitude. He reported this to his superiors in the bank, and they said he could keep it. To refuse a gift in these circumstances would be a slap in the face for the donor, a loss of face which could be damaging for the bank. But corruption is a crime. Medlycott was prosecuted and acquitted, but the bank now places a limit on the value of gifts which its employees may receive, and this limit is of course known to prospective givers.

There are thousands of such cases. It was said, for example, of the notorious George Tan of Carrian Corporation, that, 'if you talked business with him, there would be a present on your desk by the time you got back to your office'. A successful import-export company manager was about to go to Japan on business some years ago. At a dinner given by one of his manufacturer clients, he mentioned that he had booked his passage through such and such travel agency, adding how much he would love to take his wife as well. An airline ticket for them both was delivered to his house the next day.

One more representative incident. A foreman was nailing a new sign on the outside wall of a factory when a policeman interrupted him. 'You realise,' the policeman said, 'that you are contravening the Building Regulations putting up that sign without a licence.' He was invited inside to discuss the problem, complimented on his vigilance and thanked for the warning – and as he left, he was slipped a small envelope. But minutes later he returned (it being impolite to open a 'present' in front of the donor), waving the envelope and murmuring in disgust, 'Only twenty!' A new envelope was quickly presented with a $50 note inside. 'If I did not pay him what he wanted,' the foreman explained afterwards, 'he would walk in during the night shift and find the women workers here. Or we might be in trouble the next time one of the vans unloads goods on to the pavement. It is cheaper to keep him sweet.'

The police are a perennial problem on this matter of corruption. 'Corruption in Hong Kong,' said a former Superintendent of Police, Ernest Hunt, 'is as natural as going to bed at night, as waking up in the morning and brushing your teeth. When I was there, about 95 per cent of the force was bent.' He should know, having allegedly made $500,000 out of corruption (and having been present, incidentally, when a firework was put into a suspect's anus as a stimulus to interrogation). He was gaoled for a year, but then turned Queen's evidence and spoke these comments from the comfort of Spanish exile.

Other police officers have explained that if you join the force in Hong Kong, you either get on the bus or run beside it (which is pretty exhausting), or, if you try to stop it, you get run over. Honest novices who try to refuse gifts can be sent to Coventry, and if they persist in their puritanism they usually resign. The general belief is that most Chinese police constables are corrupt, and more than half the officers, including the Britons. A judge investigating the question in the 1970s noted that the whole of Hong Kong operated on a commission basis. 'If even half of what is reported is true,' he concluded, 'I despair of the chances of any law enforcement agency operating a British-type system of criminal investigation and court procedure, of being able to consistently break into, much less smash organisations of this kind.'

The 'Curry King' was Chief Superintendent Peter Godber, who came from Hastings to join the Hong Kong force in 1952. Twenty-one years later he was arrested on similar charges to Hunt's, was convicted on the evidence of Hunt and gaoled for four years – after which he flew to join Hunt in Spain. These two cases infuriated the higher echelons of Hong Kong society, and a new organisation was formed in 1973 called the Independent Commission Against Corruption (ICAC). It was given as much rope as the British system allowed to detect and root out corruption, not only in the police force, but everywhere in Hong Kong.

It immediately ran into the problem that no one would take the witness stand. And it quickly had to rule out of its programme the many 'satisfied customer' cases, where both the briber and the bribed were very pleased with the transaction and its result, and would not cooperate with any legal proceedings. It tried to track down more renegade policemen, turning now to the Chinese officers and constables, some of whom were living a life of luxury in Canada or Taiwan, and usually managing to avoid deportation. In 1977, several policemen, feeling victimised by ICAC, stormed its headquarters. The Governor, Sir Murray MacLehose, fearing a total breakdown in law and order, declared an amnesty that greatly reduced ICAC's workload, but also damaged its prestige and future success.

Across the border justice is swifter and more brutal. In the 1980s a cigarette factory manager in Guangdong was executed by a firing squad for having accepted a bribe to take inferior tobacco from the Hong Kong salesman, in a swindle said to be worth $3 million. Hongkongers are torn between envy and apprehension at this kind of advertisement of what it would be like if Chinese politics were to prevail after 1997.

Actually, in spite of all the well-publicised cases, the Hong Kong civil service is the least corrupt in the region. Vice-Chancellor Wang Gungwu, who has lived in Singapore and Australia, praises the Hong Kong bureaucracy for being resistant, not only to corruption, but also to the temptation of intervening in business and overregulating it. 'They have both tolerance and integrity.' That may not be so true of the police, who frequently find themselves in one-to-one situations of privacy, but it does apply to immigration, trade and legal officials and others whose work is more out in the open.

The broad differences in political tradition explain why the British were so tardy in introducing the Hong Kong Chinese to the British political system. Only in the very early post-war years were such inhibitions abandoned. The political reforms unveiled by Governor Sir Mark Young in 1949 at the instance of the British Labour government envisaged a strong municipal council and an unofficial majority in the Legislative Council, intended to allow the inhabitants to express their wish 'to remain under British rule and resist absorption by China'. The Guomindang and the Chinese Communists both welcomed the Young reforms: the Communists called them a 'contribution toward democratic development in China'. Business opinion also favoured the plan.

But then China changed governments. Refugees flooded into Hong Kong, and British officials decided that the political reforms would lead to disorder. They were formally dropped by the Conservative government in 1952. Decision-makers had to ask themselves what democracy could mean to a Hong Kong where Cantonese were historically free to cross the border at will and were doing so in large numbers, and where only the articulate few had the time to worry about more than filling their rice bowls.

The new factor was Chinese Communist policy towards Hong Kong. When Chairman Mao proclaimed the People's Republic in 1949 and the Red Army arrived at the Shenzhen River, which forms the border of Hong Kong, alarm filled the city. It was presumed that Chinese Communist troops had stopped at the border because China was not ready to absorb Hong Kong, and perhaps feared that such an action would provoke British and American retaliation before the civil war in China was even complete. The Hong Kong issue could perhaps be dealt with later. That 'later' proved to be a very long time, initially because the Korean War and the consequential American embargo on trade with China made China temporarily dependent on supplies of equipment and materials via Hong Kong. Hong Kong, meanwhile, depended on China for food and simple consumer goods and, later, water, and this led by the end of the 1950s to a chronic and growing Chinese trade surplus. China began to earn millions of Hong Kong dollars which she could freely convert into any hard currency, including US dollars (of which she was short).

Meanwhile, the People's Republic began to spell out to the British the conditions under which their colonial rule would continue to be tolerated. The UK should not, for instance, allow Hong Kong to become a Guomindang base. There was a small Guomindang presence, which suited the Communists' book because of the occasional need for communication and even negotiation, but anything more would be provocative. It was added that it would be better not to have a Soviet presence either, and this hardened after the Sino-Soviet split in 1960, when the Chinese did not hesitate to specify that 'neither Soviet revisionism nor Chiang Kai-shek's clique' should be allowed to come and 'destroy' conditions in Hong Kong. For years afterwards the British duly excluded the Russians and East Europeans, and kept the Guomindang down to a harmless size.

But the most important condition, which liberal-minded Britons had least anticipated, was not to move towards self-government. A foreign colonial regime which China could expel at any time, 'with one telephone call', as it was often put, was something that could be tolerated (especially in view of the dollar earnings). But the emergence of a charismatic non-communist local Chinese leader in Hong Kong, perhaps in the mould of Singapore's Lee Kuan Yew, would send shivers down the spines of central and provincial authorities trying to maintain China's national unity and suppress separatism, not to mention preserving communist orthodoxy. This reasoning was not widely understood, certainly not in the West or in the newly independent states of Asia and Africa. But it made sense to the Chinese and to the British Foreign Office and Colonial Office officials who had studied Chinese history and culture. (The status of the border with China after 1949 and these initial attitudes of the People's Republic towards Hong Kong, are discussed more fully in Chapter 19 below.)

The big test of this tacit pact came with the Cultural Revolution in 1967, which produced an intense shouting match between normally urbane pro-communist newspaper editors and trade union leaders, on the one hand, and pale and sweating Hong Kong officials (mainly British, but also Chinese), on the other. The majority of the population was against the Communists but prudently avoided making a public stand. That crisis was overcome because the embattled leadership in Beijing would not give full backing to its hopeful Hong Kong disciples – a decision doubtless influenced by the dollar earnings. The violence came from relatively small numbers, yet it marked the end of the docile acceptance of things in Hong Kong. Neither the government, though vastly preferred to the Reds, nor the Reds themselves, could any longer count on unquestioning obedience from the man in the street. This was a big step along the road to the later political reforms.

The Observer's correspondent, Dennis Bloodworth, wisely said of the Cultural Revolution incidents, that Hongkongers yearned for a political alternative to their arid choice between Victorian British paternalism and suffocating Chinese maternalism – yet there seemed nowhere further for them to go. Knuckling under to foreigners appeared to some Hongkongers a high price to pay for avoiding communism. In the 1960s, it used to be said that the Executive and Legislative Councils were the 'lapdogs' of Britain, but by the 1980s they had turned into terriers, if not Alsatians.

The flowering of Hong Kong politics in the 1980s must be traced back to the seeds that were sown earlier in the field of local government by British officials. That story begins in the rural New Territories, whose inhabitants had formed village associations in the 1920s similar to those being set up in China as part of the new republican revolution. This system was more or less continued by the British, and in the late 1940s each village was electing representatives to rural committees by universal male suffrage. The chairmen of each committee formed a body called the Heung Yee Kuk, a primitive 'parliament', which was the main interface between government and people in the New Territories and was openly courted by the Communists in 1990.

In the 1960s, the government began to consider ways of modernising these committees and extending them to the urban areas. But the riots over the increase in the cross-harbour Star Ferry fare, closely followed by the spilling over into Hong Kong of China's Cultural Revolution, produced great disruption and business recession. Political reforms were postponed.

Only at the end of the 1960s were the district officers, who had been administering the New Territories in the traditional British colonial way, extended into urban Hong Kong and Kowloon, to act as colony-wide eyes and ears of the government and to explain government policies. In the streets themselves the traditional *kaifongs* (neighbourhood associations) gave way to a new mutual aid group structure, enabling the government to respond more promptly to emerging demands and grievances. In the rural areas new District Boards were created alongside the old rural committees, with the latters' chairmen sitting on them. These also spread into the urban areas, so that by 1980 Hong Kong was covered by a network of nineteen District Boards.

By that time, even Conservative ministers in London were asking, what about democracy and elections in Hong Kong? Governor Sir Murray MacLehose's response in the early 1980s was to hold direct elections to the District Boards, and create a Regional Council for the New Territories, with some members directly elected and others indirectly elected from the District Boards and the Heung Yee Kuk, so that all interests were represented within it. Another 'regional' Council – the Urban Council – already served the urban areas. There are thus nineteen District Boards at the grass roots level, and two Regional Councils with elected representatives from the District Boards. The Legislative Council was also made more representative by the addition of two kinds of elected seats, those representing Hong Kong-wide functional constituencies (lawyers, doctors, chambers of commerce, the trade unions, etc.) and 'geographical' representatives from the Regional Council and District Boards.

Until the late 1980s there was no passionate demand for political reform in Hong Kong. Frank Ching, the liberal newspaper columnist, has argued that for the British to defend their withholding of political reforms for so long on the grounds that there was never any demand for them, was like a man, accused of killing his parents, pleading for mercy because he was an orphan. The fact is, however, that there was nothing like Ching's barbed columns in the 1960s or even in the 1970s. Whenever Hong Kong residents had been given the right to vote a representative on to some local body, they had advertised their apathy by consistently low turnouts.

In the three consecutive Urban Council and District Board elections in the 1980s, the electoral turnout wavered between 30 per cent and 37 per cent. One pre-ballot opinion survey showed that 93 per cent of the people canvassed did not know who the candidates were in their constituency, and 97 per cent did not know the name of the sitting representative elected three years earlier. The standard reply to this by the pro-democrats is that bodies without power cannot be expected to engage people's interests. It is a good point, but it does not augur well for the future direction of a community whose political control over its environment must necessarily be limited.

Going back to the factor of tradition, the Chinese have never taken to their hearts the system where individuals have to go forward under the public gaze and vote for one of several candidates, knowing that the others for whom he does not vote may well take it out on him afterwards. It is the fatal combination of doing something as an individual, and doing it publicly, that turns most Chinese off. In another opinion poll in 1985, some 30 per cent thought that politics were dirty, and 45 per cent thought that politics were dangerous.

Some of these problems would be eased, perhaps, if there were fewer British faces in the administrative field, and fewer British minds in the decision-making chairs. Chinese tradition, communist conditions and local apathy help to explain why the British did not introduce democracy at an early stage. But those factors cannot explain the slow pace of 'localisation', as the replacement of British by Chinese faces is called, in the civil service. Out of the more than 1,100 directorate officers – the highest echelon – in the Hong Kong government almost 500 are expatriate. In a community where international business and manufacturing is carried on by executives who are very largely Chinese (except in a few special cases of foreign management, like the Hongkong Bank, or foreign ownership, like the Swire group or Jardine, Matheson), it seems to be asking for trouble to have such a large expatriate element in the government.

A very senior British banker told me in 1989 that some of the Chinese in their forties in the government were 'streets ahead of the British, tougher, and better in public' – and he named Joseph Yam, John Chan and Anson Chan. Naturally, the government claims that its localisation programme proceeds by leaps and bounds, although it is now about to face the problem of resignation by prospective emigrants in the run-up to 1997. The government had intended to stop recruiting British civil servants by now, but the unexpected current shortage in many technical areas makes a dent in that policy. And still half of the sixty departments of government are run by expatriates.

The contradictions can be seen in the police, where the first Hong Kong Chinese Commissioner took office in 1989 to run a force which still has documents classified 'for British eyes only' – not out of racialism, but because of the risk of Chinese police officers being compromised by China pressurising their families. Here is another example of how British-style government does not neatly transplant. People still remember with horror the case of the senior police officer John Tsang who was found to have been spying for the People's Republic and giving them inside information on the Hong Kong Police Force and its personalities.

Another difficult area is the legal branch of the government. There are few Chinese lawyers with both the linguistic and the legal ability to adorn the judicial bench. Clever barristers make far more money at the bar, and all but the most westernised are deterred by the Englishness of the judicial atmosphere – a case of cricket versus *mah jong*, as someone put it. Of the thirty senior judges only three are Chinese, and lawyers expect that by 1997 two-thirds of the junior judiciary and about a half of the magistrates will still be expatriate.

The leisurely domestic debate over political reforms was suddenly galvanised in 1984 by the knowledge that China would resume sovereignty in 1997. An official Green Paper on the future development of representative government set as a goal the development of a system of government in Hong Kong 'the authority of which is firmly rooted in Hong Kong and which is able to represent authoritatively the views of the people of Hong Kong, and which is more directly accountable to the people of Hong Kong'. It hastened to add that this should be achieved by building on existing institutions and preserving such good habits as consensus. Direct elections had not, it noted, been 'universally successful in producing stable representative government'. The Hong Kong system was not adversarial, hence the reliance on the electoral college, comprising the Urban Council, Regional Council and District Boards, to elect members to the Legislative Council. In the particular circumstances of Hong Kong, weight needed to be given to the representatives of those mainly responsible for producing the wealth from which the rest live, notably industrialists, traders and professionals. The Green Paper suggested a Legco for the end of the 1980s which would have 16 appointed, 10 official, 12 collegiately elected and 12 functionally elected members.

Despite its careful wording, the Green Paper opened the dam for all kinds of new political demands. Intellectuals supported the document with enthusiasm. Dr Lau Siu-kai wrote that reforms were necessary, first, to make the élite feel that it had a stake in the system, secondly, to choose qualified administrators, and thirdly, to demonstrate the true autonomy that was promised by China. Martin Lee teased out the message that, 'Only a truly representative government which has the mandate from, and therefore the backing of, the people of Hong Kong' could achieve effective autonomy. Indirect elections would not produce legislators who would speak for the Hong Kong people if a conflict of interest arose involving China, Britain and Hong Kong, though Lee himself was a legislator voted in through indirect elections by the legal professional constituency.

Peter Shore, of the British Labour Party, threw his weight behind these views, observing that elections confer authority. 'It is the business of persuading people,' he told Hong Kong's budding politicians, 'which elected members have to develop. They develop authority, but inevitably members of Legco do not have it.' Theoretically, it need not be so. Martin Lee is indirectly elected, and yet he has more authority, in Shore's sense, than any other Hong Kong politician. Would it really make a difference if he stood for a directly elected seat in the future? But theory aside, politicians of the stature of Sir Szeyuen Chung and Baroness Dunn do encounter prejudice on their visits abroad from foreign politicians who sneer as if they were still 'lapdogs'.

To this litany of delight at prospective reform, Fleet Street added a heavy bass line. Leader-writers vied with each other to deride the old-fashioned Hong Kong government and its timid Foreign and Commonwealth Office mentors for not bestowing Britain's great gift of democracy on these few Chinese still in the empire. *The Times* said in 1987 of this duty on Britain's part, 'A respectable electoral system is something it has usually tried to leave behind – whatever may happen subsequently.' *The Times* perhaps was insensitive to the feelings of 6 million Hong Kong Chinese thus consigned to such doubtful experimentation. One of the arguments in the reform debate was going to be whether Hong Kong needed to follow the grisly paths of British African democracy including 'whatever may happen subsequently'. If you suspect that something other than what you intend may happen later, is it not wise to analyse and investigate and, if possible, guard against it? To say, 'There you are, take it or leave it', regardless of local circumstances, national character and tradition, and political and diplomatic constraints, is callous and shortsighted.

The People's Republic took a detached view. Britain was in charge of reform for representative government, said Xu Jiatun, and China would not interfere. Britain had a rich experience in withdrawing from colonies, although some of those experiences carried 'negative elements'. What kind of elections were best should be decided later, after study, although 'no reform should be allowed to destroy the economic base'.

That put in low key what the Chinese were to say in *crescendo* over the following years. They were only echoing what many Hong Kong businessmen and professionals felt. Louis Cha, the publisher, said that direct elections were not the only kind of elections, and liberty was more important than democracy. 'Democracy is the means, liberty is the end.' Cha Chi Ming reported what he had seen of Nigerian disorder when plunged into the direct election game, and he took the trouble to prepare detailed proposals for Hong Kong's future political system drawing from his experience in Africa with the textile industry. A polytechnic lecturer, noting that political groups in Hong Kong were new and inexperienced, suggested that direct elections would risk the monopoly of power by deep-rooted traditional forces. Another plank in the conservative platform was the prediction that a democratic multi-party system, where votes had to be competed for, would lead to higher spending on welfare and the expansion of bureaucracy to administer it; things which tiny Hong Kong could not afford.

With the arguments on both sides rumbling on, the government put out another Green Paper in 1987 inviting the public to choose from a formidable set of political options, and send their replies to the new Survey Office. This was an uncomfortable episode. The burning hopes of 1984 had been dampened by cold spray from the Chinese side of the border. The elaborate façade of options and survey results allowed the government to say in the end what it thought in the first place, that the rush to democracy had better be slowed down, from everybody's point of view.

The business lobby agreed. Billy Yung, manufacturer of electric fans, said that democracy 'would open the way for self-seeking politicians to abuse the situation. People could be influenced because they are not sufficiently educated.' Leung Chunying, the surveyor, warned that agitating for democracy served British interests, not Hong Kong's. Some businessmen said that they would prefer to have the government after 1997 run by appointees of Beijing, because that would at least make it easier to conduct a dialogue with Beijing, and such people, precisely because of their close links with Beijing, would know better how to stand up to mainland pressure. These views were couched in a more neutral way by an independent journalist who said that a directly elected system would allow Hong Kong to be manipulated by both communism and capitalism.

But public opinion was running past the conservatives. As the *South China Morning Post* said in an editorial, in 1987, 'There is evidence of a surging political consciousness of the people, especially the young and the educated, whose pride and identity with Hong Kong as their home cannot be stifled.' The liberals were angered by Britain's back-pedalling on reforms. Some of them lapsed into crude language. 'They say that we Asians . . . cannot import Western democracy. The truth is that they do not trust us to be able to handle it properly. Somehow they must think that we Asians are inferior to the Caucasians.' A Shanghainese woman writer denounced Britain for denying democracy to Hong Kong, when it had been freely granted even to those laggards in the Commonwealth whose 'electorate could only recognise pictures of frogs or crocodiles as emblems of the contesting parties'. The liberals gleefully publicised letters from the late Premier Zhou Enlai in the 1920s supporting direct elections in Hong Kong during the great strike of that time.

The British took advantage of the 'cultural factor' to question why Hong Kong should change its political system 'simply to fit into the mould of a western-style democratic system'. Its officials put it about that a one-man one-vote election system would be an 'open sesame' for the Communists to take over, for their sympathisers to enter the government structure. Martin Lee, not showing for once his customary acumen, contradicted this, saying that Hongkongers so hated communism that they would always vote against communist candidates. He even argued that if there were a democratic system in place in 1997, China would allow it to operate – surely a triumph of hope over experience. But he fell foul of family divisions when his sister-in-law, the accountant Nellie Fong, also elected to the Legislative Council, took the opposite view. 'Direct elections,' she declared, 'would not produce a fair and true representation of the opinions and the interests of Hong Kong at our present state of development.'

There were diametrically opposed opinions on whether elections would favour the Communists. Many visitors, like Auberon Waugh, said that handing over an undemocratic system to the Chinese would make it easy for them 'to impose their hideously incompetent apparatus in its place'. It would be harder to take away a free election system once it had been granted. There were many such wild stabs into the future, based on superficial analysis of Chinese behaviour. More realistic voices, like that of Andrew Wong Wang-fat, asked why people should think that reforms would insulate Hong Kong from Chinese control. 'If they want to control, whether or not there are direct elections, indirect elections, or functional constituencies, they can still do that.' Sir David Akers-Jones, the most experienced officer in the Hong Kong government until his retirement in 1987, put it in five words: 'Dictatorships can be elected too.'

Gradually, the voices in the middle began to establish their ground. Lydia Dunn asserted that representative government was 'not a weapon to be used to confront China, nor a shield to protect Hong Kong from interference'. In 1989, the Legislative and Executive Councillors produced a consensus for one-third of the Legco to be directly elected by 1991, and they held to this view in spite of opposition from Chinese officials, who said it was too fast. Soon afterwards the Hong Kong Alliance founded by Lo Takshing, the Eurasian lawyer, suggested a bicameral structure with separate chambers for the district elected and the functionally elected members, each with a veto. This borrowed from some aspects of Irish and Norwegian practice, but critics predicted that it would polarise the differences between the liberals and the conservatives. (The Hong Kong political reform question after the Tiananmen Square massacre of 1989 is discussed in Chapter 20 below.)

By now there were the forerunners of political parties gearing up for elections, when and if they came. The oldest of these groups was the Christian Industrial Committee, with liberal views and labour union ties, followed in 1975 by the Hong Kong Observers, a group of thirty-five young professionals interested in public affairs. The early 1980s saw the arrival of Meeting Point, later led by a young Hong Kong University lecturer, Yeung Sum; the Hong Kong Affairs Society, led by Albert Ho, a liberal lawyer; and the Progressive Hong Kong Society, led by Maria Tam, the Legco lawyer. The list is completed by the Association for Democracy and People's Livelihood, led by the school teacher Lee Wing Tat; the Hong Kong Foundation, brainchild of Stephen Cheong Kam-chuen, industrialist and legislator; the Hong Kong Democratic Foundation, led by Dr Leong Che-hung of Legco; and the Hong Kong Alliance of T. S. Lo.

These groupings are still tentative. Everybody is afraid of the day when the Communist Party comes into the open and says: 'If you are going to have parties contesting elections, then we shall contest as well' (and it is inconceivable that the Communist Party would ever allow itself to lose face by losing an election). That was the state of play in Hong Kong politics when the Basic Law to govern its future after 1997 was promulgated in the spring of 1990. The final text of the Basic Law is more conservative than anybody had feared, and it had the effect of making many people feel that there was no point, not at present anyway, in trying to fight it. Most articulate Hongkongers would hope to get a more liberal interpretation of it, or even an actual amendment, agreed in the future, when the pendulum in Beijing politics swings back from the conservatives to the reformers within the Chinese Communist Party. They earnestly hope that this will happen before 1997.

Despite many outward signs of modernisation, Hong Kong Chinese individuals retain enough of their traditional family-centred culture to make any superstructure of Westminster-style democracy both vulnerable and ineffective. The politics of deference to authority, of discreet consensus, of giving 'face' by mutual compromise, come more naturally than voting or continuous open discussion in the highest councils. The Hongkongers do not yet know, however, how to preserve their present civil liberties and rule of law under a 'Chinese' system.

Chapter 7

Licence to Enjoy

The absence of puritanism in the Hong Kong Chinese is not confined to displays of wealth, to working hard, or to bestowing and receiving gifts. In matters relating to human passions, the Chinese start with a fairly strict system of family relationships, yet outside the family they enjoy in some respects greater freedom of expression and freedom from social criticism than Europeans.

The duties within the family are considered virtually sacrosanct, especially those to one's elders. It is no longer the norm, of course, for parents to choose their children's partners, as happened in the old days. What usually happens today is that a young couple will meet and date, and then decide to marry, but 'face' may be given to the parents by allowing them to pretend that they have 'chosen' their child's partner. Even so, sexual propriety asserts itself at the critical moment, when a modern Hong Kong Chinese wedding, even if largely western-style, is consummated by a mutual bow rather than a kiss.

These traditions of sexual restraint die hard. A survey of young single women in 1989 showed disapproval of premarital sex, of displaying affection in public, and of making divorce easier. Intolerance is surprisingly strong in the treatment of homosexuals. So scandalised does public opinion profess to be about this phenomenon that the government has not felt able to follow the UK in decriminalising private acts between consenting adults. A few years ago, a law reform commission comprising both British and Chinese leaders of society recommended that Hong Kong come into line with Britain, stressing that this did not mean promoting or encouraging homosexuality. It was something known in the old China, after all, and even romanticised and tolerated. But the guardians of Chinese morals in Hong Kong were outraged. Homosexuality 'not only runs counter to traditional Chinese moral standards, but is also a perversive path of behaviour condemned by the public', a Chinese newspaper commented.

There was a *cause célèbre* in 1980 when a police inspector, John MacLennon, was found dead just as he was about to be arrested on charges of homosexuality. Controversy has raged ever since about the nature of his death and the reasons behind it. The climate of opinion may be gauged from the fact that during one of the radio phone-in discussions about the case, a caller who admitted to being gay telephoned later to say that he had been sacked because his boss recognised his voice.

And yet, on the hill rising back from the Central district of Victoria, there is a magnificently equipped and extensive nightspot called Disco Disco owned by a young gay Eurasian, which is tremendously popular among young men and women and appears to suffer no backlash for being largely gay in character – although strictly speaking only Thursday is 'Boys' Night'. In this respect social tolerance is perhaps enlarging gradually.

There are exceptions to the strict rules even within the family. Any reader of novels about the Hong Kong Chinese will know that no stigma attaches to a Chinese man who takes several wives or concubines or both, provided he can afford to maintain them. That was the position in law, as well as in local morality, until 1967. Reform was delayed by respected leaders of Chinese society, and even young Chinese felt uneasy at the change. Henry Lethbridge, an English university teacher, remembered a conversation with Chinese students at that time in which they insisted that Chinese had the right to take concubines. And should Chinese wives, he asked, also be allowed to have relations with more than one man? This the students found shocking and disturbing. What they were really complaining about was the British trying to change Chinese traditions.

Since the 1960s concubines have had no rights, and only monogamous marriages are valid in law. But there are still collisions between legal requirements and social expectations. One businessman died leaving a wife, a concubine and six children of whom the concubine was mother. Because of this the concubine qualified under Chinese custom as 'equal wife', and she took the wife to the High Court for half of the estate.

Even the archaic and illegal custom of *muitsai*, or child slaves, leaves traces in Hong Kong society today. One case which was recently written about concerned a *muitsai*, owned by an infertile wife for the purpose of bearing her husband's children. When the slave-surrogate disappeared after this arduous servitude, she left behind six children who neither acknowledged her nor knew her name. That was in the late 1960s.

Those are the demarcation lines for repression and licence within the family circle. Beyond the family lies the vast world of entertainment, for which Hong Kong has an international reputation, but which the Hongkongers themselves probably enjoy even more than the foreigners. And there the sparring between restraint and indulgence is equally complicated.

If you inspect the centrefold of the Chinese-language *Penthouse*, you will find the same nudity as in the American version, but with pubic hair presented more discreetly. This matches the inhibitions of readers in Hong Kong who almost never write those heavy-breathing letters to the editor about their sexual exploits (the editors have to translate from their American edition for this section). Yet nudity in public need not be distressing: such sights were not unknown in the primitive life of South China within living memory. After the Tiananmen Square massacre of 1989 a Hong Kong artist expressed his disgust by setting out spittoons on the pavement to represent China, and then lowering his trousers to pee or shit into them, and inviting the public to do likewise. The police told him to pull his pants up, but they did not arrest him.

The recent rural reality lying behind the Hong Kong personality may perhaps condition people to accept such occasional sights on the street, but the stage or screen is a different matter. When Peter Schaeffer's *Equus* was staged recently in Hong Kong, it was without the nude scenes. 'We are not allowed to perform nude,' said the Chinese director. 'The actors will be wearing basic clothes. They don't need to be naked.' Indeed, he made it clear that there would be no reference to sex at all. 'There is no need to perform anything like that on stage. It is not so important in my approach. I am concentrating on the religious element in the play.' Predictably, the nude scenes with Jeremy Irons and Diana Quick in *Brideshead Revisited* were completely cut in the Hong Kong showing, though they were integral to the story, and so was the controversial footage in *The Singing Detective*. Meanwhile, sex films without full nudity are very popular, and not just in the 'red light' districts.

At the height of the Vietnam War, when American troops came to Hong Kong for rest and relaxation, there were said to be 250 'girlie' bars. New ones are still being created. Club Volvo was opened – by businessmen, for businessmen – in 1987 at a cost of $130 million. It is the largest Japanese-style nightclub in town, with 800 hostesses. It presented such competition that the triads protecting fourteen rival clubs in the area pooled their resources to harass or poach its staff. What a customer spends for a few hours in this beguiling atmosphere can exceed what an average Chinese on the mainland earns in a year. 'Let's face it,' said the Australian *mama-san* in charge of the girls, 'most of the men come here because they want to go to bed with the girl.' Because Club Volvo was sponsored by wealthy and influential men like Ronald Li, even the communist representatives in Hong Kong gave it 'face'. A senior Xinhua official and Wang Guangying, brother-in-law of a former Chairman of the People's Republic, together cut the ribbon at the opening. But visitors from the communist mainland are said to be nervous when sitting at a table with the girls, and 'are afraid to take a girl home'.

77

Where morals meet the economy most spectacularly is where money is gambled on a game of chance or a race. There can be few people around the world among whom the gambling itch is so endemic. In neighbouring Macao, which is too small to be choosy about economic options, gambling provides the government with at least a quarter of its total income, and if visitors were not attracted to the casinos, the Macao economy would collapse.

Even at *mah jong*, which can be played at home or in one of the 200 public *mah jong* parlours, millions of dollars can change hands in Hong Kong. But it is the turf which hypnotises even the poorest and most parsimonious Hong Kong Chinese. British punters admire them as 'sportsmen who like a hefty bet and don't beef when they lose'. The figures run past belief. Bets on the 1989 races totalled $4.5 billion, which is almost $800 per head of population, or $15 per week for every man, woman and child. What Hongkongers spend on bets is already more than the People's Republic of China receives in foreign loans and investments. The figures are hard to credit, and the comparisons are cruel. These days $80 million can be bet on a single race.

The Royal Hong Kong Jockey Club, which has a monopoly over all this, is Hong Kong's second largest employer after the government itself, serving 10,000 members (there is a long waiting list) and dispensing huge amounts in tax to the government and in charity to many worthwhile causes. While others worried about the effect of 1997 on Hong Kong's quality and standard of living, the Jockey Club built a completely new and luxurious race course in the New Territories to complement the existing one at Happy Valley on Hong Kong Island.

The popular demand for information about the races forces most Chinese newspapers to carry full reports and tips. Their sales invariably drop sharply after every racing season. One communist rag, *Cheng Wu Pao*, which built up a circulation of 60,000 based on racing tips, had to close down altogether when its Communist Party mentors ordered it to stop publishing race tips – and the circulation fell to one-fifth.

Now betting has become fully computerised. You can plug your hand-held betting terminal into any telephone socket to communicate your bet directly to the mainframe computer (though there were language difficulties about this at first). You can also bet off the track in countless legal betting shops. In 1989, the idol of the punters was a 25-year-old worker in a garment factory who had never even been to a race. She put $1.40 down in a double trio wager in her first season and won $1.8 million. That was well calculated to keep the other hundreds of thousands of hopeful gamblers in the game.

Some races are fixed, controlled, it is said, by four big betting syndicates who arrange for the jockeys to produce a pre-agreed result. Yang Yuan-loong was one of the respected Shanghainese textile manufacturers of Hong Kong. The British admired him because he was so helpful in the 1960s and 1970s in putting Hong Kong's case at international textile trade negotiations. Yet in

1986 he was convicted of race-fixing, confessing to being the brains behind the Shanghai betting syndicate, and to fixing six races with two Australian jockeys. Senior British officials in the Hong Kong government testified to his character.

Yang was given a suspended gaol sentence, having cancer at that time, and commented afterwards from the USA that race-fixing was by no means easy: his attempts often went wrong. Racing, he said, would never be clean, and maybe it was time to scale down the operations of the Jockey Club which had become worse than a casino. 'You will never stop some jockeys hustling, it's their life. Why do you think some of them want to come to Hong Kong?'

The Communists do not know what to do about gambling on the horses. The betting offends their consciences, yet the government revenue is attractive, and the horses keep people away from other less harmless pursuits. Officially, they say that racing will be allowed to continue after 1997, and they say the same about the casinos in Macao, but they have not actually guaranteed the survival of betting on the races on the present scale in Hong Kong. When Deng Xiaoping's son, the disabled Deng Pufang, visited Hong Kong in 1984, he went to the Happy Valley races and bet on a couple of horses, and one of them romped in first. The resident Xinhua leaders have also attended race meetings. They would probably like to see equally enthusiastic crowds at their party ideological meetings, but do not know how to achieve it.

The other excess in which the Hong Kong Chinese indulge is the table. It is not gluttony, because the portions in which Chinese food is served are small, and even a formal dinner lasting several hours might not be found filling. True, there are occasional gourmet banquets in Hong Kong, like the one given in 1946 by the warlord Zhang Fakui, of thirty courses. Annie Wu catered for gourmets in the 1980s and considered a menu of bear paws and pine seeds, braised elk trunk with boiled turtle, snow frog fat and moose nose to be a good starting point. She was annoyed at being given only forty-five minutes in which to serve a nine-course banquet for Queen Elizabeth. When the Mandarin Hotel celebrated its twenty-first birthday, it gave a dinner which stretched over three consecutive evenings, and included wild ducks' tongues, snow frogs' ovaries with ginseng, sturgeon maw, civet, sea cucumber, crane and cordyceps (the latter being a worm in winter, and a plant in summer).

Other delicacies that occasionally figure in formal banquets for serious students of gastronomy are elephant trunk, stork, seal, deer tail and sturgeon bowels. Government inspectors investigate restaurant kitchens regularly, and in one year recently they found 12 bear paws, 16 scaly anteaters, 25 giant salamanders and 117 birds of prey waiting to be cooked and served.

These are dishes valued for their rarity, but the conflict of values between Briton and Chinese is sparked by more common candidates for the kitchen knife, particularly dog and snake. The Royal Society for the Prevention of Cruelty to Animals in Hong Kong is split over the long-standing Chinese custom of eating dogs. It is hard to find a logical reason why dogs should be regarded differently from many other animals that man eats. With snakes, it is straightforward revulsion that puts Westerners off. But in the Regent Hotel's Lai Ching Heen Restaurant the 'snakeman' will cut the gall-bladder from a live serpent for you to drink at your table with wine, and will then cut off the head and prepare the meat. That is for the rich, or very special occasions. What is happening with the menus of everyday life is that Hong Kong Chinese are eating less rice and more bread, are developing an unexpected taste for fast foods, and appear to have overcome their long-declared distaste for cheese – in the sense that Pizza Hut and similar chains have developed large followings. At the time of writing, Hong Kong boasts the largest single Pizza Hut restaurant in the world.

Tastes in the liquor to go with the food do not seem to change much. The French have somehow convinced the Chinese that whisky interferes with sex, and to many Cantonese it tastes cheesy. So Hong Kong has become the world's highest consumer of brandy per head of population. It works out at four bottles a year per head. Westerners are surprised to see their Chinese friends drinking brandy steadily through a meal. Beer and wine have only recently found favour.

These are the not-so-secret vices of the Hong Kong Chinese. Fei Yiming, the late Hong Kong communist publisher, used to tell me in the 1960s and 1970s how China would root out gambling, corruption, prostitution and drugs when it took over. Now, I am not so sure that he was right. By 1997 China will have become more permissive, and less easy to govern, and the ideological puritanism which informed Fei's attitudes seems weaker in communist ruling circles today. The Chinese Hong Kong has good hopes of survival.

PART II

The Cosmopolitan Hong Kong

Chapter 8

The Role of the Gwailos

Considering what a gold-mine it became, the British were singularly unpossessive about their Crown Colony. From the beginning, they permitted all nationalities to try their luck on the 'barren island'. The *gwailos* (literally 'ghost-people'), as the Chinese called the British and the others with white faces, were never very numerous, never numbering more than a few thousands. But over the decades they exerted considerable influence over individual Chinese and the Chinese community of Hong Kong. Adventurers and administrators, drug runners and doctors of law, medical practitioners and missionaries, writers and merchants, Russian and Dutch, Australian and Belgian, American and Jewish, all have contributed something to the sum of Hong Kong's collective wisdom and experience.

Many Western individuals have spent a career or a lifetime in Hong Kong, but few can point to a continuous family line of three generations spanning a whole century there. Sir Elly Kadoorie arrived in Hong Kong in the 1880s to found a modest stockbroking firm and turn it into a China trade fortune. Today, his grandson has just begun to take control of the most powerful family business group in Hong Kong, covering electricity, hotels, textiles, property, carpets and many other activities.

The Kadoories are Iraqi Jews, British educated and very British-oriented. Sir Elly came to Hong Kong from Baghdad in 1880, and worked as a warehouse clerk for the Sassoons, to whom he was related, for 37 rupees a month. When he was ready to start his own firm, it was with a capital of only HK$ 500. He founded China Light and Power Co. at the beginning of the century, and today it is the most efficient electricity producer in Asia.

Lawrence, now Lord Kadoorie and over 90, is Sir Elly's son, and, with Sir Y. K. Pao and Li Kashing, one of the richest men in the world. So much did he appreciate British rule and its influence that he made sure that equipment for his power plants was supplied by British manufacturers, despite the procedures of tender. He succeeded in this even when his partner in the biggest power station of all in Hong Kong was an American corporation, Exxon.

Lawrence was dropped from the Board of Directors of the Hongkong Bank when it developed significant business in Muslim countries. He never seemed to bear grudges for that kind of thing, and he has probably helped more people in time of need than any other rich man in the Territory. 'He did a lot of good by stealth,' a colleague remarked. Despite his huge wealth he answers his own telephone. His brother, Sir Horace, is the art lover, collector and philanthropist, especially active in agricultural aid for New Territories' farmers. Now Lawrence's son Michael is the heir to the Kadoorie fortunes.

The Sassoons also hailed from Baghdad. David Sassoon began to trade from Bombay in the early nineteenth century, and by mid-century his son Elias went further, to Canton, and formed his own company in Hong Kong. Four other sons of David each directed their father's business there. None of them gained full acceptance in the stuffy Hong Kong society of that time, although one of them was appointed to the Legislative Council.

Because David had the foresight to pay off the gambling debts of the Prince of Wales (later Edward VII), however, his children found places in the demi-monde surrounding the Prince's court in England. Arthur Sassoon became particularly close to the future monarch, and one of the English courtiers sneeringly described him as 'the Jew page boy . . . who gets up after each course to make bets for the King.' In more recent times. the family's interest in Hong Kong has waned. The English in Hong Kong do not lend themselves to dynasties on the Kadoorie model, but there are a few who can go back a couple of generations. Richard Darkin, who has just retired from the Hong Kong Police Force, was born in Hong Kong, his grandfather having sailed in a tea clipper from England.

The pre-war and post-war chapters of the Hong Kong story, so very unlike, were linked by the saintly figure of Bishop Ronald Hall. Before taking the mitre, Hall wrote a remarkable book, *China and Britain*, which showed, for a man of such English reticence, a rare knowledge of the real trends in Chinese life and Far Eastern affairs. After the war he threw himself into the social uplift which Hong Kong badly needed. He started the Hong Kong Social Welfare Council, the Children's Meals Society, the Street Sleepers Society and an orphanage. But he became controversial on two counts.

In 1944, he ordained Deaconess Florence Lei Tim-Oi to the priesthood, so that her congregation of about 150 Christians in Macao could receive the sacraments. In the restrictive conditions of wartime this little community was cut off from others and could not find a priest who could travel every week to give communion. Bishop Hall's view was that the needs of such a congregation should take priority over problems of a priest's sex, and that ordaining a woman was better than allowing either an unordained person to give communion or a congregation to go without the sacrament. The *Church Times* in London called Bishop Hall's action 'outrageous'. Archbishop Temple 'deplored' it, and the Chinese House of Bishops labelled it 'uncanonical'. But Hall, ahead of his time, was unrepentant and the ordination of Florence Lei gradually gained support: Archbishop Runcie later paid tribute to her.

The second problem was political. Hall was very critical of the Guomindang rule in China in its final years, and welcomed the new communist regime in 1949. He preached a sermon just before the communist victory, suggesting that God might have raised up communism in order to destroy the evil of accumulated property, just as He had raised up Rome in Christ's lifetime in order to destroy the evil of lawless banditry in Europe. He wrote home that year to say: 'We are all so glad the Communist armies have reached . . . the Hong Kong border . . . I don't want communism in England – but I do not see how anything else could have happened in China.' Later he was instrumental in shaping the three-self Christian movement in the People's Republic of China, under which the Christians were to support themselves, govern themselves and propagate themselves without foreign help.

Bishop Hall's dinner with Premier Zhou En-lai, in 1956, provoked furious envy among the Hong Kong British, but his personal integrity protected him from criticism. Once, looking at the menu in a Hong Kong hotel, he said, 'No one should spend all this on food.' He ordered coffee and rolls to last him until the next day. Hong Kong was lucky to have a man of such moral stature and the capacity to influence people in a very dramatic and lasting way. His impact is still to be observed in the city.

Other larger than life characters in the Western business community after the war were the bluff big-hearted Irishman, Sir Arthur Morse of the Hongkong Bank, and those two seat-of-the-pants merchant adventurers, George Marden and Douglas Clague. Marden was the rough diamond of the three, feared for his sardonic ruthlessness, respected for his First World War Military Cross, but disliked for what most of his colleagues and competitors perceived as unprincipled behaviour. In particular he appeared to treat his Chinese partner from Shanghai meanly. But he built up the Wheelock Marden Group almost to vie with the much older *hongs* of Jardine and Swire. Colonel Clague was in a similar mould, with a record of heroism against the Japanese in the Pacific War, liaising with the Chinese underground network in the New Territories and Guangdong. He took the credit for expanding the Hutchison Group, which became one of the big four in Hong Kong.

Most Britons retire to the UK, but some have settled in Hong Kong, the doyen being Austin Coates, son of the composer Eric Coates, who writes elegant books on East Asian affairs. His first book, *Myself a Mandarin*, is an amusing and affectionate account of his work as a New Territories magistrate. A pattern may be detected in the later post-war years for retired officials, especially those with local Chinese or Eurasian wives, to remain in Hong

Kong and even, in the case of Jimmy McGregor, to enter local politics. Sir David Akers-Jones, the former Chief Secretary, is the most distinguished of those who 'won't go home', but there are many more and they contribute to Hong Kong development by staying. The same applies to some large corporations. Jardine in particular boasts more than a score of resigned executives still working in Hong Kong for other companies or public bodies. They recently had a 'reunion dinner'.

Leo Goodstadt arrived at Hong Kong University in 1962 for further economic studies after his Manchester University degree and never went back. Father Harold Naylor, a Jesuit priest from Dublin, came in 1960, and is still teaching in Hong Kong. Bill Blaauw, leader of the Dutch community and king of the toy exporters, has been away from his homeland for more than forty years. Hong Kong has that kind of effect on people.

Of the many European professionals with long service in Hong Kong, two stand out. Father Ladany is a Belgian Jesuit priest who devoted his life to the application of Chinese scholarship to current politics. He started *China News Analysis*, an idiosyncratic periodical which is informative, wise in judgement and caring for the Chinese people if not for Marxism.

The other personality is also religious, starting life as a missionary and then turning to social work, especially basic education. Elsie Tu (better known in earlier years as Elsie Elliott) has acted as the conscience of Hong Kong in the last quarter century, rather as Bishop Hall did for the first two post-war decades. It is a measure of Hong Kong Chinese timidity and Hong Kong British conformity that in case after case of corruption, abuse of power by the authorities, or police misbehaviour, Tu has been the only voice to call for justice and for the full investigation of facts. She also did a great deal for the schooling of the very poor in Kowloon and for the rescue and treatment of drug addicts. And she did what many British professional men did in Hong Kong: she married a Chinese.

A grandfather of President Franklin D. Roosevelt was a partner in an American-owned *hong* called Russell, in nineteenth-century Hong Kong, though it did not seem to stop FDR from supporting the Chinese Nationalists against the trading interests of the European powers. But the Americans have not played a big part in post-war Hong Kong: after all, they had Taiwan as well as their dominating position in Japan and Korea to occupy them. In the early years of the People's Republic, the colonial government was embarrassed by the strong American partisanship for Chiang Kai-shek. Some Americans seemed to think that their hero would stage a return via Fujian in the style of Bonnie Prince Charlie. Embarrassingly, the American community, led by their diplomats, actually evacuated Hong Kong in 1952–3, when there were fears about a possible communist attack. They came back a year or so later with their tails between their legs, having lost much face among the Hong Kong Chinese. One of the American banks did not return for decades.

This chequered history did not prevent a Filipino businessman from forecasting that the Americans would be running Hong Kong by 1997. American residents overtook the British in numbers in 1986, although such figures have to be treated with care because increasing numbers of Hong Kong Chinese now have British or American citizenship (about half of the American figure is thought to be ethnic Chinese). The United States accounts for more than half of foreign investment in Hong Kong manufacturing, and Hong Kong has become the thirteenth best market for American goods. With a large business presence, with prospective increases in immigration by Hong Kong Chinese to the United States, and with the British absorption in European Community affairs, it is tempting for American enthusiasts to urge Washington to become more involved in protecting Hong Kong's future, and even to replace Britain as the 'pre-eminent western player' in that game. Congressmen John Porter and Stephen Solarz lead an active band of American politicians who are knowledgeable about and ambitious for Hong Kong. But somehow the American role seems more likely to remain a supporting one than a substitute lead.

From Australia came the most famous denizen of Hong Kong's bars and grillrooms, the journalist Richard Hughes. His reporting, for the *Sunday Times* and other Western newspapers, was distinctive, crisp and well-informed, so much so that he sometimes seemed to be ahead of the news. In Hong Kong, he indulged an eccentricity of character which endeared him to all, and at the end he became an institution, even having busts and plaques put up and rooms named after his memory. His good-heartedness led him to help many young cub reporters or bewildered visitors from Fleet Street, and it could be said that he was the real inspiration behind the James Bond novels of Ian Fleming. Dick Hughes's reward was to appear as the hard-drinking, hard-womanising head of the Australian Secret Service, Dikko Henderson, in Fleming's *You Only Live Twice*: he also appeared quite recognisably in John Le Carré's *The Honourable Schoolboy*. In real life Hughes' great scoop was the flushing out of Burgess and MacLean in Moscow. In Hong Kong he married a Shanghai refugee, the daughter of a Guomindang general, but he always warned his companions, 'Never marry a Chinese – they rule you with a rod of iron, disguised as flowers.'

An interesting question is how far these Westerners related to China, to Chinese culture and Chinese individuals in Hong Kong, and with what results. Jan Morris talks about the Hong Kong Britons being fused in a furnace with the Hong Kong Chinese, and made colleagues of them by cash. But the two sides seem ready to part easily enough when their joint venture is over. Before the war the lines of control and territory between the Westerners and the Chinese were well marked. When Somerset Maugham's heroine Kitty in *The Painted Veil* considered whether to marry her Hong Kong-based British bacteriologist, she reflected that, 'Life in Hong Kong sounded quite jolly: there were clubs and tennis and racing and polo and golf.' Indeed, when she got there, hardly a Chinese swam across her horizon, save to serve her tea.

When Kitty had an affair outside her marriage, it was with the 'Assistant Colonial Secretary', a development which brought the threat of a lawsuit from the real Assistant Colonial Secretary of that day, causing Maugham to recall the first edition and change the setting of the story from Hong Kong to an imaginary 'Tching Yen'. Later editions were allowed to revert to the original text.

There always were, still are, and perhaps always will be Britons who prefer their own company in Hong Kong to the stimulation of bicultural Chinese. The Hong Kong Club, membership of which is the pre-eminent social badge, began in the 1840s by excluding 'shopkeepers, Chinese, Indians, women and other undesirables'. Bishop Hall left the club when his Chinese lunch guest was barred. Only in recent years, and after some bitter struggles between the two groups of British members, one cosmopolitan and the other culture-bound, did the club open up to Chinese. Since then it has become even more exclusive as the sanctum of the privileged of all races.

Some of the distasteful prejudices of British colonial life persisted into the post-war years. It has been suggested that two outstanding government officers, Ken Barnett and Ronald Holmes, missed the promotion they might otherwise have expected because of their marriages, in one case to a Chinese who was not even middle class, in the other case to a Eurasian. That was in the 1960s. Today one sees a far more natural and permissive atmosphere. The *Hong Kong Standard*, always quick to spot an Anglo-Saxon fault, once lashed out editorially at the 'paternalistic paladins who have abused our hospitality while treating with contempt our culture and our people' – and to whom God 'was, of course, an Englishman'. The *Standard* looked forward to 1997 as a time when the Anglo-Saxons would at last have to accept an equal footing. Incidentally, if one is considering the image of Hong Kong as prejudiced against Europeans, it is worth noting that Jimmy McGregor, the vocal Scot, not only contested a seat on the Legislative Council, but won it against a Chinese opponent.

What does continue is the harmless manifestation of popular British culture. At the Bull and Bear pub, aptly named for its proximity to multiple floors of stockbrokers' offices, a thoroughly English decor is offered of knotty beams and brass bedwarmers. The menu is mainly braised beef and Brussels sprouts. As the manager proudly said, 'It took a long time to teach the Chinese chef how to make gravy like that.' A mile or so away in Happy Valley is another British hideout which used to be called the Traps Bar, until it was acquired by Scottish residents who decided to give it a tartan feel and change the name to Wee Jock's. The *South China Morning Post*, professing neutrality on the name, crushingly commented, 'Why didn't they just call it "Wee Jock's Traps"?'

One cannot pretend that westerners mix happily with the Chinese in Hong Kong, even today. Public schoolboys innocent of university experience continue to be recruited by some firms, and it is only to be expected that some of them should form defensively isolated clusters of white in a yellow sea. The further up you go, however, the more extensive, natural and mutually invigorating the cross-cultural contacts become. Because China is so unfree and Taiwan so uninviting, Hong Kong's value as a ground for East–West encounter remains at a premium. There is a fear that the general acceptance of Europeans which has prevailed in Hong Kong for most of the time may deteriorate as 1997 approaches – and as many individual Hongkongers come to feel aggrieved or betrayed by Britain. The occasional cry of 'Not them, they're our own', when violence hits the streets (which it does only rarely) means that foreign devils, not rich Chinese, are the targets of local hooligans. But the Britons who have retired there are not altering their plans.

There is every possibility that Westerners may continue to do useful work and enjoy life in Hong Kong for the next seven years, and it is still not to be ruled out that enough of that atmosphere may be retained afterwards for friendships and collaborations to survive long after the resumption of Chinese sovereignty. The presence and contributions of Westerners are one of the important reasons why China accepts Hong Kong's colonial status today and wants the same sort of structure to continue after 1997. China needs the presence of some Westerners, but better have the *gwailos* all together in their cherished Hong Kong than causing endless trouble and spreading social 'pollution' living in various parts of the mainland. In Chinese terms, Hong Kong is a Western invention, despite its being largely built with Chinese labour, and China has by no means exhausted its exploitation of it. The Western inputs will be needed for the foreseeable future, at least until Chinese players are able to command the same depth and breadth of business expertise.

Chapter 9

Indian Sunset?

In 1985, K. Sital presented a petition to the House of Lords in London for the Hong Kong Indians to have the right of abode in Britain. 'Indians,' he remarked, 'have a history of being in Hong Kong for 140 years, ever since the day the Union Jack was hoisted.'

Indeed, when the British annexed Hong Kong, they took it with 2,700 Indian troops. Abdoolali Ebrahim set up a business in the new colony within weeks – even before Jardines. Indian traders proved eager to take advantage of Hong Kong's new commercial opportunities, first the Parsees (to whom Jardine and other infant British enterprises owed much in getting started), then the Gujeratis, and then the Marwaris. In the 1860s when the colony was hardly twenty years old, two out of five of the firms in the Hong Kong directory were Indian. Sikhs were brought in by the British for artillery or other military duties, and later for the police force (and are even today employed as guards in many shops and banks). After 1900 most of the new arrivals from India were Sindhi traders. There are some Indian families in Hong Kong today – Ruttonjee, Kayamally, Tyebkhan – which can boast of having been there for more than a century.

By 1900, some of the Indians had become wealthy enough to claim positions of leadership, undertake important projects and practise philanthropy. Sir H. N. Mody, a Parsee who had arrived in 1858 at the age of 19 to work for an Indian bank, endowed Hong Kong University in 1911, and donated the buxom statue of Queen Victoria which now stands in Victoria Park. Another Parsee, Dorabji Naorojee, started the Star Ferry which still plies across the harbour, one of the few features of that stirring seaboard landscape which has not changed.

Sir Paul Chater, whose family was Christian Armenian but who was born in Calcutta and came in the 1860s to Hong Kong at the age of 18, as a bank clerk like Mody, was worth more than HK$50 million at his death. He pioneered the development of Kennedy Town and Kowloon, and was a founder of the Hong Kong Land Company: when he was lobbying for the urbanisation of Kowloon, against the views of many British who felt it was unhealthy ground, he personally took a sampan to plumb the water for proof that berths could be built on the Kowloon side of the harbour.

The Chinese sometimes accuse the Indians of having collaborated with Japan during the war, and of bringing cheap labour from Bombay to compete unfairly against Chinese businesses. In fact the Hong Kong Indians achieved a good record in the war: 200 of them served in the Chindits with honour. Now the 16,000 Indians and Pakistanis control about one-eighth of Hong Kong's foreign trade, which would appear to mean that they are about forty times more enterprising than the Chinese. It is remarkable enough that they survive in the middle of a Cantonese community which is adroit in trade, let alone outdo it. One of their assets is the ability to open up markets in the Middle East, Africa and Latin America where the overseas Indian network is stronger than the overseas Chinese. But the main explanation lies in sheer hard work and perseverance.

None has demonstrated those qualities more than the astounding Harilelas. A young Sindhi named Naraindas Mirchandani went to work for an Indian firm in Singapore in the 1920s. News came that his mother had fallen ill. He abandoned his job and rushed home to India to find that he was too late, the relatives had already cremated the lady. Mortified, he renounced his family name and invented a new one for himself – Harilela, a combination of his father's and mother's given names. Its meaning is translated by a family member as 'the frolicsome fancies of Lord Vishnu'. Thus redesignated, the young man struck even further afield to shake off the memory of his filial lapses. He began a new life in Shanghai and then in Canton, selling jade and amber. But he lost everything in the Great Slump of the early 1930s and in 1934 he brought his wife and children to Hong Kong.

Of his six sons, the second, called Hari Harilela, was the leader. Hari had no easy childhood. At 11 he had to leave school and spend his days hawking at the army barracks. Hari was taking British soldiers' measurements at the Shamshuipo camp before he was even a teenager. 'That was hard times,' he recalls. Sometimes Hari sold newspapers on the street. The family set up a tiny shop behind the YMCA in Kowloon, selling clothes to servicemen. Then Hari got an office job, and his salary, with his brothers', helped keep the family going.

When the Japanese seized Hong Kong, Hari was fired. The family survived by selling local goods to the Japanese army. In the final wartime years when food was short they took rice from the Japanese as payment, and sold it to Hongkongers. Sometimes Hari was beaten up by the Japanese.

VJ Day found Hari a hardened 23, with scant education but volumes of lessons in the school of life. The family started a ground floor custom tailoring business. All the Indian shops were selling silk, but Hari argued his father into diversifying into clothing, and they were the first to start manufacturing. Hari learned cutting from two old Indian tailors, the Din brothers. The post-war influx of British soldiers helped their turnover, especially in made-to-measure suits, which they completed in twenty-four hours. The follow-up mail order business from soldiers who had gone home was also a bonanza. The Harilelas were soon making 600 suits a day, and when the Korean War broke out in 1950, they had American GI's buying as well. They moved their tailoring shop up the Nathan Road to where the Imperial Hotel is today, and Hari diversified again into ladies' clothing. Eventually shops were opened outside Hong Kong, in Okinawa, Guam and Bombay.

Hari used the profits from his clothing business to buy properties, beginning with one on Salisbury Avenue. The family raised half the price itself and borrowed the rest from the bank. 'The Hongkong Bank was very good to us right from the start,' Hari recalled. 'Even without security they used to give us facilities that I had never imagined. It is the bank that is behind our success.' Later he struck up a partnership with a Chinese businessman, allowing Hari to concentrate on the financial side of the real estate business, while the Chinese dealt with the actual properties. When the present Imperial Hotel site came up for development Hari had an arrangement to keep the ground floor for a new Harilela shop, while Chinese partners built a hotel above. But they pulled out, so he was left with the hotel, and that was the beginning of his hotel business.

Later, having another site in Mody Road, he talked to several American hotel chains, and liked the people at Holiday Inn. So in 1975 he became the owner of Hong Kong's first Holiday Inn, followed by the Harbour View Holiday Inn, and then by other hotels, in which Hari shared the equity with partners in Singapore, Penang, Dhaka, Bangkok, Montreal, etc. In the course of this miraculous ascent to wealth in a variety of fields, Hari Harilela spared some time for public duties. He led most of the Indian community associations and bodies, and also helped the Boy Scouts and numerous welfare bodies, and funded scholarship programmes. His regret is that the British never invited him to serve on Legco. He presumes that his lack of education must be the reason. Like all successful overseas Indian entrepreneurs, he is now an investor in India itself – notably in a $4 million electronics software joint venture with American partners in New Delhi.

Hari is the leader of the Harilelas, but the other five brothers all play a part. Hari looks after the hotels and property business which he initiated, and the fifth brother Gary helps him in this. George, the self-effacing eldest brother, manages the exports, and Peter, the third brother, represents the family at the Stock Exchange. The fourth brother, Bob, helped by the youngest, Mohan, is responsible for the restaurant and travel business.

The amazing fact is that all these brothers and their wives and children live with their mother, the matriarch of the family, in a single house in Waterloo Road. Every morning, and every night the six brothers pay their ritual respects to their mother. The house is new, in the Mogul Palace style. Housing more than thirty members of the family and a similar number of staff, the house sports the luxury of bedrooms decorated all over with pearls, and a dining table made of gold-leaf glass. Twenty or thirty cars are parked in the drive, several of them Rolls-Royces.

In spite of all this, Hari remains an unpretentious and accessible man. 'He is perpetually charming,' a visitor reported, 'perpetually smiling; his manners are always as smoothly impeccable as his tailoring.' He and the eldest brother George are fluent in Cantonese because of their childhood in Canton, whereas the younger brothers and the next generation of Harilelas are less interested in the Chinese and more on the look-out for business and pleasure opportunities on the international circuit. Yet they still live with Mama. Hari speaks for all of them, and all of his fellow Indians, when he says of Hong Kong, his adopted city, 'The beautiful part of it is, that you are free to do whatever you like, you are not questioned, you are not arrested.'

After the Harilelas come the Murjanis. The elder Murjani arrived in Hong Kong in the early 1930s at the age of 16, and took up work as a sales assistant with an Indian firm. He followed the familiar pattern of saving up to start his own business, including a clothing factory. His son was born in 1946 in Pakistan, but was raised in Hong Kong and educated in Britain and the United States. In the 1970s the younger Murjani toured the United States to identify the best products for the family factory to make. He concluded that jeans were 'the single most important garment in the Western hemisphere'. But all the jeans makers, he found, 'had been producing jeans that were cut the same as jeans for men'.

He had the inspiration of making jeans specifically for women, and, supersalesman that he was, he negotiated Gloria Vanderbilt's name on the pockets, spent a million dollars on advertising, and next day Bloomingdales was sold out. Murjani's Gloria Vanderbilt jeans were an overnight sensation, and they brought the Murjanis $400 million worth of annual business. Then Murjani went into Coca-Cola clothing, which ran into legal complications and was not quite so successful. Meanwhile, as if surprised by its own success, the business ran into financial difficulties.

The Chinese do not like the Indians. There was a deep-rooted racial prejudice long before the two countries became rivals and went to war over their Himalayan frontier in the 1960s. The Chinese Robert Tang Po married his Indian employer's daughter, but such successful marriages are rare and the communities keep to themselves most of the time. A product of one such union was Jimmy Cotwall, whose father was Parsee and mother

Chinese. The Japanese tortured him to death in the war (his widow was refused permission to live in Britain afterwards).

The business on which the Indian traders founded their success was with Westerners, especially tourists and soldiers. When they diversified it was either into mail order, custom tailoring or prestige label garments. In all these cases the customers still were Westerners, and mostly overseas Westerners. The Indians did not depend on the Chinese market. A few of them rose in government service, for example the Barma brothers Tyebjee and Haider. But they were the exception.

They kept on coming. The three Sams, father and two sons, arrived from Bombay in 1957 and still occupy the tiny Kowloon shop where they set up, making three-day suits for such VIPs as Prince Charles and Richard Nixon for about $200. Engagingly, they refuse to divulge their family name.

The Chinese have gradually increased their share of Hong Kong's population, and the non-Chinese ratio has fallen from about 6 per cent at the beginning of the century to 3 per cent in 1930 and less than 2 per cent today. What will the Indians do after 1997? The successful ones are already beginning to make their arrangements: Lachman Narain, for example, has already waved his son and his son's family off to Toronto.

The early Indian arrivals (you can tell by their names – Rumjahn, Rafiq, Khan) have least to worry about. They speak Cantonese fluently, and because of that they can assimilate and be accepted, if they wish, in spite of the India–China friction. But the Westernised Indians will not find it so comfortable. Hence the flurry of activity to secure British right of abode. Of all the Hongkongers, they have the most difficult nationality problem. They do not wish to be Chinese, the British will not have them, and they do not think that Indian citizenship will help them to live in Hong Kong and use it as a base once it is joined to China.

Of the other Asian communities in Hong Kong, only the Filipinos are more numerous than the Indians; indeed they constitute the largest foreign community of all with around 50,000 residents. This is because of the Filipina maids who are hired on contract to work for Hong Kong families. A maid in Hong Kong can earn three times what a teacher can in Manila, and most of these women save desperately in order to remit money home to their families. Because they are spread about, usually only one in each household, they are not easily organised, but if you walk through Statue Square in the Central district on a Sunday, you will find thousands of them congregating to talk, exchange delicacies from home, get news from the Philippines and learn about each other's work adventures and misadventures. It is chilling to feel the collective loneliness and homesickness that these out-of-context figures express at the feet of the Hong Kong skyscrapers.

If you ask Hongkongers to think of Indonesians in their midst they are likely to talk of the Zecha brothers, especially Adrian. Actually, great-grandfather

Zecha was a Bohemian sculptor who these days would qualify as a Czecho-slovak. He emigrated first to Holland and then to the Dutch East Indies, where he married a Chinese lady from Xiamen. Another great-grandfather was head of the Chinese community in Sukabumi, in Java, who married the daughter of the local Dutch Colonial Officer. Zecha's grandfather went round the world three times – no mean feat for his generation.

If Adrian Zecha is being thorough, he will tell you that he has Chinese, Dutch, Malay, Czech, Thai, German and Indonesian blood running through his effervescent veins. The five brothers, of whom two live and work in Hong Kong, maintain their connection with Indonesia, but Adrian has a Dutch passport and is Western-educated. He had one career in publishing in the 1960s, and now has another in hotels around the region.

The Japanese were allowed back into Hong Kong only in 1954, since when they have come to be one of the larger business communities, with their own club and Chamber of Commerce. Japanese investments are very large. They have their own problems of tolerance, especially when Japanese couples encounter Japanese men with foreign wives or Japanese women with foreign husbands. In the 1960s the Japanese wives of non-Japanese husbands were excluded from the ladies' Japanese Club, so they formed their own separate club and called it the Cherry Blossoms Association – whereupon the Japanese wives of Japanese husbands relented and allowed their errant sisters in.

It would be difficult for all these Asian nationalities to live in a city in China – say Shanghai. In China, politics and diplomacy are taken with utmost seriousness, and if there is some minor tiff between your government and the Chinese government, you can expect the Chinese authorities to take it out on you, even though you have nothing to do with it. If the cosmopolitan flavour of Hong Kong, resting on the British institution of equality before the law, survives after 1997, these Asians will still be found there. If not, Hong Kong will be the poorer for becoming a largely Chinese city, with only a small Western minority.

Chapter 10

Political Refugees

When the family of José Rizal, the father of Philippine nationalism, came to join him in exile in Hong Kong in 1892, his mother gave 'thanks to God to find herself in a free country'. They were, Rizal wrote, 'very happy with the English government . . . all at peace, far from the persecutions they suffered in the Philippines'. 'I want to die here,' his father declared, 'I don't want to go home any more.'

Rizal's was not an isolated case of refuge from the turmoil and strife of the countries surrounding Hong Kong. The political refugees it received often became extremely important later, and Hong Kong benefited from having offered a vital resting point for many of the region's political leaders during the times when they were out of tune with their own governments. Although it was a little island of Asian soil, Hong Kong provided the only convenient example in the continent of a Western-style rule of law and governmental forebearance, enough to inspire visitors from other Asian countries like Rizal.

The first interesting political refugee came from Korea when that country was still ruled, though falteringly, by the Chinese Emperor. When Beijing sent General Yuan Shikai to reinforce Chinese control in Korea towards the end of the nineteenth century, one of the earliest Korean nationalists, Min Yong Ik, tried to discredit him with forged documents, and for this he was exiled and fled to Hong Kong in 1887. He obviously would not go to China, and Japan was too intimately involved in Korean intrigues: if Hong Kong had not existed, it is hard to know where Min could have found shelter.

A few years later came Su Man-shu – 'a Sino-Japanese genius', as a British historian described him – from Yokohama. Child of a Cantonese comprador and his Japanese mistress, Su found himself unaccepted socially in either China or Japan and became a fiercely patriotic (Chinese) journalist in Hong Kong. He was probably at school in Hong Kong in the 1890s.

Rizal was also there at that time, to be followed by his parents and sisters, all victims of Spanish harassment because of his talk of political reform and independence. He began to practise medicine and ophthalmology in Duddell Street in Central Hong Kong and thus earned a name as the 'Spanish Doctor'. But his heart was in his patriotic novels and tracts, and the Liga Filipina, through which he planned to bring Filipino intellectuals into a cohesive organisation to wrest ultimate liberty from the Spanish tyrants. Rizal left Hong Kong later in 1892.

One of his followers, Emilio Aguinaldo, used Hong Kong a few years afterwards as a staging point in his campaign to create the first Republic of the Philippines, of which he became President. At the age of 28 he sailed into Hong Kong harbour as part of a truce arrangement with the Spanish authorities in the Philippines. The revolutionaries laid down their arms and its leaders went into voluntary exile in Hong Kong, while the Spanish were to pay them a large sum of money and undertake reforms. Aguinaldo grasped the opportunity of the visit of the US navy flagship *Olympia* in Hong Kong harbour to talk to Commodore George Dewey and the American consul, as a result of which he returned to resume the independence struggle against Spain in the expectation of American help. One of his first acts in 1898 was to proclaim the Philippine Republic, and at a colourful ceremony the first new Philippine flag, handmade by Filipina wives in Hong Kong, was unfurled. Aguinaldo lost that struggle, and had to submit to the Americans taking over the country from Spain, but he lived to the ripe old age of 95, dying only in 1964.

The other Southeast Asian countries also sent their exiles and itinerant revolutionaries to the Hong Kong oasis of calm and stability. Tan Malaka was the best known Indonesian visitor, a left-wing nationalist who challenged the Dutch government. Exiled in 1920, he conducted insurrection at a distance, from Europe and east Asia. In the course of this he travelled through Hong Kong and was arrested there in 1932, held for seven weeks and then released. The British rejected Dutch (and American) requests for his extradition, finding no offence. From his cell Tan wrote letters to the British labour leaders George Lansbury and James Maxton arguing against deportation. On finally sailing from Hong Kong, Tan told a British Special Branch officer, 'when the roles are reversed, I will remember your courtesy'. Tan became the only credible rival to Sukarno for the first Presidency of the Indonesian Republic, and as such was mown down by Sukarno's supporters in 1949. Another important Indonesian politician, Djoko Harjono, was exiled to Hong Kong for seven years in the 1970s.

The most famous arrival of all was a little man with a wispy beard who was to inflict astounding defeats on the Japanese, French and American armies and become for many people the world's 'Mr Revolution'. This was Ho Chi Minh. In June 1931, he was surprised by the British police living under a false name at a Kowloon address. The Vietnamese communist revolutionary's whereabouts had been discovered from a European Comintern agent arrested in Singapore carrying Ho's Hong Kong address on him. The Hong Kong government wanted to deport him, but a banishment inquiry was first necessary to determine where he should be deported to. Although he denied being a Communist, Ho had attended the First Congress of Indochinese Revolutionaries which was held in Hong Kong in 1930, and presided over the creation of the Vietnam Cong-San Dang in a Kowloon football stadium.

The French pressed for extradition, but a young anti-colonialist British lawyer in Hong Kong, Frank Loseby, happened to hear of the case and helped to secure Ho's release on legal technicalities. 'Just tell me what I must know,' he said to Ho, 'to defend you successfully. Say no more than is necessary, for all revolutionaries have their secrets.' Those are not words often heard in European colonies in Asia, nor in some independent countries, come to that.

Loseby applied for a writ of habeas corpus. He was refused, but two appeals to the Privy Council in London on grounds of abuse of executive power won Ho a guaranteed twelve months asylum, during which time the Hong Kong government was responsible for his safety and upkeep and the police could not use the Comintern documents found in his possession because they were *sub judice*. He was kept in the Bowen Road hospital, where he was visited by many leading personalities including the Colonial Secretary of the time, and he wrote a book in English expounding his political philosophy. Unfortunately, Loseby, his lawyer, in whose charge it was left, lost it in the Japanese occupation.

When the case came to the Privy Council the following year, Stafford Cripps for the government agreed out of court to a compromise, whereby Ho would leave Hong Kong as the deportation order had specified, but under his own steam and without any particular ship endorsement – and the Hong Kong government would pay $1,000 for the cost of his appeal. Ho had suffered from tuberculosis during his stay in Hong Kong and the Comintern decided to muddy the trail by announcing, as the *Daily Worker* of London did in August 1932, 'the death of Nguyen-ai-Quoc [Ho Chi Minh's alias], founder of the Communist Party of Indochina, secured by imperialist terror in the prison hospital of Hong Kong'.

In fact Ho was whisked from hospital, disguised as a Chinese teacher, to sail for Singapore. He presented himself again in Hong Kong the following January and was rearrested, released and taken on a government launch to a ship bound for Xiamen, joining it under cover of darkness in the Lyemun Strait. From there he travelled to Shanghai and Moscow to take up the future which the whole world knows, of leading the Vietnamese nationalist movement first against Japanese invasion, and then against French colonialist obstinacy, and finally against American intervention – in order to create a

Communist Vietnam, which his successors have now shown to be one of the most economically backward and politically repressive regimes to be found anywhere in the world.

There was one more possible appearance by Ho Chi Minh in Hong Kong, towards the end of 1948, when Yang Hsaonan, father of the present Chief Justice of Hong Kong and then a merchant in Shanghai, received a caller – 'a man with a young face but white hair and a long beard'. His calling card, Yang wrote in his diary, 'showed that he was Ho Chi Minh. He asked me for a free passage and money . . . I . . . presented him with $20 and a free ticket for *s.s. Sheng-ching* bound for Hong Kong. In return Mr Ho gave me his photograph and some of his recent works.' This was a time when Ho was directing a guerrilla campaign against the French, and it is strange to find him hat in hand for his transport from China to Hong Kong – though he was known to have conferred with communist colleagues in Guangzhou.

It cannot be overemphasised how unusual it is in the Asian context to find idealistic young lawyers like Loseby, and a system of legal checks and balances allowing an able lawyer to prevent arbitrary actions against individuals. This is a major reason for the choice by disaffected Asian leaders to be exiled in Hong Kong rather than anywhere else. Ho Chi Minh was certainly impressed by the workings of British law, and so grateful to his young lawyer Loseby that, although there was no further communication for almost thirty years, Loseby did receive in his office, after Ho Chi Minh had assumed the Presidency of North Vietnam, an invitation to go to Hanoi and be Ho Chi Minh's guest with all expenses paid. Loseby and his wife and daughter took up the invitation, and were amazed at the warmth of Ho's feelings towards them.

Ho Chi Minh was not the only Vietnamese Communist, and may not have been indispensable to the emergence of a communist state there. But it is a legitimate speculation that, but for the altruistic efforts of a libertarian young lawyer and the safeguards of the British legal system, Ho might well have been returned into French hands in 1931. In that case, he would probably have been executed, and it is just possible that Indochina might have taken a less revolutionary road of more gradual change – which in turn might have spared hundreds of thousands of lives and prevented the Vietnam War's becoming such a monstrous burden on American society.

Hong Kong played host to another Vietnamese head of state in 1946–8 when Bao Dai, Emperor of Annam, spent his exile in Hong Kong. The French colonial authorities sent envoys to Hong Kong to try to persuade Bao to become the leader of an effective Indochinese opposition to Ho Chi Minh, whom Bao had earlier been assisting on a nationalist platform. Bao also discussed the Indochina situation with an American diplomat in Hong Kong, William Bullitt, the first intimation of the fatal US involvement. Ngo Dinh Diem, the future President of South Vietnam, made the journey to

Hong Kong to persuade Bao not to sign any agreements with the French, but without success.

At about that time one of Thailand's post-war dictators, Pridi Phanomyong, arrived in Hong Kong in disgrace, having been forced out of the country which he had ruled with such a strong arm. Pridi was the leftist in the Thai leadership of his generation, and had often had to work underground or in exile in Paris. In 1944–7, he became the most powerful figure in the entire country. But the death of the Thai king, a surge in inflation and corruption scandals undermined Pridi's position. His government and his power collapsed after a successful *coup d'état* by his opponents, and he went into exile, via Hong Kong, initially to Guangzhou in China, but later again to Paris. When you are in a hurry, Hong Kong is the best place to arrange your onward travelling.

The asylum of Hong Kong was invoked by groups of politically motivated migrants, as well as by individuals. After 1917 some fervently religious Russians fled from communism to China, and when the Chinese brand of communism caught up with them there in 1949 they mostly filtered out from China via Hong Kong. A typical group was the congregation of more than 100 'Old Believers', a sect of the Russian Orthodox church, who travelled from Xinjiang down to Hong Kong *en route* to Argentina. They strode about Hong Kong during their short stay in nineteenth-century peasant costume – billowing trousers, high-laced boots, the women in kerchiefs and ankle-length skirts. They had asked to make a new start in Canada, but the Canadians proved too individualistic and would not accept immigration by a group, even of political refugees.

The case where Hong Kong's hospitality as a place of refuge was strained almost to breaking point was that of the boat people from Vietnam. As a direct result of Ho Chi Minh's extending his communist power to South Vietnam after the American withdrawal in the early 1970s, large numbers of overseas Chinese who had won a living in south Vietnam from petty capitalism and trade found their prospects so drastically reduced that they opted to leave. Taking their families and possessions in necessarily small and not always seaworthy boats, they sailed either northwards to Hong Kong or southwards to Malaysia and other Southeast Asian destinations. In May 1975, the *Clara Maersk*, a Danish freighter, dropped anchor in Hong Kong harbour with more than 3,740 Vietnamese refugees, whom it had rescued at sea. They were admitted temporarily on humanitarian grounds.

From then onwards there was a steady flow. The most popular route was from the vicinity of Hue, the port roughly midway along the Vietnamese coast, across the open sea to the Chinese island of Hainan, and then skirting the coast of Hainan and the south Chinese mainland, going ashore sometimes for water and provisions, to Hong Kong – a journey of about 800 miles. Hong Kong, the easiest 'stepping stone' for these desperate boat people to reach, has received more than 178,000 refugees since then, only 112,000 of whom were resettled elsewhere. Hong Kong's temporary and inadequate refugee camps, made squalid by the sheer numbers involved, were left – literally, in some cases – holding the baby. There are now more than 56,000 Vietnamese boat people languishing in Hong Kong's thirteen detention centres, and most of them have no option but to return to start their lives anew in Vietnam.

In the 1970s, when this sad story began, Hong Kong accorded refugee status to all the boat people who reached its shores. At an international conference convened in Geneva in 1979 by the United Nations High Commissioner for Refugees, Hong Kong agreed to act as a place of first asylum for the growing numbers of boat people, on the understanding that they would eventually be resettled in various Western countries. Their favourite (or easiest) destination was Malaysia, where 30 per cent of the boat people setting sail since the Geneva conference have gone. But Malaysia is a country with an unpopular Chinese minority and a government which cannot afford politically to allow new Chinese immigration, and it soon took the tough attitude of not allowing these refugees to land. Sometimes they were forced out to sea again, perhaps to starve or drown or be robbed and raped by pirates. Hong Kong was the second favourite destination, where a quarter of the Vietnamese refugees arrived, followed by Indonesia, Thailand and the Philippines with smaller numbers. Seasonal prevailing winds were an important factor in deciding where to go.

And then a change was observed in the boat people. Up to 1979 the great majority of them were overseas Chinese, but after 1980 they were almost all ethnic Vietnamese. Hong Kong could try to cope with overseas Chinese settlement, but large numbers of ethnic Vietnamese attempting to live in an already overcrowded Hong Kong would create damaging racial tensions on top of all the other difficulties. Furthermore, the new refugees after 1980 were increasingly from North Vietnam, the old bailiwick of Ho Chi Minh, rather than from the formerly capitalist south, and could no longer be described, therefore, as refugees from a newly imposed communism. Many of them came overland through China. These changes clouded the prospects of resettlement in the United States or Europe. It was obvious that these people were leaving to get a better living rather than to escape political persecution.

The Hong Kong government suspended automatic refugee status and started screening new arrivals to determine whether or not they were fleeing because of, in the United Nations definition, a 'well-founded fear of persecution on grounds of race, religion, nationality or membership of a particular social or political group'. If not, they were economic migrants who were unlikely to find asylum in third countries, and would therefore have to be repatriated. An agreement on voluntary repatriation was made with the Vietnam government, through the United Nations, in 1988, and another international conference at Geneva with forty-six countries represented followed the Hong Kong government's lead in ending the automatic refugee status of the boat people and adopting screening processes for them in future.

When it came to the point of making the first repatriations, there was an outcry by public opinion in Britain and America where sympathy for political refugees is deeply ingrained. But there is no other solution if the Western countries will not themselves take further quotas of boat people. Already there are more than 1,300 Vietnamese boat children who were born in Hong Kong refugee centres and have seen no other home, and there are another 4,000 refugee children living in these centres. Since they do not have political or religious differences with the Vietnamese government, the only problem in repatriating them is the possibility that they might be punished by that government for having left Vietnam illegally.

This is why the Vietnamese government has to be involved in the new arrangements, and its agreement has been secured not to punish them. The initial monitoring by British diplomats in Vietnam has indicated that this commitment is being honoured. In practice, it boils down to a question of money and prestige. If enough new economic aid can be provided to Vietnam, and goodness knows it needs it, then some leverage is created whereby repatriated refugees should face few problems. But it hurts Vietnam's self-respect if the international media publicise the fact that Vietnamese people refuse repatriation, not wanting to live in their own country. It is necessary somehow to find a small area between voluntary and involuntary repatriation where these sensitivities can be accommodated.

It is difficult for the Hong Kong government to say so, but its room for manoeuvre is limited by the fact that it has been routinely repatriating illegal arrivals from China for many years, since the early 1960s. If Chinese from China who sneak into Hong Kong without a visa in search of a better material life can be unceremoniously escorted back to the frontier and handed back to the Chinese guards, why should Vietnamese arrivals by boat be treated better? It is a question which any Chinese would ask, including the 98 per cent of the Hong Kong population who are Chinese and share the Chinese dislike of Vietnamese, and also including the Chinese in the People's Republic, who probably feel that a tougher policy, á la Malaysia, would be both equitable and more effectively deterrent.

Now the Hong Kong government senses that it faces a 1997 deadline, because Chinese officials have said that the problem of the boat people must be settled by then – including those already in Hong Kong and those who may still come in the next seven years. China would not allow them to be treated as residents, it was said, and the UK was too 'lax'. It was hypocritical and a use of double standards to treat the Vietnamese better than the illegal immigrants from China, and that could lead to racial conflict between the

Vietnamese and local Chinese. If all that could be said in public by a senior official of China, one could imagine how differently the matter is likely to be treated after the British have left. The likelihood is, therefore, that the UK will make every effort to clear the decks in the next seven years, initially by repatriation, mandatory or otherwise, and then perhaps as a last final resort by pleading for the residue of the Vietnamese to be accepted in America, Australia and Europe before the Union Jack goes down.

This liberal record of the Hong Kong government towards Asian refugees is not likely to survive the change of sovereignty in 1997. British mercy was not, of course, extended to every case. Asylum was never carried to the point of jeopardising the necessary practical relations with the Chinese authorities, for example. The Hong Kong government generally aligned itself with the view that the international communist conspiracy should be clobbered at every opportunity, even if it differed with its Dutch, French and American counterparts over individual cases like Ho Chi Minh's or Tan Malaka's. But the record is better than that of other places in east Asia.

Will there be anything left of the asylum after 1997? It is doubtful, if only because the Hong Kong leaders will have enough of a challenge keeping themselves free from total dictation from Beijing, and in that context will give priority to other issues of far greater importance to Hongkongers. If Hong Kong autonomy goes well, many Chinese might like to enjoy that overt superiority over other countries which comes from hosting their exiles in your own little enclave. There is also a practical diplomatic advantage in gaining access to foreign intrigues the easy way on your own soil instead of having to go to other countries for it. But if British colonial rule scored seven out of ten on asylum, a realistic prediction for after 1997 might be only two out of ten.

Chapter 11

The People in Between

'We,' said the senior civil servant high in the government ranks, 'are the only genuine Hongkongers.' The small and subdued Eurasian community is indeed the only group of people in Hong Kong with no motherland to return to. They are heirs to many traditions, owners of none.

For years after the founding of the colony, unaccompanied Western men found themselves in close proximity to the Chinese, and the Eurasians are the natural product of that proximity, mainly through the system of concubines, but also through intermarriage. There were Chinese who married English wives, like Sir Ho Kai, one of the first Chinese to be educated in England. He came back in the 1880s with not only degrees in law and medicine, but also a wife from Blackheath called Alice. For that period it was a bold match. But few followed Ho Kai's example, and the overwhelming majority of Eurasians trace their ancestry back to a Western father and a Chinese mother.

The greatest leader of the entire Hong Kong community in the first half of the twentieth century, Sir Robert Hotung, was a case in point. His father was a Dutch merchant, Charles Bosman, and his mother was in the category of 'protected woman', that is to say that she belonged to a brothel, but if the police raided it she could establish immunity by declaring that she was 'protected' by Bosman. Some people used to think that Hotung was Chinese, but the 'Ho' was borrowed from the first two letters of his father's homeland, Holland. When he first went abroad to the United States during the First World War, he travelled on a passport bearing the name Bosman.

It follows from this kind of union in the early days of Hong Kong that the first Eurasians were usually brought up by their Chinese mothers. The parents, living in separate worlds, did not normally cohabit, and the fathers did not join the household of the mother and the children. The first generation Eurasian was invariably Chinese-speaking, therefore, not bilingual at all. Some of them became reabsorbed into the Chinese community, losing their potential separate identity. We see them today only in the occasional suggestion of a European feature on a Chinese face.

If the father were Chinese then, of course, the children would be regarded as Chinese and identify themselves as such. Han Suyin, the novelist, was in this position, having a Chinese father and a Belgian mother, and when her first husband, a Chinese, took her to Europe before the war, he told her sternly: 'Your blood is Chinese, blood comes from the father, the mother is only a receptacle.' Chinese male chauvinism overlaps with racial exclusivism to ensure that any doubts about an individual's identity are kept to a minimum. Yet Han Suyin, asked as a child how she would choose between being European and Chinese, had said firmly that she would like to be both.

Eurasian children of European fathers in Hong Kong followed their mothers' lead and became more active in the Chinese community than in the European. The Eurasian Sin Tak Fan, who led the Chinese community in the 1900s and 1910s, was also known as Stephen Hall, but the Chinese of that day did not apparently feel awkward about having a man of mixed blood to lead them. On the contrary, since the main business of the organised Chinese community was to compete with the Europeans and gain concessions and facilities from them, a person like Stephen Hall with some access to European society was an ideal figure.

Sir Robert Hotung's large family was tragically divided on this issue. He himself wore Chinese dress, claimed Chinese nationality and tried to bring his children up as Chinese. The times when he summoned the family to assemble were at the Chinese New Year, not at Christmas, and again at the Ching Ming Chinese festival, which the more westernised members of the family called 'Chinese Easter'. Some of his children followed his lead, others did not. His son Robin joined the Chinese army and became the representative of the Republic of China at the United Nations. But his daughter Jean publicly regretted her father's 'retreat' into Chineseness. 'I used to feel sorry that he threw in his lot with the Chinese.' Although she gained fame as the 'first Chinese baby' to be born on the Peak, where Sir Robert was the first non-European to be allowed to buy a house, she found her complicated antecedents to be 'a continual source of embarrassment'; she even suffered at the university where she was classified as Chinese. Chinese students could only matriculate with a pass in the Chinese language, which she could not manage, so she failed her exams – yet her English friends, with whom she fully identified, did not need it at all!

Such tragedies of brothers and sisters, parents and children turning against each other because of the accidents of physical feature and cultural preference are common among Eurasians. But the same factors make them eminently qualified to act as go-between, intermediating between the European and Chinese communities. The Eurasians may not be fully accepted by either side, but they are usually more acceptable to the Europeans than the

Chinese are, and more acceptable to the Chinese than Europeans are – at least that used to be the case in the nineteenth century and in the earlier part of the twentieth century, and even today one can still see evidence of it. A surprising number of the 'fixers' who are so prominent in Hong Kong business turn out to be of Eurasian origin.

It is largely a question of confidence. A Chinese may well lack the self-assurance to act confidently in dealing with Europeans, and vice versa, but a Eurasian, precisely because he is in the middle and has had both streams of cultural influence bearing upon him since birth, can manage it either way. So the Eurasians became useful in Hong Kong's commerce. The big Western trading companies and banks frequently called on an able and well-connected Eurasian to act as a middle-man in dealings with the Chinese public.

From about the 1890s onwards, the Eurasians became important people to know in banking. After the First World War, Sir Robert Hotung was the *comprador* for Jardine Matheson, and others with Chinese names masking a Eurasian identity fulfilled the same function for the Hongkong Bank, the Mercantile Bank, etc. If a Chinese businessman wanted a loan or credit from a foreign bank, he would usually have to go through Eurasian *compradors*, and this made them, as a class, extremely rich. In Hong Kong wealth almost automatically brings political power, and the Executive and Legislative Councils have usually had a Eurasian member, sometimes more than one, even if disguised behind a Chinese name. From Man-kam Lo in the 1930s, through Alberto Rodriguez, Roger Lobo, Oswald Cheung, Tak-shing Lo and John Swaine, this distinguished roll-call testifies to the contribution made by Eurasian leaders.

The complexity of a Eurasian family can be astonishing. Jean Hotung felt herself pulled apart by the various elements in her ancestry. Where the cultural road to follow is unclear, and there are competing racial models within the family, the tug-of-war can be most painful. Eventually, however, the strife and competition may be looked back on as an enriching legacy. Sir Roger Lobo, now a retired businessman, can point with pride to the fact that his great-great-grandfather was an Englishman in the East India Company, and that one of his grandfathers was the Belgian merchant Henrique Hyndman. By now, many Eurasians have married Eurasians so that the mixture of race is on both sides. This is what happened to Jean Hotung, who complained about her family pushing her into a Chinese mould; she married into another leading Eurasian family in Hong Kong.

Men like Sir Robert Hotung were creatures of their time, and further gradations of status and identity were caused in his family by the fact that he not only had two wives at once, Clara and Margaret, but also supported a number of concubines. (His youngest brother went even better, with more than twelve concubines and over thirty children.) The convention was established that Sir Robert's descendants through his wives took the name Hotung, while those who came from the concubines took the family name Ho. But when Jean wrote a book about her childhood, she could not bring herself to mention the concubines and her brothers and sisters who sprang from them.

The Hotung wives actually coexisted rather amicably. The only awkward moment was when Hotung was knighted and one wife had to be selected as the official consort. Even then, both were accorded the courtesy title of Lady, so face was saved. Another of Sir Robert's sons, Eddie, caused a furore in the family when he married an Irish girl called Mordia O'Shea without waiting for his father's approval. Eddie, who had both legs amputated in the war, had two sons, Eric and Jo, who are active today in Hong Kong. Eric founded the Chinese gold and silver exchange, and has built on his antecedents ('my grandfather was a schoolmate of Dr Sun Yat Sen, and was a close friend of the philosopher and reformer Kang Yuwei') to become a valued participant in the US–China relations business, having founded his own Hotung Institute for International Studies.

Another daughter of Sir Robert, Irene, neatly closed an awkward chapter of European–Chinese relations by marrying a chemical engineer who was the great-grandson of Commissioner Lin Tse-hsu of opium war fame. The union of the families of a European trade and the highest Chinese official to seek to eject the West from South China makes an appropriate foundation for Hong Kong's new role in China's modernisation.

Sir Robert's younger brother was Ho Fuk, among whose grandchildren in Hong Kong may be named Elaine Ho (a long-time aide and confidante of Jardine *taipans*), E. P. Ho (a civil servant who is the only one left among his brothers to remain in Hong Kong, the others being spread in every continent), and Stanley Ho Hung-san, emperor of Macao and king of the casinos. Stanley, a tall handsome businessman who is nervous about his personal security, could hardly have failed in a business career, his father having been a *comprador* for Sassoon's, and his three uncles and grandfather being *compradors* for the Hongkong Bank, Jardine, and the Mercantile Bank.

As a child Stanley Ho lived halfway up the Peak in conditions of affluence, but that life collapsed when his father bought the wrong shares and went bankrupt, sneaking away to Saigon in disgrace. The young Stanley could hardly afford a bus fare, and when he reached Hong Kong University on a scholarship he could hardly scrape up the money to take a girl for coffee. His university career was in any case interrupted by the war, at which point he took a junk to Macao with only a dollar in his pocket. There he found his great-uncle Sir Robert Hotung sitting out the war, so he sat at his knee and learned many things from the old man.

Stanley Ho began his business career by selling wood oil to the Japanese in return for food and textiles which were needed by the Western refugees in Macao. At one point he was almost captured by pirates, escaping only by a rapid change of flag. He continued trading during the war, selling precious metals and even aeroplanes to China, and during the Korean war in the early 1950s he helped the Chinese to get round the American embargo by using his Macao connections to sell rubber tyres, corrugated iron, Vaseline and other goods to China.

At 24 Stanley was already a millionaire, using his profits to buy property and to win the casino franchise in Macao. He was the man in the middle when China negotiated with Portugal for the mutual recognition of the status of Macao in the late 1970s. He built up the casino in Macao to an annual turnover of $400 million, of which 10 per cent went to the government, and another 10 per cent to charities in China. Sometimes his judgement failed, as when he lost $50 million on a race course which he built for the Shah of Iran just before his downfall. Now he is Hong Kong's socialist multimillionaire, going snipe shooting in China where they call him *gwailo*. His elder son was killed in a car crash a few years ago, leaving a schoolboy as the heir to his remarkable fortune.

Another important family which has intermarried with the Hotungs is that of Sir Man-kam Lo, a solicitor and tennis champion, who married Victoria Hotung, another of Sir Robert's daughters. He encountered controversy in the war when he was forced to work for the Japanese administration, and there were the usual arguments about whether such orders were to be resisted at all costs, or whether it was best to bow before the storm and retain at least a little control of events on behalf of the defeated community. His son, Tak-shing Lo, is also a lawyer, very anglicised and a keen contender in the stakes for the political leadership after 1997.

Many Portuguese names are to be found in Hong Kong, and some of their bearers are fully ethnic Portuguese. But the majority imply a Eurasian or Sino-Indian background. The Portuguese settlement at Macao dates back long before Hong Kong, and there were also active Portuguese communities in Goa, Malacca and Timor. The Portuguese were always less stand-offish than the Anglo-Saxons about matters of colour and race. 'Portuguese' can mean, in the Hong Kong context, Portuguese from Macao who have intermarried with Chinese and often speak a unique mixture of Portuguese and Cantonese at home. The so-called Portuguese in Macao today are in fact mostly Chinese, most of the 'real' Portuguese having already left for the United States. The Portuguese in Hong Kong were a big community until the 1950s, being particularly strong in the middle reaches of the Hongkong Bank and at such institutions as St Joseph's College and Lasalle College. These days the community is somewhat depleted. Two of its leaders are Sir Roger Lobo, whose English and European antecedents have already been mentioned, and A. de O. Sales, who was born in Canton, and is 'Mr Olympic Games' in Hong Kong.

Eurasians are constantly being hurt by the outside world's uncomprehending racialism. When the Japanese were about to invade Hong Kong in 1941, the government evacuated all foreign women and children, but some Eurasians were turned back from Australian ports because of the 'white Australia' policy of that time. Jean, the daughter of Sir Robert Hotung, went to visit her children at Sydney just after the war and reported this conversation with the immigration officer:

'You are partly Chinese, are you not . . .? What percentage?'

'Fifty.'

'Are you sure it is 50 per cent? Couldn't you make it a little less?'

'No.'

'In that case, I'm afraid I shall have to take some action in the matter.'

In the end, she did not have to report regularly to the authorities during her visit, as the letter of the law seemed to require, but the exchange at the airport was enough to arouse buried memories of prejudice. James Marshall, a civil servant, recalls reproachfully how his father was buried at the Hong Kong Cemetery because he was white, while his mother had to be buried elsewhere because she was not.

It is perhaps too early to talk of overseas Eurasian communities. The numbers are still small, and Eurasians are more individual than the Chinese and do not necessarily stick together. Yet there are some who have acquired fame or fortune in such new lands as Britain, Australia or America. Timothy Mo is one example in Britain, son of a wealthy Chinese businessman and an English mother, educated in England and taking England as his physical and cultural home – while still retaining in his novels (*Soursweet*, *The Monkey King*, and *An Insular Possession*) that itchy and half disdainful curiosity about China and things Chinese which most Eurasians have.

Given the gradual relaxation of racially exclusive attitudes, one would guess that there would be more Eurasians in future. The long-term trend must be towards more racial intermarriage. There are probably more Eurasians in Hong Kong than any statistics suggest. They are more prominent in business and public life than might appear on the surface. They will continue to be an important group in Hong Kong in the future, and leaders like Stanley Ho and Tak-shing Lo, with their access to Beijing, should be able to take the community into the twenty-first century provided the Chinese do not insist, after 1997, on a fumigation of European culture.

Chapter 12

The Asia–Pacific Neutral

The only war in which Hong Kong was actually invaded was the Pacific War or Second World War. For three years and eight months a much reduced population of under 600,000 trembled at the command of Lieutenant General Rensuke Isogai. The episode produced a fund of well remembered atrocity stories. Liang Yen describes a near collision in Garden Road near the present American Consulate-General, where a Japanese officer instantly beheaded the offending Chinese driver, and the head rolled downhill spouting blood. It was a time of deprivation, humiliation and isolation. The extraordinary thing was that throughout the period of Japanese occupation there were small bands of Chinese guerrillas actually holding parts of the New Territories of Hong Kong, and there were numerous escapes from the prison camps where more than 9,000 British and other Western prisoners were interned.

Some of the close friendships and professional trust forged in this deadly game of outwitting the foreign soldier who did not know the terrain were to endure into the post-war era and create an unexpected, if discreet, camaraderie between the British and the Chinese. Before General Isogai's intrusion, the British and the Chinese were politically on opposite sides. One was the colonial power, the other the colonial subject. One was the Western imperialist, the other was the Chinese victim of imperialism. But in 1945 when the two parties gratefully emerged from their enforced togetherness in the face of a common enemy, it took some time for them to sink back into their old antagonisms, and some of the common anti-Japanese spirit survived the renewal of colonialism.

British administrators, soldiers and businessmen hastened back to Hong Kong in 1945, brushing aside the universal anti-colonial mood, to start rebuilding the city, tidying the streets, controlling prices, redeeming bad money, imposing law and order, and offering what soon became scarce commodities in Far Eastern centres, namely, political stability, good shipping services and no inflation. To most people's surprise, Hong Kong's business went into rapid boom and by 1948 trade was hitting record levels.

Less commendable was the legitimising of hostility towards persons and things Japanese. The Chinese already disliked and despised the Japanese before 1941, but after the war they showed a more open antagonism in which the Europeans acquiesced. The ghosts themselves took a very long time to lie down. I. M. Pei, the architect, experienced unease when he first inspected the site for the new Bank of China building in Central Hong Kong. Japanese had tortured Chinese there forty years earlier, and people living and working nearby still claimed to hear the shrieks and groans. Because of this, Pei altered the site a little, bartering a piece of adjacent land with the government in return for building an extra road. The Reuters office had also been used for torture, and the night desk man claimed, years after the return of peace, to hear moans and cries in the building.

On the other hand, many Hong Kong Chinese had profited commercially from the Japanese occupation, even if they did not collaborate politically. Nobody liked to investigate this kind of allegation thoroughly, in case it brought out too much that was best left forgotten. Only the Chinese Communists were exempt from such innuendoes.

The Korean War in 1950 renewed political uncertainty about Hong Kong's future and disrupted trade. An American journalist visiting Hong Kong in 1951 called it 'a dying city', perhaps influenced by the evacuation of all the American diplomats. The Hong Kong Chinese felt pulled in different directions: as capitalists, they did not support Communist China or North Korea; but as Chinese, they sympathised with Communist China's determination to resist American armed force. For many of them, the American embargo was an invitation to indulge their patriotism and line their pockets at one and the same time – by supplying materials to China in avoidance of the embargo.

Several Chinese traders, like Poon in Timothy Mo's novel *The Monkey King*, made a fortune this way. Men like Fung King Hey and Stanley Ho arranged a supply of goods which they claimed were not war-related and could not possibly help the Chinese military effort, but which were scarce in China because such a very broad embargo list had been drawn up. There is no doubt that China was extremely grateful to these Hong Kong merchants and that some of them benefited later with contracts, honours or special treatment.

The Vietnam War followed, bringing a new trade in materials with the American side, by way of military procurement, and a boom in spending by American soldiers on rest and recreation in Hong Kong. By 1969, Hong Kong was earning more than $500 million a year from Vietnam procurement and 'R & R'. Wars also need correspondents, and Hong Kong became the Far East base for the West's war correspondents, like Ian Morrison of *The Times*, the real-life model for Han Suyin's hero in *A Many Splendoured Thing*.

In between wars, and in the remarkable extended peace of 1975–90, Hong Kong stays neutral. It does not take sides in the region's political conflicts, but rather helps to mediate the quarrels of others in the region. Leo Goodstadt called Hong Kong Asia's honest broker, and although honesty is not the first quality which people might associate with Hong Kong, there is certainly a fund of experience in broking and Hong Kong can show a clean sheet in political affiliations. Lord Kadoorie defined Hong Kong as the 'fluid flywheel' which takes up the difference between East and West to avoid friction.

Many examples could be cited where Hong Kong has played the neutral intermediary. There is one long-running dispute for which Hong Kong has had a grandstand seat since the 1920s, and that is the Communist–Guomindang rivalry in China. Dennis Bloodworth of *The Observer* has been reporting secret meetings between Communist and Guomindang representatives in Hong Kong for decades: his stories are always denied, but no one can think of any other place where such discussions could be held, and most people agree that they probably are being held somewhere.

The development of indirect trade between China and Taiwan via Hong Kong, which has now reached an astonishingly high level, has led to a need for mediation of commercial disputes, and this is now met in Hong Kong. When the usual differences over specifications, delivery dates, condition of goods, etc. arise, arbitration is not appropriate because the legal departments on each side cannot acknowledge each other. Mediation is therefore required. Even though it lacks legal effectiveness, it has publicity and moral value at least.

Turning from commerce to the world of ideas and literature, two of the most famous contemporary writers of China and Taiwan, Liu Binyan and Chen Ying-chen, were invited by Hong Kong University together, and they embraced each other at Kai Tak Airport in 1988. Although they had admired each other as dissident writers who had been imprisoned by their respective governments, this was their first actual meeting – in Hong Kong, at the initiative of Hong Kong.

In the world of shipping, Hong Kong is used as a 'cover' destination for ships running between Taiwan and the mainland coast of China. People's Republic ships, owned by Chinese companies and manned by Chinese seamen, sail to Taiwan from Chinese ports under Hong Kong registration flying the Panama flag. They return with Taiwan goods for which the bill of lading says Hong Kong, but the actual destination is the Chinese mainland – another example of the usefulness of Hong Kong in a world where ideology, national sovereignty and pride are so important. When China and the Portuguese authorities in Macao agreed to settle their border conflicts which had broken out in the early 1950s, the details of the agreement were settled in Hong Kong.

In many ways Hong Kong would seem to follow a Swiss model of international behaviour. Sir Y. K. Pao has long advocated that Hong Kong should become the Geneva of the Far East, by which he meant in particular that Hong Kong should develop its shipping registry to become a fully fledged flag of convenience, as well as a banking centre in which Far East customers will have as much trust regarding confidentiality as the world has come to hold for Switzerland. In some respects Hong Kong already goes further than Switzerland in the practice of international neutrality. If, as a resident of Hong Kong, you abide by the law of Hong Kong, you are protected from other governments – more than would be the case in Switzerland. Foreign citizens living in Hong Kong are not deported, except in the special case of China. 'We do not take in other governments' laundry,' an official explains.

Hong Kong can thus serve as a place to launch good causes. When China was attacked by Japan in 1937, it needed to mobilise world opinion and support, and Soong Ching-ling, Sun Yat Sen's widow, launched the China Defence League in Hong Kong in 1938, as a prelude to rallying world support in the war which had just broken out. Since Hong Kong has a free press, the rival propaganda machines of the Guomindang and the Communist Party in China and Taiwan made much use of Hong Kong before 1949 as a base for spreading the good word to other parts of the world. When the Communists gained control of the mainland, their international propaganda organs used to mail political material to many countries of the world through the Hong Kong Post Office, because a Hong Kong postmark was less controversial. Sending things via Hong Kong meant that the recipient was more likely to be untroubled in receiving the material than if it had a Chinese stamp. This was certainly so in America, but also in a number of other Western countries and in Southeast Asia and even the USSR. British Commonwealth status proved its worth once again.

Outside the world of China, in which Hong Kong is an obvious neutral point, there have been disputes in East and Southeast Asia where Hong Kong has played a similar role. In the 1960s, for example, the British-initiated creation of the Malaysian Federation was bitterly opposed by Indonesia, as a result of which normal trade between Indonesia on the one hand, and Singapore and Malaysia on the other hand, was interrupted. The fact is, of course, that overseas Chinese families are the principal shippers of goods from Indonesian ports as well as from Singapore and Malaysian ports, and these families have branches in Hong Kong. So it seemed only a natural precaution to make arrangements so that goods left Indonesian ports with shipping documents showing that the goods were destined for Hong Kong, and to have these documents changed on the high seas, so that the ship could sail directly to Singapore. This was the kind of service which Hong Kong was glad to perform, and it was a major contribution to the economies of Southeast Asia.

The same thing happened when South Korea had a dispute with Japan, resulting in the prohibition of direct trade. Once again, ships left Japan with goods consigned to Hong Kong, but sailed directly to Korea with the documents being changed *en route* – and vice versa. One may deplore the political and legal deception, but everybody involved in the actual transaction was extremely grateful to Hong Kong for playing the role of the silent middleman.

Such instances could be multiplied, and there is a great deal of evidence to support the idea of Hong Kong as a kind of Pacific Switzerland. Hong Kong is an open city which specifically does not restrict its facilities and benefits to nationals of particular countries. Indeed, it is used as a centre for information gathering and semi-diplomatic activity by countries as varied as Singapore (whose government developed substantial trade and political links with China during the long period when it had no formal relationship with Beijing, through contacts developed and conducted in Hong Kong) and Vietnam, which has a government presence in Hong Kong that is formally a trade office but is presumed to conduct semi-political functions as well with countries not fully represented in Hanoi.

Hong Kong is a press and communications centre, one of the freest in the world, according to *The Economist*, with more than 500 regular publications (more *per capita* than Britain). Hong Kong needs a variety of newspapers and periodicals for its domestic consumption, and its publications also serve the Chinese-reading public in neighbouring countries, including China itself as well as Southeast Asia. What may appear a little more surprising is that Hong Kong has become a centre for regional English language publications for the whole of Asia, including India and Japan. This was already the case with a few specialist journals in the 1950s, but the major step forward was the transformation of the *Far Eastern Economic Review* into a full-scale comprehensive regional news magazine at the beginning of the 1960s. More specialist periodicals also appeared, dealing with industry, construction, engineering and medicine, for example, all carrying Asia-wide sectoral information for an Asia-wide readership.

In the early 1970s, a rash of new publications hit the stands which fully exploited Hong Kong's advantages as a regional press centre. In 1970, *Orientations*, *Business Asia* and *Textile Asia* all made their appearance, bringing for the first time in Hong Kong a fully modern professional touch. Then came *Insight*, edited, as its publisher Adrian Zecha declared, 'not for any single national audience, but for all decision-makers in Asia'. Its early issues carried translations of the main articles into Thai, Malay, Chinese and Japanese, but that could not be sustained.

In 1972, *The Asian* began its brief but influential career, a Sunday newspaper published in Hong Kong and other centres in Asia for circulation in nine different countries, along with the leading existing national English language Sunday newspapers. It was edited by Tarzie Vittachi, the most brilliant of the post-war crop of Asian journalists, who had fled Sri Lanka some years earlier. For well over a year, *The Asian* circulated 80,000 copies, and was beginning to dent the Anglo-Saxon grip on English-language media in Asia, being a wholly Asian-manned and Asian-owned publication, able to take a firmly rooted regional view of events instead of the UK-oriented or American-oriented habits of mind that had prevailed before. It broke entirely new ground, bringing home to many Asian readers for the first time the possibility that kinship with Asian neighbours might be more important or more interesting than the attenuating ties with the old colonial powers of Europe or the new superpower overlord, the United States. But *The Asian* ran aground on finance, with disappointing advertising support. The final blow was the imposition of martial law in the Philippines (where most of the finance had been raised) which put a stop to the flow of working capital.

But the idea of fully Asian publications did not die. Later in the 1970s, an Indian, T. S. J. George, with one or two colleagues, left the *Far Eastern Economic Review* and founded a rival weekly news magazine, *Asiaweek*, a little brasher, a little more exciting and a little more Asian than the *Far Eastern Economic Review* (which remained the superior product in spite of all that, though the circulation figures ran close). Amit Chowdhuri, another prize-winning Indian investigative journalist, launched *Asian Finance*, and later in the 1980s came the *All-Asia Review of Books*, *Billion*, and numerous others, testifying to the fact that Hong Kong was the best city in the whole of Asia from which to finance, publish, edit and distribute English language publications for continent-wide readership.

Newspapers outside Europe trying to build up readership within Asia also used Hong Kong. *The Asian Wall Street Journal* was an Asian version of the US original, and the *International Herald Tribune* began printing an Asian edition in Hong Kong in 1980. *The Financial Times* of London at one time bought into the *Far Eastern Economic Review* but sold out again, and the journal is now owned fully by the Dow Jones group of the United States. Only 15 per cent of the *Far Eastern Economic Review*'s 75,000 readers are in Hong Kong itself. What had not been fully anticipated earlier was the thirst for reliable non-partisan English language news about Asia in countries like Singapore and Malaysia, where there was a degree of censorship or self-censorship about domestic events.

But the logic was that if you built up your readership in those countries, you would in turn become subjected to censorship pressures, and this is what happened to the *Far Eastern Economic Review*, *International Herald Tribune* and *The Asian Wall Street Journal*. Similar problems will occur after 1997 if the Chinese authorities insist that Hong Kong publications refrain, for example, from advocating independence for Taiwan or Tibet, questions which are subject to severe censorship within China itself on public security grounds. There are also worries in case Hongkongers employed by magazines or

116

newspapers of this kind become subject to arbitrary arrest in China while working for their publication.

The *Asia Magazine*, which was begun as an insert in several English language newspapers in Asia, also faces these censorship problems. Two of its issues were banned a few years ago in Taiwan because it said that the ruling party in Taiwan was structured on a Leninist model, besides which a small flag of the People's Republic of China was featured in the travel section, and a story on the film of *The Last Emperor* referred to 'the new progressive communist China'. The political sensitivities of Asia make it likely that someone is going to be offended by whatever you say about current events. At least publishers and editors in Hong Kong have now accumulated a great deal of wisdom about this.

It is not just a question of English language publications. There is a vigorous Chinese press in Hong Kong which distributes outside the territory. Indeed, the very first Chinese language newspaper in the whole of China was brought out in Hong Kong – the *Chinese Foreign News*, in 1860. Today, newspapers like *Ming Pao* distribute not only to Chinese readers in East Asia but also to the overseas Chinese in North America. Its editor is Louis Cha Liang-yung, the author of best-selling martial arts novels which are read by political leaders in Beijing and Taipei in spite of being banned in both countries. Albert Cheng is bringing out a Chinese language version of *Forbes* magazine for Chinese businessmen worldwide.

The spiritual centre of this press activity is the Foreign Correspondents Club which was built up by Hessel Tiltman (*The Guardian*), Tillman Durdin (*New York Times*), Richard Hughes (*The Sunday Times*) and their friends. For some years it occupied a splendid if slightly decaying house on Conduit Road, which had earlier belonged to the *comprador* of a leading trading company. The story goes that he invited his employer to his house-warming party; when the man arrived he looked at the property in surprise, and enquired, 'Is this all yours?' The *comprador* replied, 'Yes, Sir'. 'Then you're fired,' his European boss declared. This was the house where *A Many Splendoured Thing* was partly filmed, appropriately enough since Ian Morrison of *The Times*, on whom the hero was based, was an active member of the club before his death in the Korean War.

It may seem a somewhat artificial function to serve as the centre for foreign language materials to neighbouring countries, but of course English is rapidly becoming the *lingua franca* of Asia, and Hong Kong derives great advantage from being so advanced in its press and book publishing facilities for the region.

Hong Kong is also a centre of tourism, with 5.5 million visitors a year in 1988 – one to every resident. Many of those are Asians, particularly Japanese and Chinese. The total number of tourists has doubled in the past five years. Hong Kong is the only city in the world to have had two of its hotels, the

Regent and the Mandarin, named among the world's best ten in recent years. The Regent is entirely new and wholly elegant, while the Mandarin is more conventional in its luxury. Then there is the Peninsular Hotel, the oldest and most famous, the kind of hotel that cheerfully tore out half a floor of lavatories at the request of Emperor Haile Selassie of Ethiopia and replaced them with squat toilets.

In the last three years the Hong Kong hotels have begun to expand internationally in order to compete with the American chains which had already spread all over Asia. Now the New World Group in Hong Kong has bought Ramada of the US, the Wharf Hotels Group has bought Omni, William Hunt has bought Southern Pacific Hotels, the Regal Hotel Group has acquired half of the Aircoa Hotel Management Group, and such prestige hotels in the West as Maxim's de Paris in New York, and the Churchill in London have also been acquired by Hong Kong owners. Can they digest these purchases? Do they know enough about the foreign hotel business? Are they paying too much for their acquisitions? Such questions are eagerly debated in Hong Kong bars. Certainly, Hong Kong has taken a big leap forward in becoming the New York of the Pacific by consolidating its central position in tourism and hotel operation in the Far East.

From time to time an important international company moves its headquarters out of Hong Kong to Singapore or somewhere else, and from time to time other companies set up such headquarters in Hong Kong. It is a moving picture, but over the years there have been a large number of corporations from various countries which have chosen Hong Kong as a base. The motivations are varied. Costs used to be low, but are no longer so competitive. Wages and rents are now a reason why some companies are leaving. But the availability of services, the ease of communications, the knowledge of English, the low taxes, and lack of regulation are all attractive. When ICL, the computer firm, split its Asia–Pacific office at Sydney, it was Hong Kong which won the Asian division. AT & T has a regional headquarters in Hong Kong, 'the best place to service the Far East and Asia/Pacific area', its manager said. US West International, Worlds Of Wonder, Yaohan Department Store, the Korea–Japan Finance Company, and Singer–Nikko are among the companies which have set up such headquarters in Hong Kong in recent years, and General Motors did so in 1990. *Time* Magazine and RCA also have such offices. As Adrian Zecha said, 'Once you've done business in Hong Kong, it spoils you for anywhere else.'

For companies in high-cost Australia and New Zealand, especially under Labour governments, Hong Kong is a place to push out their boundaries into the northern hemisphere, escape domestic restrictions and reconnoitre a world strategy. 'If you want to expand elsewhere in the world,' said Bill Wyllie (Hong Kong's senior Australian), 'Hong Kong is probably the best location for an Australian.' Alan Bond, Rupert Murdoch and Ronald Brierley were the pioneers.

Sotheby's has tried hard to capitalise on Hong Kong's position for art auctions, recognising that Chinese buyers and sellers prefer the secrecy of the behind-the-screen deal; there have now been a number of successful auctions where Chinese have been persuaded to bid in public if only through proxies and representatives. There are mountains of money in Hong Kong for the kind of works of art which a good auctioneer like Sotheby can provide. There has also been a series of vintage wine auctions.

Could these aspirations for universality of role be crowned by Hong Kong's becoming a headquarters for international organisations? This is one of the dearest ambitions of many Hongkongers. Despite its colonial status in international law, Hong Kong has been acquiring a degree of international autonomy. As early as the 1950s, when local conditions and fast-moving events just across the border made it impossible for the Hong Kong government always to follow the instructions of distant mandarins in Whitehall, the nickname heard in the Colonial Office corridors in London was 'Republic of Hong Kong'. One Member of Parliament visiting from London listened glumly to the Governor's arguments against restricting Hong Kong textile exports, as the UK was then requesting, and finally asked, 'Do you realise how many marginal constituencies we have in Lancashire?'

Unusually for a colony, Hong Kong sends its Governor to lobby for its trading interests in Washington, in London, in Geneva or wherever the action might be. London allowed Hong Kong much rope in matters about which UK officials were largely ignorant, for example, persuading Southeast Asian governments not to discriminate against Hong Kong Chinese visitors, or collaborating with other governments in the region against drug running. The Hong Kong government still maintains its own police representative inside the British Embassy in Bangkok for the latter purpose.

At international meetings or negotiations the Hong Kong representative always had to sit behind the British delegation, and was technically a member of it. But his interests increasingly diverged from those of his British colleagues, especially on international trade in textiles, where the British were protectionist but Hong Kong necessarily took a free trade stance. In the early post-war years Hong Kong's trade negotiations with other countries were handled by an official from the UK, and even when Hong Kong officials from Hong Kong began to take part, they did so under a UK official who technically headed the 'Hong Kong delegation'.

This became so absurd, and the requirements of the British officials so intolerable, that one Hong Kong Trade Secretary, David Jordan, refused to work with the British official in Washington who was obstructing his strategy on textile trade negotiations with the Americans. 'I take my instructions,' he indignantly declared, 'from the Governor of Hong Kong.' There was a truce in 1967 whereby Hong Kong was granted *de facto* autonomy without having to work through British officials. And in the early 1980s the Hong Kong government began to send its own man to head a Washington office. 'We began to have an existence as a country,' a senior Hong Kong government officer suggested, 'which had never happened before.' Even then, and even after the Colonial Office was absorbed into the Foreign Office, London tried to run Hong Kong's fiscal affairs and budget. Sir Philip Haddon-Cave nearly resigned as Financial Secretary on more than one occasion because of this kind of straitjacketing.

Meanwhile, Hong Kong joined some of the Asian regional organisations as a matter of practical need. It became an associate member of the UN regional organisation, ECAFE (Economic Commission for Asia and the Far East), now renamed ESCAP (Economic and Social Council for Asia and the Pacific), and in 1969 Hong Kong joined the Asian Development Bank, headquartered in Manila. Hong Kong hoped to get associate status with the European Community, but the British request for this was spurned because Hong Kong was thought to be too big a trading nation to be favoured in this way.

Similarly, the UK sought to have Hong Kong qualify for the international Generalised Scheme of Preferences, but again the European Community and the United States opposed this on the grounds that Hong Kong was already sufficiently developed industrially and did not need such special treatment designed for developing countries. When the EC countries finally accepted Hong Kong two years later as a developing country entitled to these trade preferences, they excluded textiles and footwear and reserved the right to impose quotas on sensitive items (and Japan and the US followed suit) so that Hong Kong effectively lost the benefit of the scheme.

The paramount international trading organisation is the GATT (General Agreement on Tariffs and Trade), and this was always the major target for Hong Kong. When two of Hong Kong's biggest markets, Britain and the United States, demanded restrictions on exports of textiles at the end of the 1950s and early 1960s, Hong Kong had to negotiate with them bilaterally. Whitehall often butted in to assert its own policies over the heads of Hong Kong representatives, though the reins were gradually let slip. When the bilateral restraints came to be enlarged in a proposed international regime for the international textile trade under the GATT, Hong Kong had for the first time to perform under the arc lights of the GATT in Geneva with the rest of the international community. Initially, the Hong Kong position was presented by John Cowperthwaite as Trade Secretary, later Financial Secretary, in the Hong Kong government. His cool grasp of the arguments and intellectual command of the debate made a formidable impression.

Hong Kong began by submitting reluctantly to particular restraints in particular markets, but by the late 1960s had grudgingly to go comprehensive.

In the conduct of the many tedious negotiations on textiles in the GATT Hong Kong achieved a high degree of autonomy. One of its officers, William Dorward, was sent on a six-month United Nations fellowship to the GATT in 1963, and a Hong Kong government office was set up in Geneva, under a Briton from the Foreign and Colonial Office in London. Only in 1974 was the post filled by a Hong Kong government official, Dorward. When he first put his flag up to ask for the floor and said that he was speaking on behalf of Hong Kong, a frisson ran through the delegates in the Palais des Nations.

Ironically, Dorward was able on this occasion to disagree publicly with the British without the British being able to reply directly, because they now stood behind the European Community flag. When a British point of view about Hong Kong needed to be put in these negotiations, it had mostly to be put through a continental European spokesman. Even so, the French suspected that the whole thing was a device for the UK to get a voice behind the back of the European Community, while the Third World delegations presumed that Hong Kong, as a colony, must be loyal to the UK and was not therefore to be trusted in the substantive negotiations.

In 1986, Hong Kong won its own membership of the GATT, as its ninety-first member. Sovereign power has never been a requisite for GATT membership, unlike the position with all the United Nations bodies. Once the British declared that Hong Kong was a separate customs territory applying GATT rules, Hong Kong could be accommodated. It sat proudly between Haiti and Hungary, no longer tucked in behind the large British delegation. Some delegates wondered if they were not making a gift to China of two votes after 1997, but that was looking far into the future. Actually, China could not win her own membership because of her restrictive trading system, and when in the 1980s the Chinese had to discuss with the British how to deal with Hong Kong's separate membership of GATT after the reversion to Chinese sovereignty in 1997, the Chinese showed a great interest in Hong Kong's success. Several senior Xinhua officers grilled senior Hong Kong government trade officials privately but at great length, on the circumstances in which Hong Kong obtained its separate seat in the GATT without upsetting anybody else, including China. Chinese trade officials responsible for reconnoitring the GATT in Geneva had earlier found the Hong Kong experience, as retailed privately by senior Hong Kong officials, extremely informative and helpful.

The main use to which Hong Kong first put its GATT membership was the international textile negotiations. After the first multilateral agreement of the 1960s, another follow-on regime was insisted upon by the major importers (the US and European Community). By that time Hong Kong had made its number with other developing countries interested in the GATT textiles debates. After the speechifying for the benefit of home constituents, the negotiation of the Multi-Fibre Arrangement (MFA), as the new system came to be known, finally came down to the seven or eight delegates with a large stake in the outcome – including Hong Kong, which thus elbowed its way past Australia, Latin America, and most of the other Asian developing countries which were textile exporters.

The sheer size of Hong Kong's export trade made Hong Kong important to the Americans and Europeans in creating the new restrictive structure. Hong Kong was not represented by a generalist civil servant, for whom textiles was something he happened to be doing this year but might not be doing another year. Instead the Hong Kong man was a trade official who knew the entire technique and business of textiles in his own territory and was usually more on top of the technical problems in the Geneva smoke-rooms than his colleagues from other countries. In the end, the Africans, Latin Americans and Southeast Asians and others came to appreciate the detailed grasp of their Hong Kong colleague, and came to trust him sufficiently to be willing to allow him to represent their interests in certain respects. So it was that the MFA came to be constructed finally by hardly more than half a dozen men – an American, a European. a Japanese, an Indian, a Brazilian and the Hong Kong delegate.

After William Dorward the next Hong Kong representative was Lawrence Mills, the 'golden-haired blue-eyed boy from Lewisham'. He found himself in the extraordinary situation of becoming locked in debate on behalf of the entire Third World with his opposite number from the European Community representing the industrialised developed countries – who happened, in a reversal of ethnic roles, to be the French civil servant of Vietnamese origin, Tran Van Tinh, speaking for the European Community. Tran had risen in the French civil service and then been lent to the European Community, making his mark in negotiations with the Third World on various trade matters. Mills and Tran used to joke about their mutual fate of leading, as it were, 'the wrong side', Mills speaking for the Asians, Tran for the Europeans.

Carried away by these successes in international bodies, some Hongkongers began to float the idea of their city becoming a headquarters for one of them. Stanley Ho conceived (while listening, he says, to Schumann's Fantaisie) the idea of leasing Hong Kong and Macao to the United Nations for a 100 years and hosting the UN Headquarters in Hong Kong. He tossed the idea out as early as the 1960s to a group of Hong Kong Chinese businessmen and Xinhua officials and they all applauded. Chinese sovereignty could be assured, Ho explained, and China's prestige would be boosted, while Hong Kong would be enabled to make a larger contribution to China's modernisation – besides which the brain drain would be plugged, and even Taiwan could be attracted to the concept. The Ho plan was backed by a group of businessmen looking for ways to transform Hong Kong into the Switzerland of Asia.

Ho's dream even got to the point of being quantified, as is common in Hong Kong. Someone calculated that it would cost $770 million. Stanley Ho was asked if he would support a new UN building in the way that Rockefeller had given $8.5 million for the New York building. 'Yes, I would,' he replied. To the same amount? 'That isn't very much money,' he said, 'I am sure I could afford that.' A journalist muttered afterwards, 'He probably keeps that much in his back pocket.' But nobody had done any homework into the actual possibilities of the UN's moving or the factors involved, and there is very little chance of Ho's dream being realised.

The idea of hosting an international body remains most attractive, for the same sort of reasons that led Stephen Cheong to lobby so hard for Hong Kong to host EXPO 97 during the period before and after the hand-over date, thus putting China under the glare of international limelight at that crucial moment. Since China had already designated Hong Kong as its 'international city', Beijing might not object to such moves in future. They could be credited to China as the sovereign power. But not many international organisations, certainly not the UN, would even consider a headquarters site in China, because of the combination of communism and the shock waves that went out from Tiananmen Square in 1989.

It is worth remembering that the United Nations' regional commission in Asia, ESCAP, was first set up in Shanghai. Only when the Communists were about to take over Shanghai did it migrate to Bangkok. It is unlikely to want to migrate again, and there are now vested interests on both sides in the Thai locale. But new bodies proliferate from the United Nations system from time to time, and there are entirely new organisations likely to be formed in the years to come, such as a Pacific Rim Organisation. It would be natural and sensible for Hong Kong to lobby for the headquarters site of such bodies, even though the international community is unlikely to take such suggestions seriously until the Chinese government alters its outlook.

The main fear in Beijing regarding the internationalisation of Hong Kong after 1997 is not the creation of a bigger stake for the international community in the territory as such. China is more worried lest the British plan to extend their influence beyond 1997 with a presence in Hong Kong to look over China's shoulder all the time in its handling of Hong Kong issues, whether through Pacific Basin institutions or in any other way.

As the would-be New York, or Geneva, of the Pacific, Hong Kong's main rival is Singapore, another city-state which depends entirely on its international performance and image, and is therefore sufficiently outward-looking to meet the requirements of being an international city. Singapore has high taxation, about double that of Hong Kong, and some of the other costs of living and working and carrying on business there are higher. But at least rents are lower, and in the end there is not much to choose between them.

The characteristics of the two populations differ. The Singapore Commissioner in Hong Kong recently commented: 'Hong Kong people appear more aggressive, they are used to a *laissez-faire* life-style. Singapore people don't spend money so openly; Hong Kong people have no inhibitions about showing wealth. But they have a particular entrepreneurial skill. We tend to be more conservative in Singapore, whereas Hong Kong people go for broke.'

Behind such contrasts lies a common work ethic, the shared heritage of Confucian values, the same emphasis on education and family ties. One speaks here of the majority of the population in both cases, Singapore having a 25 per cent non-Chinese population which filters these qualities, whereas Hong Kong is, of course, 98 per cent Chinese.

Sometimes the differences and rivalry are magnified too much. Neither Singapore nor Hong Kong is capable of taking over the other's role or business. Their manufacturing strategies differ and their international banking business has developed to allow each its own speciality. Until very recently, Hong Kong had the great advantage over Singapore of not having the constraint of a Malay–Indonesian presence all around to limit the options of the international city-state. But now Hong Kong is entering into the same kind of constraint with China, by actually submitting to Chinese sovereignty, and that will diminish this particular advantage. All the same, one is left with a final feeling that Hong Kong has a more Pacific-facing situation and would be the more natural choice for an international city in the west Pacific, Singapore being slightly distracted by Indian Ocean considerations.

When the Kiel Institute of World Economics established a Pacific Rim Institute of Comparative Economic Studies in 1988, it did so in Hong Kong. The internationalisation of Hong Kong is already proceeding along tracks laid down in earlier decades, but it is bound to gather force in the 1990s and in the next century, even if interrupted by harsh repressive policies from Beijing from time to time. The use of Hong Kong by business corporations of all kinds from all countries will appear in the next section of this book. A relatively new development is the expansion of Hong Kong-owned corporations into the regional and international scene. The hotel owners have most recently been in the news for this, but it is also true of ship owners and in the machinery sector. Stanley Ho and James Ting, Chairman and Chief Executive respectively of Semi-Tech, acquired the US Singer Sewing Machine Company in 1989 for $220 million, the largest Hong Kong take-over of any American company to date. There will be more of that kind of thing. There are many multinationals operating worldwide from a Hong Kong management base, like First Pacific, which has trading, banking, pharmaceutical and manufacturing companies in Australia, Britain and India, to mention only a few.

Even in manpower terms, Hong Kong is going to become more international, not less. The brain drain of emigrating professionals will lead to more international replacements. In 1997, there are likely to be more Westerners and other foreigners, but fewer Chinese, in Hong Kong. This is the irony of the return to Chinese sovereignty.

Under the rule of a European power not identified with any big Asian country, or with either of the superpowers, Hong Kong offered neutral ground where antagonists in the region could meet. The North and South Koreans discussed in Hong Kong the details of their fielding a joint team in the Olympic Games, something quite impossible for them to do in their own countries or anywhere else in East Asia, where every country is an ally of one or the other. Opposing sides in many East Asian confrontations utilised Hong Kong to meet and parley discreetly and without embarrassment, rather like meeting in a well-appointed railway station waiting room where allegations of pressure from either side could be excluded. This function of neutrality is needed in every region, and in Asia it is performed by Hong Kong. But it is not a role which is likely to survive after Hong Kong becomes a part of China, however autonomous, because China is too big a player on the regional scene and no one will believe that China would not bring pressure to bear upon one or other side in such clandestine meetings.

The other side of the Swiss neutrality idea is more durable and that is Hong Kong's function as the business, social and communications centre of Asia–Pacific. Cut off from its real 'home country' – China – by communist isolationism, and unexpectedly endowed by Britain with a 'neutrality' in Asian affairs, Hong Kong has seen its international character fortified. British institutions and administration are superimposed on a Chinese social base to create an open city without official discrimination by nationality, race or religion. Apolitical, awash with money, polyglot and *laissez-faire*, Hong Kong is a natural choice to be the 'New York' of the Pacific, or unofficial headquarters of the Pacific Basin. It is the place which citizens of all neighbouring and regional countries most want to visit, the place where corporations in the region would most like to operate.

Hongkongers seek to intensify this quality of Hong Kong as a protection against excessive interference from China after 1997. As Jack So, chief executive of the Trade Development Council, fervently declares, 'Let's get this damn place internationalised.' Not every aspect of this ambition is likely to be approved by China, but China also needs Hong Kong's internationalisation for her own economic and social reasons, and some slightly slimmed-down version of this role in Asia is likely to continue into the next century.

PART III

The Economic Miracle

PART III

The Economic Miracle

Chapter 13

Playing the Oceans

In barely half a century, from 1945 to 1990, Hong Kong vaulted from devastated squalor to glittering prosperity. When the Japanese surrendered in 1945, the 600,000 inhabitants were almost starving. Their municipal and productive facilities were derelict, their zest for life and work all but stilled. Today, a population ten times bigger inhabits a gracious and affluent city with a standard of living equal to that of the southern half of the European Community and expected to overtake Britain's by the mid-1990s. From that unpromising backwater of 1945, Hong Kong has become the eleventh largest trading economy in the world, controlling the fifth largest merchant fleet in the world, and exporting more clothing – to name only one commodity – than any country in the world bar none.

These are stupendous achievements if one looks back to VJ Day in 1945. Everything then was in chaos and disrepair. Just before the Japanese took possession in 1941, the China Light and Power Company staff had systematically sabotaged the generating plant so the Japanese could not use it fully. Lawrence Kadoorie returned in 1945 to find his main power station 'in a deplorable state – dirty, unkempt, overrun by giant rats . . .' There was no coal, so logs had to be thrown into the furnace. Electricity was resumed in October but gas did not flow until January 1946.

When Jardine opened its private office safe, it was delighted to find all the files intact, together with a bottle of brandy which someone had thoughtfully left there in 1941. Those first few months of rehabilitation were a time for resourcefulness and working without the book. For the young officials who rolled up their sleeves and got down to work, it was an exhilarating time 'because we had no old men to tell us what to do'. There were very few cars on the road, so drivers gave lifts wherever they went. Kadoorie knew that things were 'back to normal' a few months later when a young lady outside the Peninsula Hotel refused his offer of a lift in his Sunbeam.

Hong Kong had been grabbed by Britain in the first instance because it was the finest deep-water port on the China coast, and Hong Kong's name, history and economy all reflect the sea that washes around its coasts. With the return of peace, Hongkongers turned gratefully to the business it knew best, maritime trade.

The port was slow to modernise because low wages allowed unloading and loading by lighters, with the ships remaining in mid-harbour, but the opportunities of the container age were grasped with vigour. The container port is the largest in private ownership in the world, and by the late 1980s Hong Kong overtook Rotterdam to become the world's busiest container port. The old entrepôt function of Hong Kong was to take goods from ocean-going ships in bulk, and break them down into smaller shipments for onward consignment by smaller coastal or river shipping, or overland transportation – to all parts of China, and to Northeast and Southeast Asia (and vice versa). The containers have carried on the tradition, the Kwaichung container port in Hong Kong being used by exporters and importers not only in Hong Kong but in South China and even further inland.

Hong Kong was used for transhipment because the smaller ports lacked facilities for large-bulk trade, but there was another kind of trade. Japanese goods restricted by the British government in the 1950s, for example, were sometimes shipped through Hong Kong, and even today about a quarter of Japan's exports to China are transhipped via Hong Kong, that being found most practical and convenient by both sides. The same, of course, goes for China's trade with two other important economies where political recognition is lacking, namely, South Korea and Taiwan. The shipments through Hong Kong of those two trades have already exceeded the annual level of $5 billion.

There is also smuggling, which is, after all, only a bad name given to trade which is desired by both buyer and seller but which some political authority seeks to thwart or tax unduly. One of the features of the early post-war years was serving the China market for imports that were restricted by the Guomindang government. It was quite common in the late 1940s for armies of 300 or 400 loaded coolies to cross the New Territories border at night quite illegally, carrying flares to light their path. Or for river boat passengers on the Hong Kong–Guangzhou run to swarm ashore just before docking with armfuls of contraband. There was one engineer on the Hong Kong–Guangzhou railway express who used to be paid $50 just to slow down at a certain point where trucks could pick up smuggled goods thrown from the carriages.

The most abused creature in this story was the pig. Cantonese farmers earn foreign exchange by exporting pigs to Hong Kong. When foreign exchange became scarce, the Guomindang authorities took the foreign exchange and gave the pig exporters import permits up to the value of the pigs. These permits became so valuable that the pigs were smuggled back into China again in order to qualify for another import permit, and so the Chinese customs officials began to cut off the tails of the pigs to indicate that they had received their permit. Undeterred, the traders exchanged these tail-less pigs in Hong Kong for pigs with tails, smuggled those back and put them through the works again. In battles between bureaucrats and traders, the traders are usually a move ahead.

Because of the Korean War, the Americans, at the end of 1950, banned shipments of strategic goods not only to China but to Hong Kong and Macao as well – and a wider United Nations embargo followed in 1951. The Hong Kong textile manufacturers, who had only just set up their mills, were deprived overnight of Chinese materials which they needed to export products to markets outside China. 'To plunge the sword into the delicate texture of international trade and finance,' Sir Arthur Morse of the Hongkong Bank told his annual general meeting in 1951, 'may cause irreparable injury and shatter faith in the sanctity of contract. We cannot therefore see eye to eye with the US authorities with regard to the embargo.' To have the embargo imposed on top of the refugee influx was 'like a man who is sacked by his boss,' one industrialist said, 'and goes home in turmoil, to be welcomed by his wife introducing the new baby – an extra burden just when the income is slashed'.

Fast launches started to run from Hong Kong into China loaded with kerosene or rubber tyres or whatever other commodity was the demand of the moment, this time with the full official blessing of the Chinese authorities. The Americans banned shipments of cobalt oxide, for example, which the Chinese use for the blue colouring on enamelware plate rims, and sodium nitrate which is a glowing agent for gas lamps. Neither the Chinese nor anyone else had any compunction in helping such items to reach China, some doing it for patriotism and some for cash. In those early years, the Hong Kong customs service had many corrupt officers. It was 'riddled with corruption, blatant beyond belief', one young trade officer from Britain found on arrival.

The gold trade was another semi-illicit activity from which many Hong-kongers made their fortune. It was centred, not in Hong Kong but in Macao, across the other side of the Pearl River estuary. Macao, being Portuguese, had been neutral in the Pacific War and did not belong to the International Monetary Fund, so it was perfectly in order for it to allow a free trade in gold. Every few days in those early postwar years a plane-load of gold in big bars would land at Macao, officially exported from Bangkok or other Southeast Asian cities. Macao would process this gold into smaller bars which would then be dispatched to Hong Kong for onward consignment to private customers in the region at much higher prices. At this point it became illegal, because Hong Kong officially regulated the trade in gold, and its officials were supposed to stop it entering.

131

In practice, there was sympathy for Macao in those early years, because Macao's neutrality had enabled many British or Chinese escaped prisoners or refugees from the Japanese to take refuge, and Macao had provided some cloak for Sino-British intelligence activities. Macao was tiny and had no other important means of earning a living, so no one in Hong Kong wanted to stop or spoil its gold trade. In any case, Hong Kong's instincts were always in favour of free trade as against regulation. Nevertheless, the smuggling of gold into Hong Kong exercised the imaginations of the Chinese for many years. They even sewed gold into the bodies of live ducks or chickens. But the export of gold from Hong Kong remained legal. Roger Lobo operated a fleet of Catalina flying boats between Kaitak and the Macao outer harbour, as well as coastal ships to ferry bullion on to Southeast Asian destinations, especially Saigon.

Hong Kong later relaxed its policy on gold imports and became the third biggest gold market after London and New York. There is a gold and silver exchange which is very physical, in that soft-shoed traders clinch deals by grabbing arms, legs or feet – 'more like a rugby pitch,' an observer remarked, 'than a market.' About 300,000 one-kilo bars are imported every year from Switzerland, Britain and the United States. About a quarter are retained for local producers of jewellery and tael bars for the overseas Chinese market, while the rest is unofficially re-exported to black markets, notably Thailand, Taiwan and Korea, where large profits await the merchants because of official restrictions.

The banning or restricting of a commodity immediately increases its value to a businessman. Despite its distance from the places of origin, Hong Kong has become the world trading centre for ivory, and it is mostly poached. Two well-known Hong Kong families dominate this trade which is worth about $50 million a year. They say that it is completely legitimate, being covered by import licences which have gone through international checking. Other reports say that hardly 1 per cent of the relevant containers arriving in Hong Kong are inspected by customs, and it is generally believed that at least one Hong Kong trader buys illegally from poachers, takes the ivory to Dubai for rough carving and then legally exports it for final carving in Hong Kong, there being no controls on worked ivory. Now the world is up in arms about the killing of elephants for their tusks, and the ivory trade is banned in Hong Kong.

Another case is South Africa, boycotted by every true green liberal, but treated among Hong Kong business circles as just another trading partner. South Africa is in fact Hong Kong's twenty-second biggest trade partner, supplying coal for the China Light power stations and steel for the construction industry. There are about 135 South African companies in Hong Kong covering the region as a whole, able to operate freely and meeting little repugnance. South Africans have bought into one or two Hong Kong trading companies, and Jardine, Matheson used to have investment interests in South Africa.

There was a time when Hong Kong seemed to be inheriting Japan's reputation as a copier of other countries' designs, patents, and inventions. But legislation was enacted to protect intellectual property in the early 1970s, backed by prison terms vigorously enforced, and Westerners now see Hong Kong as having virtually the best record in Asia on copyright.

From being in the early post-war years a place renowned for counterfeiting and smuggling, Hong Kong, from the 1960s onwards, has joined the front line in protecting the international free-trade system. Being the custodians of a *laissez-faire* policy, Hong Kong government leaders felt able to use strong language about this. John Bremridge, the Financial Secretary and a former Swire executive, complained in 1982 how vulnerable Hong Kong was to 'hypocritical governments' which stopped people buying what they wanted to buy, at the instance of 'crooked politicians . . . intent on screwing small countries like Hong Kong . . . to get themselves re-elected'.

But the price of being so successful in making the goods that consumers in other countries want (even undercutting traditional domestic suppliers, as was the complaint of Lancashire about Hong Kong's cloth and, later, garments exports to the UK), was finally to incur the penalty of physical restriction in the form of quota controls. It is a sad commentary on international free trade that whereas two officers and six clerks were sufficient to supervise Hong Kong's export quota control system thirty years ago, there are now 200 full-time staff backed by mainframe computers. Well over half of Hong Kong's exports are on quota restriction today, and need to be administratively measured, at great expense, before being shipped.

The forerunner of quotas was the system which the United States instituted in the 1950s, to make sure that goods being exported from Hong Kong to the United States were not actually Chinese, and evading the embargo against goods from China. The famous instance of this, which jiggled the grey cells of officials on both sides of the Pacific, was the pressed duck which Hong Kong exporters traditionally shipped to San Francisco to be hung in the windows of Chinatown. Obviously, it is hard to be sure where a duck may have come from, so American officials, unwilling to run the risk of being branded in Congress as soft on communism, ruled that such ducks must be presumed to be of Chinese or North Korean origin, and therefore needed a comprehensive certificate of origin if they were to be allowed in. 'So we used to send inspectors out,' a Hong Kong official recalled, 'to put rings round the legs of little ducklings when they hatched, so that when they grew up and were slaughtered and pressed we could certify that they were good democratic ducks and not rotten communist ducks. Then Washington said, how can we guarantee that the eggs had not been laid in China? . . .'

The next ripple of guffaws around the Pacific under this 'lunatic system', as Hongkongers called it, concerned wigs, of which Hong Kong suddenly became a very large producer and exporter. It did not last long, but the same learned debates droned on about whether the human hair used in Hong Kong wigs was originally from Chinese heads or not. At its height the industry actually sent Chinese hair to Indonesia to be relabelled as Indonesian and flown back to Hong Kong. But American experts were able to tell by the follicle size and oil content of the individual hairs that these were not the big, coarse, flexible hairs of Indonesians with their oily meals, but Chinese. In any case, if all the hairs were Indonesian it was calculated that every Indonesian woman must be bald because Hong Kong was responsible in the late 1960s for 40 per cent of world production. Eventually, the clever Japanese produced konecolon, a synthetic hair, and Hong Kong lost the industry altogether.

Only in 1971 did the Americans lift these 'lunatic' restrictions, and now ducklings, oysters and hair can be sold to the US in relative freedom. But during that McCarthyite period of blind distrust, many other silly things were done to add unnecessary cost to business. In 1963, officious US inspectors found that the Hilton Hotel, then in American ownership, had been decorated with materials from the wrong side of some border, and $500,000 had to be spent in redoing them with democratic decorations.

Later, in the 1980s, came a rash of anti-dumping restrictions by the European Community and the United States on many products being exported from Hong Kong industries, including garments, video cassette tapes, TV sets and telephones. Strictly speaking, it is impossible to prove dumping by Hong Kong manufacturers under the GATT regulations, because its domestic market is so small. Export manufacturers in any case prefer not to dabble in the local market in case their product is copied by a local competitor. The production of a given item is almost always totally exported, and so there is no domestic price with which to compare the export price, to determine whether there has in fact been unfair practice. The European Community therefore constructed a domestic price arbitrarily which, naturally, proved its point about the Hong Kong export price being too low. It took a long time and a lot of arguing for the Hong Kong producers to even begin to counter this wave of protectionism. Some of the articles complained of, like denim, were already restricted physically under quota, so that 'even if we give it away', a Hong Kong exporter exclaimed, 'we cannot go over the quota limit'.

The irony is that Hong Kong itself, being a free port, has no tariffs or quota restrictions of its own on imports, except in a handful of cases (liquor and tobacco, for instance) where excise duty is levied on both retained imports and re-exports. American officials recognise this, and in 1987 the US Secretary for Commerce expressed the hope that East Asian countries like China would eventually follow Hong Kong's example of doing without tariff barriers and imposing stringent intellectual property laws. But Congressional pressure is not so discriminating, and the message from the US legislature seems to be that 'we cannot fault you, but please persuade your neighbours to do better otherwise we will have to punish you as well as them!' Being a free port means that you have no ready retaliation to threaten against other countries.

The sea is thus the medium through which Hong Kong industrialists have clawed their way to the top of the profitable export league. But it has also been kind, to say the least, to another remarkable group of Hong Kong businessmen, the shipowners. Starting virtually from scratch in 1945, the Hong Kong merchant fleet somersaulted over the British and Greek in the early 1980s to become the second largest behind the Japanese, amounting to 60 million deadweight tonnes – more than 1,200 ships, or one-eighth of world shipping.

There were three giants in this story of climbing from nautical rags to riches – all Shanghainese who came to Hong Kong as refugees. The first was Sir Yue-kong Pao (of World-Wide Shipping), the second was C.Y. Tung (of Island Navigation Corporation), and the third was T.Y. Chao with his son Frank (of Wah Kwong). Each is a world-class shipowner, and yet they grew and flourished together in the small enclave of Hong Kong.

Pao is a jovial, short-statured bundle of energy, whose first move into shipping was at the age of 37. He started his career as a small time banker in central China: asked what was his worst moment in life, he recalls the day when as a young branch manager in Hunan he had to travel in a lorry on top of the live pig baskets.

He and his father joined the brain drain south to Hong Kong in 1949 'in the mouth of the dragon', only just escaping the Red Army's approach. They began a trading business, bringing Taiwan sugar in for the China market, and also Chinese beans, soya bean cake, feathers and similar traditional goods for onward export.

But the young Pao had already halted his step in walking around Hong Kong to watch the ships unloading at the Kennedy Town docks. 'For an investor,' he thought, 'ships are the best movable assets.' The experience of having suddenly to evacuate Shanghai was never to be forgotten.

One thing he was very clear about. 'I did not want to be an employee.' He was looking for his own business, and both banking and trading seemed tame. Shipping he felt was 'the greater challenge for an outsider from Shanghai'. His father warned the younger man that he knew nothing about shipping and could easily lose his shirt. But by 1955 Pao had saved $200,000, and he boldly asked Jake Saunders, then the Chief Accountant at the Hongkong Bank, for a loan. As a former banker, he had come to know Saunders slightly by then, and it is an unkind invention to say that he begged on his knees for a loan, as one account would have it. He knew how to present a project. His father's blessing obtained, Pao bought his first ship.

The next big step was the alliance which he struck with the British *hong* of Wheelock Marden, with whose shipping interests he entangled himself. It began without even a formal contract. He shook hands with George Marden on the deal and the partnership was on without signature. Wheelock Marden helped Pao to break through into the closed circle of shipowners favoured with international financial support, for which otherwise he might have had to wait many years.

He quickly showed his flair for getting the best out of ships with careful financial management. He introduced a rejuvenation policy, replacing old ships by new ones wherever possible, on the argument that you get a better return from a new ship and it is a better asset – rather as one would drive a new car in preference to an old one. But his triumph was to milk the Japanese system of *shikumisen*, a complex, almost ritual maritime dance by which Pao bought new tailor-made ships from Japanese yards for only about a quarter of their true value, because as a foreign customer he was able to benefit from Japanese government export credit. Having got the contract for the ship to be built, Pao could then find an operator to commit himself to long-term charter of the ship after it was launched, and this in turn enabled him to get financing from the banks to pay for the ship in the first place.

In the end, everybody was satisfied. The shipbuilder got the order, the operator got the use of the ship, the Japanese government got its foreign exchange (very important for Japan in those days), and Pao was left by almost a sleight of hand with the ownership of the ship for very little actual cash outlay. The profit might be rather small but so was the risk in view of the long-term charter commitment. 'A thin profit from many ships,' Pao once said, 'will eventually produce more money than a quick killing.'

His friend Saunders at the Hongkong Bank recalled in 1968, by which time it had all been stunningly successful, that some experts had considered the long-term charter 'not only unwise, but also . . . the result of a lack of sound knowledge of shipping business'. Undoubtedly there would have been some in the bank warning against the loan to Pao, but the bank was used to giving its experienced officers their head on loan decisions, and were probably impressed by Pao's homework.

There were two weaknesses in Pao's scheme. What if the Japanese ship operators failed because of a weakening of the market? The Japan Line, one of Pao's important customers, came perilously near to bankruptcy in 1978, and Pao was lucky that the Japanese banks bailed it out (or perhaps, as a banker, he knew they almost certainly would). Again, the flag of convenience, which was an important part of his scheme, allowing the Japanese lines to use cheap labour and cut costs, was under growing threat from the United Nations in the form of UNCTAD (the UN Conference on Trade and Development, the Third World forum). Pao may have reckoned, correctly, that for all the speechifying UNCTAD would not be able to make an effective reduction in the use of the flag of convenience, at least in his working lifetime.

He was helped by events. The closure of the Suez Canal in the mid-1950s and again in the 1960s made the bulk carriers in which he had invested extremely viable. Could he have foreseen the Suez crises? He was totally against gambling, and preferred to get a small return on a sure bet. Like his fellow billionaire Li Kashing, Pao operated on rational analysis and not on gambles.

He once said that business was not 'an art, or even a science, it is an obsession'. A revealing anecdote concerns the breakdown of one of his early vessels, a second-hand ship. Pao had flown to Nagasaki, where the breakdown had occurred, and he stayed with his ship when it was towed back to Yokohama for repairs. Then he was ferried back to Nagasaki in a very small pilot boat, in cold weather with strong winds. 'I thought to myself,' he recalled later, 'if anything should happen, we would need to swim in this cold water.' And sure enough, he solemnly practised swimming in cold water for the next thirty years. That is the kind of man who would make a success in almost any business in any country.

Meanwhile, his corporate development ran ahead. Having made himself indispensable at the Wheelock Marden shipping desk, he won control of Eastern Asia Navigation, its maritime subsidiary, in 1963. The Hongkong Bank helped him to do this, one of the earliest examples of its new policy of assisting able Chinese entrepreneurs to take over inefficiently run British companies. Profits were more decisive than nationalism; friendships had to give way to competence.

It was not surprising that Pao became the first Chinese director and vice-chairman (non-executive) of the Hongkong Bank, or that the bank came to own a quarter of his fleet. It did not seem to inhibit him much later, in 1986, when he was one of the 'White Knights' who sprang to the rescue of the Standard Chartered Bank, the Hongkong Bank's traditional rival, in its financial difficulties. He was easily able to bring his holding up to 15 per cent. It was not a whole-hearted rescue, however, and three years later he sold the main part of his stake at a loss. In similar vein, Pao had succeeded in being a major co-founder of the new airline Dragonair while at the same time being a director of Cathay Pacific Airways, whose monopoly the new airline was setting out to undermine. In these respects Pao was perhaps a child of the Chinese cultural tradition, always seeking to bring people together, always trying to avoid the final showdown.

At the end of the 1970s, Pao took his first step into property, acquiring Hong Kong and Kowloon Wharf after competition with Li Kashing. Three years later he reduced his fleet in order to expand his property empire around Harbour City, on Wharf's land. By 1982, some two-thirds of his World-Wide International funds were in property. He cut his fleet by almost one-third in a single year in order to achieve this change of direction, anticipating the bad times which the shipping industry was about to enter.

By this time he had come to the attention of political leaders, in China as well as elsewhere. He had his first meeting with Deng Xiaoping, the supreme leader in China, in 1984, and was thanked for the way in which his shipping companies had collaborated with their Chinese counterparts. Pao made frequent large donations to Chinese good causes, particularly in education and particularly in his home town of Ningpo, where he established a school in memory of his father. He founded a university at Ningpo and gave more than $20 million to it. On one visit to China he had two meetings with Deng in only three days. Some people in Hong Kong began to say doubtfully that he had swung to Beijing too quickly and given too much. In fact his investments in China were very small compared with others, or compared with his own wealth.

Yet another new corporate career seemed to open before him when his company won the cable TV contract in 1989, opening up opportunities for a second telecommunications network in Hong Kong. Since this particular venture would not be profitable until after 1997, it was taken as a token of Pao's confidence in Hong Kong.

It is entirely in character that Y. K. Pao is a fitness fiend, who takes his skipping rope everywhere with him and is miffed if he is not the first down in the morning at the foreign hotels where he spends so much time, in order to get the best use of the swimming pool.

He would not be Chinese if he did not involve his family in the business. His brother Chi-li has a fleet of his own, but Pao has no sons. Instead he has sons-in-law. One is Chinese, Peter Woo, who inherits the main group of property companies, another is Helmut Sohmen, an Austrian who met Pao's daughter Anna while they were both students at Chicago and married her. Sohmen recently entertained Margaret Thatcher on her Austrian holiday, sharing an opera box at Salzburg to see *The Masked Ball* (Thatcher launched a ship for Pao in Shanghai in 1984, and likes to talk about Hong Kong with the family). A third son-in-law is Japanese, a fourth a New York surgeon. The Paos provide a model of the cosmopolitan family of the future.

Pao himself entered semi-retirement in 1988 and spends most of his time playing golf, especially in the US. But he keeps himself informed. His wealth is hard to estimate. His net personal income was put in 1980 at $250 million a year, and his shares in the mid-1980s were said to be worth twice that. An informed guess at his personal wealth a few years ago was $1¼ billion.

He was by common consent the greatest self-promoter on the world stage, constantly elbowing in and arranging to meet important people as if by chance. His days were filled with meetings with Margaret Thatcher, George Bush, Deng Xiaoping, the royalty of various countries, etc., and he was reputed to have chivvied the British and Chinese governments into coming to an agreement about 1997. He has an uncanny sense of timing. He worked the Japan government subsidy system to the hilt, far beyond what was perhaps expected by its authors, and then he unloaded tonnage ahead of the major collapse of the 1980s and bought property at a time when the market was nose-diving, securing bargains which are now proving their value. He would deny that there was anything uncanny about it, preferring to attribute his success to the financial homework which he always did with intense thoroughness. After all, he almost gobbled up Jardines and Hong Kong Land.

If Pao was the top financier among the Hong Kong shipowners, C.Y. Tung was the acknowledged master operator. Born in Shanghai seven years earlier than Pao, he began as a shipping clerk, married his boss's daughter, and started his own company. At the approach of the Red Army in 1949, he led a flotilla of eleven of his own ships carrying his flag to Hong Kong. More than the other two, Tung retained his Guomindang ties. Within fifteen years he had built up his fleet to be in the class of Onassis and Niarchos.

Tung was more diversified than Pao, and unlike his rival he disliked the Japanese *shikumisen* system, choosing to retain control of his ships. He made a fortune sending them to North and South America during a shipping shortage there. He built his first big tanker, *Oriental Star*, at a French yard with a Bank of America loan, and in 1959 he launched *Oriental Giant*, of 67,000 tonnes, then the largest ship ever built, engined, owned and operated entirely by Asians.

Another label for C.Y. Tung was 'Container King'. He spearheaded the containerisation of Britain's Afro-Asian liner trades with four partners in a consortium, and he pioneered Asia's entry to the container era with his own fleet serving American ports in the late 1960s. A spectacular coup was the purchase of the *Queen Elizabeth*, for which he calmly wrote a cheque for $3.2 million. While being transformed into the imaginative Seawise ('C.Y.'s') University, it was burnt out in 1972 by arsonists and Tung wept as he watched it go down. He bought two President ships for the same role of floating university.

At his peak Tung controlled more than 150 ships of more than 11 million deadweight tonnes, and by the time of his death in 1982 he was the world's largest shipowner in terms of numbers of ships, worth $130 million altogether. The family empire expanded to include banking, insurance, property and oil. By the 1970s his son Chee-hwa (C.H. Tung) had taken over the management of the business. In 1980 he bought the British firm of Furness Withy for $70 million.

But the Tung empire was not as well prepared for the crash of the 1980s as was Pao's. C.Y.'s enthusiasm for supertankers and expensive container ships, not to mention plush new offices, landed the fleet in financial difficulty in 1985, with debts of $320 million. The younger Tung secured new money from Henry Fok, the property billionaire, and also from the banks. Even the Bank of China, anxious to prove its role of potential guardian angel to Hong Kong's capitalists, lent indirectly through the Hongkong Bank (the Tungs were too close to the Guomindang and Taiwan for direct dealing). They survived the crisis.

C.Y. Tung loved the sea and his ships. Unlike Pao, he was quiet and frugal, though he did make some of the international social rounds and became a good friend of Prince Rainier of Monaco. What he was consistently good at was making the most profit out of his fleet.

The third genius in this remarkable trio of shipowners was T.Y. Chao of Wah Kwong. He arrived in Hong Kong in November 1948, slightly earlier than the other two, bringing with him 'half a ship' and leaving the others behind. He started again in Hong Kong with second-hand ships bought from Western owners, and from this modest new beginning he built up a fleet of world importance. Meanwhile, his son Wen-king (Frank Chao) had gone through Sunderland Technical College and Durham University in the 1950s and returned to help manage the business. It was he who pared the fleet to only three ships in time for the recession of the early 1980s, his feeling for the market saving the company.

The Wah Kwong chartering philosophy is that when the market goes up, you should go short term on contracts, and only go long term if you sense that rates will hold. 'When you get yourself in the water,' Frank explained, 'and the water reaches your nose, you're dead. But if the water is just below your nose, you can breathe and you are alive. There is a small difference. But that difference counts.'

But the Chaos almost stopped breathing in the 1980s. The shipping slump hit them harder than they had expected and the collapse of long-term charters left them with $850 million of debts. They barely escaped bankruptcy and the aged T.Y. at 75 was obliged to auction the $11 million collection of antique jade and porcelain which he had built up over forty years. Only in 1988, when a profit of $29 million was declared, did Wah Kwong begin to turn the corner.

The company decisions were made by father and son together, with two other directors, and all four tried to convince each other if their views differed. But the old man had the final say. He was the one who insisted on beginning to rebuild the fleet in 1987 when prices were cheap, calculating that the market had hit bottom. Now there is a grandson, Frederick, who is expected to take over during the 1990s.

Hong Kong's position on the China coast at the edge of the Pearl River estuary makes sense of its shipping exploits. It was not so obvious that this small place would produce one of the best-known and most efficient privately owned airlines, Cathay Pacific. There is not even a very modern airport, the facility at Kai Tak becoming rapidly inadequate for the growing demand. It will be several years before a new airport is in place to take over. Meanwhile, Kai Tak is right at the edge of the urban area, and landing aircraft have to fly uncomfortably close to buildings and mountain tops.

Cathay Pacific was the brainwave of two wartime pilots, the American Roy Farrell and the Australian Sydney de Kantzow. They learnt their trade on the air transport hump from Calcutta to Kunming. When the war ended, they ran chartered cargo flights from Shanghai to Australia, but in 1947, like so many Shanghai businesses, they relocated in Hong Kong. Jock Swire was interested in 'getting into the air over his ships', and the company was formed with the involvement of Australian National Airlines, P. & O. and Butterfield and Swire. Gradually, it grew into a small respected passenger airline, going into jets in 1963 and winning international awards in the 1980s, and soon to go round the world. Swire sold part of the equity to the public to strengthen Cathay Pacific's claim to be Hong Kong's airline. The Chinese banking institution CITIC later bought into it, apparently to introduce some competition for the fumbling and over-bureaucratic Chinese national airline. Today, Cathay Pacific has become the outstanding example of responsible and profitable passenger aviation outside government ownership.

The future for aviation in Hong Kong is clouded by past subordination of Hong Kong's interests to British interests over landing rights, and by prevarication over airport renewal. Gordon Wu put forward a $3.5 billion plan for a new airport at Lantau, as a private sector project which would recoup its investment from associated port and residential development. Subsequently, the Hong Kong government proposed a $16 billion development, also in Lantau, which would have a second international airport as its centrepiece, to open before 1997. This would cost more than the Channel Tunnel between Britain and France, including a suspension bridge with a span longer than the Golden Gate in San Francisco. But the project is not yet finalised and meanwhile less expensive new airports at Shenzen and Macao may steal the traffic.

Trade and transport were Hong Kong's lifeblood until the Shanghai industrialists brought in large-scale modern manufacturing in 1949. Even then, the new industries depended entirely upon exports, and so the sea has remained the key to Hong Kong prosperity – and the key to China's desire to keep Hong Kong going.

Chapter 14

Five Billion Pairs of Trousers

The first advertisement in the first post-war issue of the *South China Morning Post*, four days after Hong Kong's 'liberation', was for a textile company. Its message read: 'Reopening soon. Sooner if possible.'

Hong Kong's manufacturing industry did not start from scratch in the post-war period. The first dockyard, the Taikoo sugar refinery and the Green Island cement plant all go back to the nineteenth century. The Taikoo dock produced its first ship in 1910, and interwar years saw the start of the Nam Jam flashlight plant, Amoy Canning soya sauce factory, Hong Kong Rubber Manufactory, Cheong Lee shipyard and Union Metal bicycle factory. The first phase of post-war manufacturing was thus a renewal of this earlier activity, accentuated in 1949–52 by the arrival of many refugees, entrepreneurs and skilled workers from Shanghai, at a time when Southeast Asian markets were hungry for textiles and household articles of which they had been starved during the war, and which they were not yet producing in sufficient quantity themselves.

British officials were at first overwhelmed. Jimmy McGregor, then a government officer, recalled:

> We had at least one and a half million refugees who had come here from China, most of them with virtually nothing – except their brains and their will to work. It wasn't – as many have suggested since – a case of most people arriving here with very large sums of money, suitcases full of silver dollars . . . Very few came with money and expertise. Most came with what they stood up in. And we didn't have land and we didn't have any knowledge of production systems to help with industrial development. The people we had to help were entrepreneurs, they were not industrialists, even in cases when they had a little money. Yet they had to build their own small factories and to learn on the ground. No one was there to teach them. Our educational system was small at that time, and completely inadequate to deal with the huge numbers who needed to be trained.

Finance was the main problem, especially for the newly arrived Shanghai industrialists. Saunders of the Hongkong Bank and Bird of the Chartered Bank had known several of them from pre-war days in Shanghai, and were ready to help them, even without proper security, on the basis of the trust they had then formed. Saunders of the Hongkong Bank thought of a way round their lack of working capital. He arranged for them to take raw cotton from the wharf company and pay for it later in the form of spun yarn. This device got some of them going earlier than they would otherwise have been able to. P. Y. Tang had offloaded expensive equipment in Hong Kong, but storage space was short and he could not afford to pay the high fees necessary to get the machinery out and generate income. Again the banks came to the rescue, knowing it was the only way to get money moving.

Where the banks were sceptical of the success of manufacturing projects whose owners they did not know, the mills were left without credit. James Hsiung Lee brought his company, China Engineers, from Shanghai in 1949 with a record of successful management which the Hongkong Bank recognised. On behalf of several fellow Shanghainese, Lee formed a cotton pool system whereby a dozen or more of the mills met every day to settle their raw cotton needs, upon which his own company would go to the bank to open a letter of credit for the amount. With this piggy-back credit, the other mills were able to make a start, and in 1952 the banks started to lend directly to them.

That was the first wave. The American embargo arising out of the Korean War brought a second wave of industrialisation in Hong Kong from 1953 on. The 1950s were the decade of Hong Kong's industrial take-off, with annual production growth reaching 20 per cent. Industrial exports exceeded the value of the entrepôt trade for the first time in 1959. This was unprecedented: for Hong Kong had always considered itself a trading port and never in any important sense a manufacturing centre. During the four golden decades, 1950–90, the number of people employed in factories multiplied eightfold, while their production increased sixtyfold.

In other parts of East Asia with similar conditions industry was mollycoddled. Bureaucrats planned and organised it with varying degrees of technical advice. Singapore, suddenly deprived of the naval dockyard, sought to create new industries for itself by legislation, as it were, with little regard for the adequacy of the infrastructure to support them. Hong Kong was noticeably out of step with these neighbours. Its industry grew naturally and organically from the entrepôt foundation, emerging lopsided and biased in various directions (towards light industry, for example, rather than heavy), but deriving entirely from market forces and entrepreneurial decisions.

Some officials in Hong Kong felt it would be helpful to encourage some heavy industry, to substitute for imports and provide technical spin-off, not to mention more jobs. But this was where the obstinacy and unassailable logic of one man, John Cowperthwaite, usually prevailed. First, as Trade Secretary and then as Financial Secretary, this ardent disciple of free trade and *laissez-faire* insisted that the government should not play God. The market should decide what industries should set up in Hong Kong.

Carried to an extreme, the Cowperthwaite view would have left it to private industrialists to decide where to build their plant without any concern for public policy, merely on the price and availability of land. But critics asked if there should not be some kind of land policy? Should there not be industrial estates? The siting of steel rolling mills in Junk Bay was a triumph for the planners, next to what was then the world's largest ship-breaking centre. But within a few years the ship-breaking centre, a product of the ephemeral shipping recession, had disappeared and the rolling mills never really had a chance. There was competition from cheaper producers in China and they got into debt almost immediately after they had been talked into the project by the Hong Kong planners. It was, as an Industry Department official conceded afterwards, 'a bureaucratic decision which the market did not substantiate'.

When the Industry Department created its first industrial area at Kwuntong, the rubbish-dump-plus-reclaimed-land of the late 1950s, it made the mistake of trying to plan it in detail, letting out sites for specific industries. That proved entirely impractical, and industrialists were eventually left free to choose their sites. When it came to the Dow Chemicals polystyrene plant, the Americans explained that they needed space, and that their process could not be done in a high rise building. Cowperthaite said, in that case, Hong Kong should not have it. But the industry planners gave an island for the purpose and this time it worked out successfully.

Hong Kong's industrial success was almost entirely due to private enterprise operating with only minimal restrictions without any bureaucrats laying down what to make, for what markets, and in what quantities. They did have things to say about safety and working conditions, not so much at the outset, but increasingly as the years went on.

It was textiles and clothing which dominated this whole development. The Shanghai refugees presented Hong Kong with a ready-made industry in barely two or three years. Not everybody thought it was a good idea. Some critics said it was ridiculous to develop a textile industry in a place with no ready supply of fresh water (which the dyeing and finishing end of textiles soaks up in great quantities). There was scepticism about export markets, which were vital because the Hong Kong market was so small. At the end of the 1950s the Economist Intelligence Unit told the Chamber of Commerce in Hong Kong that there was little scope for textile exports, and the Jardine *taipan*, Hugh Barton, called on the government to restrict the garment industry because it was already producing more than the world could absorb. How wrong they all were. Since then the Hong Kong manufacturers have sold about 5 billion pairs of trousers and 4 billion shirts, enough to clothe everyone in the world!

Being export-oriented was important. There was no question here of regarding exports as a spin-off from domestic sales, or finding other people to buy what you have already designed for your home customers. It made for secretiveness, because each factory feared that someone might spy on it to steal its export market, and it made for efficiency too. One buyer on a two-day visit told T. K. Ann of the Winner Group on the first day what he wanted, and Ann was able to show him the sample from the loom on the plane just before he flew off, to his amazement. Another unexpected advantage of not having a domestic market was the contrast that eventually became drawn with Korea and Taiwan, two of Hong Kong's main competitors. Because they had large home markets, they used American government-subsidised cotton in the 1950s which kept their domestic prices down. But the condition was that they were not allowed to export products from that cotton back to the United States. Hong Kong preferred to buy the cheapest cotton on the open market and was therefore able to meet the growing American demand for cheap garments – ahead of Korea and Taiwan.

In fact a number of the early garment factories in Hong Kong were started by Americans. Linden Johnson, who had served with the Flying Tigers and came down from Shanghai in 1949, was the pioneer. He started Mandarin Textiles in 1950, making high quality women's clothes for the US market. His Dynasty was the first prestige label for Hong Kong garments, and it was always said of him that he had a tailor to man every sewing machine. Charles Bassine launched Castle Peak Industries in 1957, using what many saw as the perfect combination of American capital, Japanese management and Cantonese labour. Murjani owed his start in clothing, in 1956, to the encouragement of Herman Katz, an American garment trader.

The textile and garment makers soon ran into resistance from the domestic producers in their main markets, beginning with the UK and spreading to the US, the EC and others. At the beginning of the 1950s there was a huge demand for textiles in Britain which the Lancashire mills could not meet. Their equipment was old, they were still on a wartime footing, they took their time retooling. Hong Kong by contrast had brand new, highly modern Swiss or American equipment brought in by experts. British importers started buying up Hong Kong greycloth, finding the quality acceptable and the price cheap.

In 1957, however, an indignant mission from Lancashire arrived in Hong Kong to reconnoitre the ground for restricting this upstart new competition. Even then, as one of the Shanghai textilemen remarked, 'While the Manchester people were protesting and negotiating for constraint, they were also buying from us and bargaining over price.' The same Hong Kong industrialist concluded: 'It was worldwide free publicity for us, it did not cost us a cent. We became famous, they all came to buy from us.' There was something in that, but Britain being the metropolitan power, and Hong Kong being a colony, it was inevitable that shipments were restricted. Sales could be made only on quota and trade was cut back, albeit on an industry-to-industry than government-to-government agreement.

There was one saving grace in the whole arrangement with Lancashire: the restrictions were on volume, not value. For yarn and greycloth this made little difference, but with finished and printed fabrics, and especially with garments, there was an enormous differential. The principle was followed all through the subsequent international negotiations, and Hong Kong came out of them with an incentive to upgrade its products and make more profit from the same volume of shipments. In 1972, after restrictions had been in force in Britain for more than twelve years, Hong Kong manufacturers held almost half of the British cloth market.

The United States followed Britain in demanding voluntary export restraint, on certain textile items under the GATT, in 1960. Only eight years later, Hong Kong overtook mighty Japan to become the largest foreign supplier of cotton cloth to the United States. For a small territory operating under such political and natural disadvantages, this was extraordinary.

The other European Community countries also buttoned Hong Kong down, the worst experience being in 1977 when its demands were so restrictive that they were expected to cost 10,000 Hong Kong jobs. Hong Kong opinion was angered because the Europeans said that other Third World countries, less competitive than Hong Kong, should get more access to the European market – but at the expense of Hong Kong, not of the European producers. Europe wanted to be charitable to the Africans and South Asians at Hong Kong's expense, and it seemed so obviously unfair. No notice was taken of the fact that Hong Kong was a free-trade territory which the manufacturers of European countries were completely free to enter – unlike Korea and Taiwan which had high protective walls around their industries.

All these quota arrangements were absorbed into the GATT, culminating in 1974 in the Multi-Fibre Arrangement, and during the five-yearly renegotiations for this, Hong Kong became an important – and increasingly militant – participant. The textile export business became increasingly complex, like entering a labyrinth of dead ends and confused signals which waste immense amounts of human energy, paper and time and do no credit to the Western governments or the GATT.

Yet Hong Kong does not complain, at least not too loudly. 'The only textile industry that was protected by the Multi-Fibre Arrangement was Hong Kong's,' a retired Hong Kong trade official sheepishly admits. Once the quotas are negotiated for all the supplying countries, they become locked in time, capable of being varied only marginally, and taking no account of changes in market competitiveness. To put it bluntly, Hong Kong probably exports more textiles and garments under the quota system today than it would do if it were a free trade world. Without the Multi-Fibre Arrangement, the Hong Kong textile and garment industry, which is the greater part of Hong Kong's total manufacturing industry, would be thrust back fully on its own competitiveness and might well lose some sectors to other Third World exporters. Officially, the government still says that the restrictions are disgraceful. What else can they say, when they are supposed to be the champion of free trade?

The result is a huge business in quota-selling. Quota premia are actually quoted in Hong Kong, and some quota holders can make more from selling their quotas than from selling the textiles themselves which are under quota restriction. New entrants will pay money to hide behind quotas which old pioneers can no longer fill, or do not wish to. The whole business is a blight, a distortion, and the worst possible advertisement that anyone could imagine for the concept of managed trade. Derestriction would award the difference between free market price and restricted market price to the consumer rather than the quota holder who is yesterday's successful competitor.

Who were these Shanghai industrialists who created all this uproar in world markets? The doyen was T.Y. Wong of Hong Kong Spinners, carrying on what his father had founded. Then there was P.Y. Tang of South Sea Textiles, who was so well organised that he diverted his new machinery from its intended Shanghai destination a year before the others, and was able to transfer hand-picked workers to the new Hong Kong site only days before Shanghai fell to the Communists. He was succeeded after his death in 1971 by his son Jack, also US-educated (MIT and Harvard).

T.K. Ann of the Winner Group leads a consortium of interlocking specialised Shanghai textile companies, from trading to spinning, weaving and garments – a successful vertically integrated enterprise. Not so lucky with vertical integration was C.C. Lee, who merged his factory with Jardine and Castle Peak Industries in 1962 to form the Textile Alliance. It was laid low by the recession, and sadly became a Japanese subsidiary. One of Lee's partners was Y.L. Yang, who was most helpful in the 1960s in advising government officials on textile negotiations, travelling to various negotiations overseas for the purpose. Later, he was found guilty of race-fixing by the Royal Hong Kong Jockey Club, but one of the trade officers who worked with him commented, 'Y.L. Yang was the best of all. So whatever he did wrongly or falsely later, Hong Kong owes him a debt of gratitude.'

The dyeing side of the industry is headed by Cha Chi Ming, of China Dyeing, who had been continuously engaged in textiles in various Chinese provinces and then in Shanghai and Hong Kong, and more recently in places as far afield as Africa. Like T.K. Ann, he has taken a leading role in the negotiation with the Chinese on the Basic Law to govern Hong Kong after 1997. Another big enterprise is the Nanyang Cotton Mill run by H.C. Yung, whose father was one of China's greatest industrialists, the Flour King and Cotton King of Shanghai and a director of the Bank of China in pre-war years. Lawrence Kadoorie helped Yung and his friends to locate an old rope factory to buy for a site in Hong Kong.

This is how the migration appeared from the Shanghai point of view, as explained by a Shanghai textile magnate now in Hong Kong:

Early in 1946 'my father placed a large order for new spinning machines and power looms with a well-known British manufacturer, with delivery to be made in Shanghai around the middle of 1947. However, political and economic conditions in China failed to improve and it looked as if a civil war . . . might break out. My father thought it might be wise to transfer our operations to Hong Kong, and he spent six weeks here in the summer of 1946 to look things over.'

He liked the idea of a free port and the absence of formalities and restrictions, but he couldn't see that Hong Kong offered any market. There were no industrial workers here and no natural resources – not even an adequate water supply. Besides it was hot and humid here for most of the year and this makes it difficult to spin cotton. My father decided against moving to Hong Kong and returned to Shanghai.

A few months later he was told by the Guomindang authorities in Shanghai that he would not be allowed to import new machinery because of the foreign exchange shortage. Actually, he had enough money on deposit outside China, but did not like to say so. 'After considerable thought,' his son went on, 'he cabled the British manufacturer to ship his machinery to Hong Kong rather than Shanghai. Late in 1947 his machinery arrived in Hong Kong and was placed in storage in Kowloon. My father and two of his submanagers flew here to locate some place to set up the spinning machinery and looms. My father was able to rent an old warehouse, and by early 1948 was ready to begin operations.'

Some of the Shanghai tycoons would have preferred to go on to other places, particularly the United States. But Chinese immigration was heavily restricted by the Americans at that time, and the gates were closing in Southeast Asia too, because of the avalanche of Chinese refugees from communism. Rong Yan-ren tried to start a spinning mill in Bangkok in 1949, only to find that the government wanted a majority share, he could not bring in the technicians and skilled workers he needed, and bureaucrats controlled his production and marketing. The mill went bankrupt. Another Rong, Rong Hong-yuan, tried to set up a mill in Taiwan, in 1948, but the government would not supply electricity. The few Shanghai cotton kings who went to Taiwan found their enterprises hamstrung by the Guomindang government there.

These were the circumstances in which the majority of the Shanghai textilemen settled in Hong Kong.

The Cantonese spinners and weavers are fewer and smaller. They focused on the British market, whereas the Shanghai manufacturers (some US-educated) went all out for the American. The Cantonese were used to the Imperial (and later Commonwealth) preference system which created for Hong Kong industry a substitute for the home market it lacked. It encouraged cheap goods, however, and gave no incentive to trade up, unlike the textile restrictions that were introduced later. It was possible to sell junk duty free which could not be sold in other markets even over tariff barriers, so this arrangement was not the best foundation for building foreign trade.

Lam Kan-sing, a tiny frail man, was the stoutest defender of Cantonese interests in the textile industry. 'The Shanghainese came down,' a trade official remembered, 'and in a couple of years they spoke fluent English. And there was Lam Kan-sing who lived all his life in Hong Kong, and we had to have interpreters for him in the Textile Advisory Board.' He was only 4 feet 6 inches, yet he had four wives, in the time when it was legal to do so.

From the breathtaking amounts of yarn and cloth that were being spun and woven in Hong Kong and exported all over the world, grew a clothing industry that was also of startling dimensions. During the 1960s it overtook Japan to become the biggest supplier of garments to the United States, accounting for a quarter of total foreign supplies, and in the 1970s Art Buchwald was able to refer to Hong Kong as 'PX to the world'.

There were always a few tailoring businesses, some of them very large. Two tailors who came from Shanghai were William Woo and Ascot Chang, who specialised in English-style shirts and made them for George Bush, among others. The Indians were the leaders in this business, airmailing suits to San Francisco in profusion. A US Congressman, Gus Savage, was officially investigated recently for cutting official appointments in China and Hong Kong in order to have a three-day suit buying binge with the Hong Kong tailors.

The garment kings are not necessarily people who were trained or had a family introduction to the industry. Francis Tien of Manhattan Garments was the young engineer from Shanghai who got stranded in Hong Kong on his way home in 1949. When a friend of his in Canada asked him to act as a buying agent to ship some clothing to him, he did so, and then thought, that was easy enough, so why not do it for himself? He shopped around for more orders, and got one for a thousand dozen pairs of trousers. He found a factory to make them, shipped them off and waited for the money. But the buyer rejected the whole shipment because the seams were coming apart, the sizing was wrong and there were many other things at fault.

Tien was stunned. He determined this time to learn how to do it properly. He acquired a small factory, and he and his wife spent virtually all their time there for two years while he was taught, by a good foreman, how to carry out every single operation involved in the making of trousers. Fifteen years later he was the biggest trouser maker in the whole world. In 1988, Hong Kong exported 206 million pairs of trousers, of all kinds, mostly denim jeans, with an average value of about $6 each – enough to clothe every American adult.

Gloves were a line that was started early, in 1952, for the American market, and did very well indeed. In 1989, half a million pairs of Hong Kong gloves were barred from the French market, where glove making falls within some leading politicians' constituencies. Sweaters were also strong sellers. Frank Lin started his Milo group by making cheap cardigans in the 1950s, and has now seen it grow to occupy a modern twelve-storey factory in Kwaichung dealing in property as well as general trading. In 1985, when the Americans altered their country of origin law, Hong Kong sweater manufacturers were prevented from having the knitted panels done by hand in China and brought back to Hong Kong to be incorporated in Hong Kong garments for the US market. But instead of giving up, they invested $40 million in new Japanese computer-controlled machinery to do the job in Hong Kong, and increased their sales to America as a result.

An unusual success story is Laws Fashion Knitters. Law Ting-pong started to make knitwear in his home and built that up into a medium-size business. He could not afford to educate his six sons, but by the time Raymond, the seventh, arrived, the family was able to send him to Britain to study maths. In 1979, Raymond came home with two London School of Economics degrees and a job waiting for him in the Hong Kong University faculty. But his father demurred, saying that he had not spent all that money for the boy to waste his life teaching at a university; he should come and work at the factory. So Raymond Law took over his family business and made it into one of the biggest knitwear makers in the entire region. Now he is 33, runs two Rolls-Royces and an Italian sports car, and is a multimillionaire.

Hong Kong's shirt factories export 160 million shirts a year, more than enough to clothe every male European chest. Pyjamas and underwear are also good money spinners, and nobody remembers now the day in 1968 when many Harrods mail order catalogue customers returned the Hong Kong-made children's pyjamas – not because there was anything wrong, but because 'they did not associate Harrods with Hong Kong'. That image has changed rapidly. All the same, it was pushing things a little when the House of Commons canteen staff found itself issued with Hong Kong-made uniforms, at a time when the ladies and gentlemen inside the chamber were all supposed to be rooting for Lancashire.

Does Hong Kong copy designs? Giorgio Armani, the Italian fashion designer, believed so, and tried to do something about it. He hired detectives in Hong Kong to stamp out the illegal use of his name on locally made clothes. One offending T-shirt was sent to him to see. He liked it so much, he copied it himself! Today, Hong Kong's fashion designers are household names in many cities of Asia, Europe and America. Hong Kong labels such as Flying Circus, Reno, Sparkle, G-2000, Giordano and Esprit are as well known as its designers Regence Lam, Eddie Lau and Renée Ozorio. William Lo is now a fashion designer in his own right in Italy, and Hannah Pang, the new star of the 1980s, was the one who put silver spangles on men's black leather trousers.

Today, labour is both expensive and short in Hong Kong. A recent estimate was that factories were undermanned by about 30 per cent. It is these internal cost constraints which threaten Hong Kong's textile and garment competitiveness, not the external curbs of protectionism. The senior government official who described them as 'sunset industries' because of protectionism was premature, and he was thinking of the wrong reason. The quotas help to keep the industry going: it is the internal costs that most menace it, although fashion, computerisation, and modern efficiency still give it a vital edge over other countries. Indeed there is a new dimension to the garment success. By the 1980s Hong Kong had become the largest net importer of textile fabrics in the world, larger even than the American market. Hong Kong's garment factories expanded faster than the weaving mills could keep pace with, creating jobs and income for the mills of other countries.

After textiles and clothing, electronics was the next export industry success. It started in a private house in Prince Edward Road, where its Shanghainese owner had learnt radio manufacture in Japan. He had girls sitting in every room, even the bathroom, assembling kits from Japan, soldering them to the printed circuit boards. When the operation was found out, Japan embargoed the kits, whereupon the Hong Kong maker sent a courier with a couple of big suitcases every week or two to bring them back on a plane. Eventually, Atlas Electronics, as this operation was called, employed 7,000 workers with assets of $5 million and factories in Malaysia and Singapore as well as Hong Kong.

Meanwhile, Warren Simmons, the American pilot, decided that he could make money by manufacturing radios in Hong Kong. Since he tried to manage the enterprise from the cockpit of his Boeing 707, it was a flop, but he did recommend Hong Kong to Dr Robert Noyce, of Fairchild Semiconductors, the inventor of the planar transistor, who was then looking for a place to make transistors and semiconductors. Flying in from India, Noyce liked Hong Kong's qualifications and he started a major factory in the early 1960s. The Zau Brothers were also micro-electronics pioneers, trained in the USA.

In 1982, Elcap and ACL Semiconductor took the giant step of making microprocessor chips. Elcap had started in the 1960s making hi-fi loudspeakers with only $50,000 capital. In twenty years it had a five-storey modern factory at Taipo making custom-designed wafers for the international computer community with a capital of more than $2 million. By then there were more than thirty companies making computers in Hong Kong. And there were problems over counterfeits. Rank sued the shops selling fake Apple computers at one-fifth the price. People said they were sometimes just as good.

This was an industry for meteors like Clifford Pang, who began his Lafe Computer Magnetics in 1981 and won a contract with Control Data of the United States to supply magnetic heads for computer disc drives. His big chance came with the computer boom of 1984 when even the Japanese were unable to meet world demand. He made a point of not relying on overseas suppliers, as many of his rivals in Hong Kong did. Instead, he made his own and achieved a turnover in 1987 of $19 million. Then he began to run into difficulties.

Hong Kong companies, unlike many rivals in other countries, had to upgrade their operations without subsidy. RCL Semiconductors did it by staying in low-end assembly but spending on research and development, setting up the first full wafer fab operation for dynamic random access memories. The new climate called for more specialisation. Johnston Electronics, under Patrick Wang, became a world leader in design and production of micromotors, and Motorola produced the Dragon KAT chip with 93,000 transistors on a piece of silicon one quarter the size of a fingernail. The owner, Tam Chung Ding, who fled from Guangzhou in 1950, put seven engineers to work on this for eighteen months.

Probably the best known of all the electronics manufacturers is Swilynn International, which recently concluded a $25 million contract to supply video cassette housings to Hollywood. It hit the British headlines with its investment of $22 million in Hartlepool for injection moulding and video cassette assembly. Its net profit in 1988 was $1 1/2 million on a turnover of $23 million. It has turnkey projects in five countries and more on the way in China, India, Indonesia and Taiwan. Its policy is to supply technology for a fee, and when the operation is running and quality is assured, it buys back the supply of the product, thus ensuring both profits and a reliable source of the products. Swilynn has consistently taken a modern and sophisticated view of industry far removed from the penny-counting wiles of the early pioneers. 'Mass production,' its managing director declares, 'with low labour costs and trying to flood the market is out of date already.' With this kind of industrial enterprise, Hong Kong has a long future.

Many people associate Hong Kong with plastic flowers. This is an industry which began with the 1950s and within a few years, before the end of that decade, had become the biggest producer in the world, with men like Li Kashing cashing in. It ran into trouble in the 1960s, and had to cut back, but in 1966 it was still earning $85 million, which is a lot of plastic flowers. It was one of these factories, a typically small sweatshop, which sparked the Cultural Revolution riots of 1967. The factory where the original trade union protest was launched, which later escalated into political rioting, had manually operated injection moulding machines, where the worker jumped in the air and used his body weight to close the mould!

Some of those manufacturers went into plastic dolls at the end of the 1960s. The three Young brothers had started making plastic toys, switched to rubber sandals but finally settled on plastic dolls. They took out a five-year licensing agreement, put together their family's rice profits, the income from the rent on their properties and the proceeds of the sale of their old rubber sandal factory, and got a bank loan of $800,000. By 1968 their sales were hitting $10 million. They deserved the name of their company, Perfekta.

Many of the smaller Hong Kong manufacturers settled for supplying to world famous brand name owners abroad, and never established their own identity. When the American toy company Worlds of Wonder collapsed with the meteoric Cabbage Patch doll, it was found to owe five manufacturers in Hong Kong a total of $55 million. Yet most of the Hong Kong factories employ fewer than twenty workers.

There was a brief moment of glory when Universal International Holdings bought Matchbox Toys after Lesney went bankrupt in the early 1980s. The acquisition was for $30 million. But David Yeh, the Shanghai-born banker turned toymaker, could not turn Matchbox around to boost the image of the Hong Kong industrialist in Britain, although the toy company's Hong Kong operations went from strength to strength. The biggest toy manufacturing company in the world is Kader Industrial, created by the 'ramrod tough fellow' H.C. Ting.

That kind of problem resulting from tight family ownership and management still plagues Hong Kong. Chen Song overcame it for his injection moulding machinery enterprise: he had no son, but several daughters. One of them became a night club singer, but the others all trained as engineers and are now running the company.

A surprising area of Hong Kong pre-eminence is watches and clocks. As early as 1975 Hong Kong was selling hundreds of thousands of watches to Switzerland. Then Stelux loomed over the horizon, the brainchild of Wong Chong Po, who as a schoolboy had worked in his father's watch shop in Bangkok. He borrowed $100,000 from his mother to start Stelux in Hong Kong in 1962, and a decade later he was being written up in *Fortune* magazine. By the 1980s Hong Kong was making one in every three watches produced in the world, and one of its companies alone was making 7 million wristwatches. Now Hong Kong has overtaken Japan to become the second biggest producer after Switzerland by value and the largest exporter by volume.

Then the Hong Kong makers began an orgy of foreign buying, of factories and brand names. Asia Commerce bought Juvenia Horlogerie of Switzerland for just over $3 million, and purchased a licensing agreement to make watches with the Carven label of France. National Electronics and C.P. Wong's Stelux also bought Swiss watch makers, to be able to use their European brand names which have such selling power in world markets. The typical goal was to acquire a European luxury brand name for upper market models, keeping the Hong Kong brand names for mid-market appeal, and moving assembly to China, especially of liquid crystal display quartz watches for the lower end of the market. About a quarter of Hong Kong's watch and clock exports now come from Chinese factories.

Stelux had bought Bulova for $14 million, but it sold the company back to the Americans when Wong said he was tired of their refusing to do what he told them at board meetings. Later Wong bought Universal and Titus of Switzerland, as well as a small watch factory in Birmingham. The successful Hong Kong manufacturer is nothing if not ambitious.

Cameras have done well on the Hong Kong scene. Haking Wong and his brilliant partner Pauline Chan started making them in the 1950s. They took a wandering route via the manufacture of toothbrushes, rubber footwear, and wigs before settling into cameras. Pauline Chan, the most brilliant industrialist Hong Kong has produced outside the textile and garment field, went to Japan and other countries to learn every new process of production as it came along, from anodised aluminium and grinding lenses to making shutter metals. Their production was so good that they sold components to the German binocular industry, which was a high compliment, and they were licensed by Kodak to make instamatic cameras. Now the company is one of the world's largest producers of cameras, and it contributes heavily to education, especially universities and technical institutes.

Sir Run Run Shaw, the film mogul of the three famous Shanghai Shaw brothers, is the grand old man of Hong Kong's film industry. Their father pulled a rickshaw in Shanghai, and that is why Shao Yifu became known as Run Run Shaw. Run Run has handled the cinema side of the family business since the 1920s, and did more than anyone else to build up Hong Kong to be the third largest film producer after the United States and India.

His right-hand man was Raymond Chow, who in 1969 struck out on his own with the Bruce Lee film *Big Boss* and the popular *Enter the Dragon*. Chow can boast that every one of the three hundred films he has made was profitable. He now runs a Rolls-Royce, a Porsche and an Aston Martin, plays golf with Li Kashing and makes Hollywood films with Roger Moore and Frank Sinatra. But while Shaw and Chow have made profits from their studios, the general verdict in Hong Kong is that film-making is *pin-muen*, a side-door industry – in other words a gamble.

Once the palmy days had passed, Hong Kong had to run industries on relatively high wage levels and with much higher costs, particularly rents. And the squeeze operated from the outside as well, with growing restrictions in many of Hong Kong's markets.

What to do? There were three ways in which Hong Kong's industrialists could carve out a future for themselves. One was to spend more on research and development and make more technical advances. A second course was to pioneer new markets to supplement the old ones. Finally, production itself could be relocated in lower-cost places. All three of these strategies are increasingly adopted.

There were always enterprises which made remarkable technological advances. When Stephen Lau came back from Battersea College in the 1960s, he started a weaving mill where he pioneered not only brushed denim but also indigo dye. The denim industry generally benefited greatly from the use of open-end yarn and also cold dyeing solutions, which save dyestuff and make colours more fast. None of this was borrowed or learned from the US industry, quite the opposite. These were instances where Hong Kong industry pulled itself up by its own efforts. There was also an increasing use of Hong Kong designs, although the well-known fashion designers tended to jump directly to customers in Paris and New York rather than serve their local industry.

New markets are not easy to find in a world of competitors, but Hong Kong has recently made strong efforts in countries like Japan where there are no quotas even though there might be other difficulties of access. Meanwhile, Hong Kong is not slow in positioning itself for the European unified market in 1992, through a wide range of investments in textiles and electronics, etc., not only in Britain but also in other EC countries.

The third strategy of relocating production abroad was undertaken earlier in countries where Hong Kong had acquired a market share and needed to protect it. But the new trend is to invest in overseas production purely for reasons of cost, in order to serve third country markets more cheaply than could be done from Hong Kong. China, and especially Guangdong province just across the border with easy geographical access and a shared culture and language, was the obvious place to which Hong Kong manufacturers could move their producing operations.

By stepping across that sludgy little River Shenzhen to enter the People's Republic, you move to an economy where wages are anything from one-sixth to one-twelfth of Hong Kong levels, depending on how far inland you go. In the old days, the antagonism of communist bureaucracy prevented Hong Kong from taking advantage of these facts of life, but since Deng Xiaoping's open door policy of 1979 the Hong Kong industrialists have been welcomed. There was a big move by the spinners and weavers across the border in 1982, so much so that the chairman of Hong Kong's Textile Institute predicted gloomily: 'China will have the mills, the equipment and the expertise acquired from the Hong Kong operators, besides the land and low cost labour. There is no way Hong Kong can compete.'

Brushing aside such warnings, Crocodile Garments invested $3.2 million in a Zhongshan plant, for export to Australia and Japan, in a joint venture with a Japanese company. Hong Kong Peninsula Knitters started a joint venture knitting factory at Shenzhen in 1979, and by the end of the 1980s Novel Enterprises had no fewer than eight joint ventures in China making yarn, dyeing and manufacturing Big John jeans for export to Japan.

Asia Commercial employed 1,000 Chinese workers in Dongguan to make 7.2 million watches a year, and the toy makers joined the bandwagon. Francis Choi, chairman of Early Light Industries, explained that with production costs 70 per cent cheaper, the transport cost to Hong Kong was amply covered, making Guangdong province a 'very attractive manufacturing base.'

Much of the electronics industry also moved into China. Clifford Pang of Lafe Holdings created a new industrial park in his home town of Zhongcun 'to help the transfer of technology between Hong Kong and China, but also to play an important role in the development of technical expertise to complement the technical evolution of China and open a new phase of Sino-Hong Kong cooperation'. The county governor applauded Pang for showing 'deep feelings and concern for the modernisation of his home town'. Most of Pang's production was moved to South China by 1988. Like Gold Peak and Luks, he, too, went into joint venture with Japanese companies in Guangdong, using Japanese technology, Hong Kong management and Chinese labour to produce cassette deck mechanisms, car audio and VCR components.

Billy Yung eagerly moved his entire manufacture of electric fans to China, and Nam Tai Electronics relocated its printed circuit board manufacturing in Zhanjiang. The Hong Kong Electronics Association proposed a 10 million square feet electronics city in Nantou or Zhanjiang, an imaginative proposal which in normal times would probably have been accepted with alacrity in spite of the incipient saturation of this area of Guangdong province behind Hong Kong and a growing deterioration in the quality of labour. But the economic cutbacks at the end of 1988, followed by the Tiananmen Square repression in 1989, muted the welcome that Chinese authorities could give, and thoroughly discouraged the patriotic and mostly young entrepreneurs who wanted to create an indissoluble marriage between Hong Kong and South China.

The Hong Kong-owned operations in Guangdong province, and in other parts of China, continued largely undisturbed or uninterrupted by Tiananmen, and not every company changed its mind about the long-term attraction of relocation in China. Universal Appliances, for one, said that it would stay making television sets and telephones. 'There is still no place as economically viable as China,' its representative said, 'with other countries lacking infrastructure, or else, like Thailand, having too many Hong Kong companies already present.' Universal insisted that all its manufacturing would be located in China by 1990 as planned.

China opened up in 1979, but Hong Kong had actually begun this process of relocation before. The Hwa Chong Enamelware company began production in Nigeria in 1962 and Cha Chi Ming followed with textile plants in Nigeria and Ghana. Before long Cha had 15,000 African workers in his seven factories in West Africa, although there were some closures later when foreign exchange became short and materials and equipment could not easily be imported.

The Hong Kong deployment in Southeast Asia exploited links with overseas Chinese communities. Relocation in Malaysia and Singapore came early, with Mee Di Weaving mills in Perak, and Winsor Industries' vertical integrated spinning and weaving mill in Melaka, costing $42 million. In 1989 Tomei moved half of its hi-fi and stereo manufacturing enterprise to Malaysia and Indonesia, preferring those sites to China, and Hong Kong's watch manufacturers made their first visit to possible manufacturing sites in Southeast Asia in the same year, following the chill wind from Tiananmen Square. One important factor in Southeast Asian relocation is that Malaysia, Indonesia, the Philippines and Thailand all retain the Generalised System of Preferences, allowing access to all Western markets at lower rates of tariff than Hong Kong.

Hong Kong investments in the Philippines included textile projects by Yangtzekiang and Murjani, and a Harilela shrimp enterprise. Several electronics companies are switching from China to Thailand, including Starlight Industries, Johnson Electrical and Q P L, which has abandoned its Chinese expansion plans and is investing $1.3 million in Thai plants instead. The Hong Kong Electronics Association is negotiating for an electronics city in Thailand to substitute for the one originally intended for China. Novel Enterprises has denim factories in Mauritius producing for the American market free of quota. Indeed, Hong Kong textile manufacturers have become the biggest employer in Mauritius, and substantial employers in Egypt, Sri Lanka and Southeast Asian countries. A cynical observer in Hong Kong said that the Hong Kong manufacturers knew how to make things work in places even more corrupt than South China.

As the metropolitan country, Britain should expect to receive some direct investment from Hong Kong. Unfortunately, it has not been very successful, certainly in textiles. Although a small plant by Cha Chi Ming has settled down well, the operations of Yangtzekiang Garments and Peninsula and Sun Hing Knitting in the North of England have not been fruitful. Littlewoods, which had bought much in the past from Yangtzekiang, encouraged the Hong Kong company to manufacture on Merseyside for the UK market, but the venture lost money in spite of various management changes.

The electronics investments have done better. Swilynn's video cassette plant in Hartlepool followed the European Commission's allegations of the dumping of these products from Hong Kong. Holian built a factory for electrical goods in Dundonald in Northern Ireland for $4 1/2 million, explaining that production costs there 'were only slightly higher than Hong

Kong'. These Hong Kong enterprises do not make it easy for themselves by bringing into a country like Britain the small-time habits of secrecy which rob them of normal media coverage and local popular support.

In the US, Wing Tai (the name means 'Everlasting Prosperity') started a jeans factory in El Paso, but it closed because of low productivity. James Ting of Semi-Tech Micro-Electronics bought the American Singer Sewing Machine Co. 'Who knows Hutchison and Jardine,' he crowed, 'in the villages of South America or the jungles of Africa? But everyone knows Singer . . . for me it is a sort of romantic acquisition. It is more than a company. For once in my lifetime I have got an opportunity to touch people's lives everywhere in this world.'

Over four decades, barely one working lifetime, Hong Kong eagerly grasped the opportunities to make a living from industry, and worked hard to overcome its inherent disadvantages. Hong Kong has no natural resources at all, save its superb natural harbour, which ships can use conveniently to bring materials and take products. The population is small, boosted by the Shanghai refugees and vitally stimulated by the few experienced entrepreneurs and industrial specialists who came with them. Several intelligent people thought they were all crazy to try to make money from manufacturing, in such a small place with so few facilities and with no assured markets. But the Shanghai magnates showed the way and the Hong Kong Cantonese workers were glad to earn the wages, though often at first in deplorable conditions of the kind associated with industrial pioneering. Their reward was to win through in the end to wage rates that are now the best on the entire Asian continent, leaving aside Japan, and are creeping up steadily to European standards.

Even the wet blanket of physical restrictions on exports, first to Britain and then to the US and Europe, could not discourage the Hong Kong manufacturers, who now, some of them, sit back contentedly and sell their quotas instead of their cardigans and camisoles. In all these respects Hong Kong won the admiration of the East Asian countries, most recently of China. They would all like to follow a similar path. Industrialists need now to upgrade their operations at home instead of relocating abroad, acquiring more production technology and raising both productivity and the quality of their goods. Manufacturing in Hong Kong is at risk because of underinvestment, high rents, inflation and high wages, and the economy is twisting inexorably towards the service sector. From trade, which was Hong Kong's first rice bowl, industry developed as a second means of livelihood. Now the service industries, especially banking and business services, are taking the strain in their turn.

Chapter 15

A Bank in Search of a Role

The strongest Asian bank outside Japan is another unexpected product of tiny Hong Kong, namely, the Hongkong and Shanghai Banking Corporation (known for short as the Hongkong Bank). It was started in 1865 by the colony's merchants who wanted efficient banking on the British style, but independent from British Indian interests which at that time weighed more in London than those of the newly unrolling China and East Asia trade. It started in a very small way, but flourished in the free atmosphere of Hong Kong to reach its present astonishing eminence.

The service sector of the Hong Kong economy, including tourism as well as banking, has climbed as a proportion of the post-war economy to reach about two-thirds today. The rise of Hong Kong as a financial centre, first for its region and then for the world, is the main factor behind this: in the mid-1980s the financial sector was showing average growth of 28 per cent a year. There are now more than 400 financial institutions, including seventy-five international banks, crammed into the gregarious tower blocks of Hong Kong Island. No other cities have a more active foreign banking presence except London and New York. And Hong Kong complements those two cities very neatly in being, from the point of view of continuous trading, in the so-called 'third' time zone.

Hong Kong is among the seven largest foreign exchange markets, and has emerged as the main centre for fund management in Asia, offering low taxation (16 $1/2$ per cent on profits and 15 per cent on salaries) and minimal regulation, especially of off-shore trusts. Investment advisers are tending to drift towards Japan, in spite of higher taxation and costs and greater regulation there, because Japanese investors are their biggest customers and most of the funds which are managed from Hong Kong go to Japan in any case. But Hong Kong is the traditional primary syndication centre for Eurodollar loans to Asia, yielding to Singapore only as a funding centre.

161

The off-shore 'Asian' dollar market did not develop as its sponsors had hoped. The government continued to tax the interest, and also worried about how to exclude its own residents from the benefits of this market. It changed its mind several times on these issues. It also faced problems of bank failures, of which there were seven in only three years in the mid-1980s. Hong Kong had to nurse its currency through a period when it began by being tied to sterling in the colonial manner, and was then floated, and finally became pegged to the American dollar. At one point, Hong Kong's sterling balances represented a quarter of the total for the whole sterling area, and Hong Kong's contribution to the stability of sterling was consistently underestimated. London seemed surprised when the colony complained at losing so much on the value of its reserves when sterling was devalued or floated. Finally, Hong Kong declared economic independence, so to speak, and manages its own very strong currency in a workmanlike and autonomous manner.

The banks played a crucial role in 1945 and 1946 in getting the wheels of the economy to turn again after the wartime standstill. There was no war insurance, so how was Hong Kong to reconstruct if not through bank credit? One step was to honour the $30 million worth of bank notes signed by British bank officers under duress and circulated by the Japanese, now changing hands at well below their par value. The government could not declare them legal tender after the war, but the Hongkong Bank said it would honour them. In all these matters Sir Arthur Morse, the 'wild Irishman' who never read a book but followed every horse race, played the hero. He had saved the bank by transferring the legal headquarters to London during the war, and now, after the war, he led the recovery, presiding over the financing of the new manufacturing industry from Shanghai.

During the years since Morse retired in 1952, the bank has become the fourteenth most profitable in the world. That power is generated mostly in Hong Kong itself, where the bank and its subsidiaries hold almost 30 per cent of all deposits and are responsible for more than one-fifth of all loans. Almost a half of its global assets are in the high-growth Asia–Pacific region.

Small wonder that Hongkongers hold the Hongkong Bank almost in the same sort of awe and regard that Englishmen traditionally reserve for the Anglican Church. The bank still keeps the character that its founding statutes imposed upon it, with shares widely distributed and an independent management. The approval of the (management-dominated) board of directors is needed for any one individual's equity to exceed 1 per cent, and this gives a vital scope for manoeuvre to the bank's professional management. There are no large blocks of equity in the hands of a single powerful person, family or company. The bank can thus maintain its traditional personality of being run by 'aggressive expatriate East Coast Scots', as they were once defined. Although it is usually assumed that three-quarters of the shares are owned in Hong Kong, and predominantly by Hong Kong Chinese investors, the senior management is wholly British and contains a hard core of Scots. Young recruits from Britain are still treated in the old-fashioned way, bachelorhood being required until the age of 25 or until the end of the first tour of duty, to make sure that cadets really want a life in the East.

Whether due to Scots temperament or not, the bank established a reputation for great caution. 'We are a damned conservative bank,' said William Purves, its current chairman and a 'leathery Scot'. 'We are very liquid . . . On a group basis we are about 70 per cent lent, as against 90 per cent of most banks.' It stayed outside the trend in the 1970s for sovereign lending to Third World governments, explaining that it had better outlets for its money. Only the misjudgements about Alan Bond – to whom it was said that almost one-fifth of the bank's shareholders' funds were exposed – and the beguiling George Tan of Carrian tarnished this reputation. The bank is human and can fall for charm like anyone else, but not as often.

It finds itself in the extraordinary position of acting in some ways like a central bank for Hong Kong, without having that designated responsibility, and while continuing to operate as a commercial profit-making body. True to *laissez-faire*, the government has left most banking arrangements to be undertaken voluntarily by the banks themselves. The Hongkong Bank, along with the Standard Chartered Bank, issues the colony's currency notes, for example, and it is only recently that the government took some powers of control over the money supply and over interbank interest rates away from the Hongkong Bank, which had been exercising them all along.

Perhaps more would have been done by now to construct a central bank if it were not feared that such a body would be misused by the Chinese authorities after 1997. A study group set up a year or two ago warned that, 'The control of the Hong Kong banking system by a socialist central bank would . . . be harmful to Hong Kong's capitalist free-enterprise economy.' The Chinese, for their part, have promised that neither the People's Bank of China nor the Bank of China would try to usurp the role of the Hongkong Bank or become Hong Kong's central bank.

Sir Arthur Morse's chairmanship saw the establishment of the People's Republic of China and the beginning of the nationalisation of foreign assets, as a result of which the bank had to give up most of its network in China. Its reaction was to expand in North America and Southeast Asia, and to acquire at the end of the 1950s the Mercantile Bank, which was strong in India, and the British Bank of the Middle East, with its access to newly arrived Arab finance. Saunders, the Chief Manager in the 1960s, wisely drew the line at Africa in this international expansion but made a thrust to Australia, sensing the development of the Pacific Basin business system. That was a period of difficulty in Hong Kong, with riots, the Vietnam War, some disastrous bank runs, etc., and the bank responded by making more equity investment in its own corporate customers, seeing this as a way of ensuring more business after its loans had been repaid. But it chose companies like Sir Y. K. Pao's shipping fleet, and Cathay Pacific Airways, with offshore assets less vulnerable to the political ups and downs of Hong Kong and China.

One exception was the Hang Seng Bank ('Evergrowing Native' Bank), the most successful local Chinese bank which nevertheless appeared vulnerable in the bank crashes of the mid-1960s following a construction industry crisis. It opted for 51 per cent take-over by the Hongkong Bank and has been a great source of profit to it ever since. The Hongkong Bank has blithely ignored suggestions to release it, which seems a curious neglect of public relations.

The internationalisation of the bank continued in the 1970s and 1980s, along with modernisation and the creation of a merchant banking arm, Wardley. The equity investments were taken to a logical conclusion by deliberately using the bank's weight in some of the boardroom struggles and intercompany rivalries, especially where these allowed the bank to tip the scales in favour of Hong Kong Chinese entrepreneurs of proven ability (Y. K. Pao and Li Kashing) at the expense of older British companies which appeared to have lost their way or become over stretched, thus fulfilling a politico-sociological as well as a financial function. But executives did have reservations about the equity policy and some critics warned against the bank's turning into an industrial holding company. At one point the bank held not only a half of Pao's shipping companies and a fifth of Hutchison Whampoa and Eastern Asia Navigation, but also a quarter of Cathay Pacific Airways and almost a half of the *South China Morning Post*.

The imaginative global leap was made in the last ten years, when the bank bought the Marine Midland Bank of New York and tried very hard to match that with a comparable acquisition in the UK. These acquisitions were different from earlier ones in adroitly shifting the centre of gravity of the bank away from Hong Kong, a decade or more before the prospective Chinese take-over, without creating adverse publicity. There was an awkward moment when the New York authorities insisted that the Hongkong Bank should disclose its reserves, but the bank succeeded in arranging for Marine Midland to become a federal rather than a state bank, and the federal watchdogs in Washington were less demanding. In New York, where this was the first such take-over by a Far East bank, there were headlines saying, 'Red China Buys Midland', and jokes about Midland Marine's staff throwing the silver out and getting the chopsticks in. The irony is that their only serious misunderstanding with their new owners was a purely Atlantic problem of language, of British meanings of words versus American meanings – nothing to do with China at all.

In 1981, the Hongkong Bank made an $800 million offer for the Royal Bank of Scotland. The Standard Chartered Bank, its traditional rival in Hong Kong, already had an offer on the table. The British authorities hesitated in deciding whether the Hongkong Bank was British or foreign. It seemed to be a bit of both. The Monopolies Commission agreed that it was not a foreign bank; as William Purves insisted, 'This is still a British colony, and therefore we are a British bank.' But the Royal Bank of Scotland argued that geography dictated a dependence in future on the People's Republic of China, and the Monopolies Commission accepted that the take-over would mean a transfer of control overseas. It was therefore rejected.

Instead the Hongkong Bank bought 14.9 per cent, as much as it was allowed, of the Midland Bank, at a cost of $640 million, and with a commitment not to increase this stake for three years. The Hongkong Bank seems now to be preparing for some kind of merger with this British clearing bank. They have evidently been able to strike up a cordial working relationship, and their strengths are complementary. The Hong Kong Bank would like to take its Midland Bank stake at least up to 20 per cent, and perhaps also prefer to move its domicile to Britain, rather than have its international status downgraded by a domicile which would become that of a communist country after 1997 – however autonomous Hong Kong becomes and however liberal China may again become. Yet any such move would create a damaging loss of confidence in Hong Kong and strike at the bank's profit base. Joint ownership by a new holding company in neutral territory and perhaps 60 per cent owned by the Hongkong Bank, is now talked of. Already the Hongkong Bank has amended its statutory framework to allow it to submit voluntarily to the Companies Ordinance in Hong Kong, to allow public access to the shareholders' registry and generally to remove the impression of special privilege. All this would help it to get British approval for a Midland take-over.

In the end, the bank will probably have to reveal its reserves, and it says it is ready to do so if other banks in Hong Kong follow suit. It is usually said that the bank declares only half of its reserves, or alternatively that they amount to rather more than $40 billion.

The Hongkong Bank has handled its acquisitions gingerly, reflecting both a lack of self-confidence about the particular applicability to other parts of the world of the factors in Far Eastern success, and also a general instinct that it is better to leave the man who knows the job to get on with it. Instead of taking subsidiaries by the scruff of their neck and turning them in a different direction, the bank presides over a decentralised 'federation of banks' which is unusual and which may still some doubts in British minds about the future of Midland. The only fly in the ointment is the enormous debt portfolios of Marine Midland in Latin America and of the Midland Bank in the Third World at large: if these three major banks in different continents are to undertake a concerted strategy, then the fabulous secret reserves of the Hongkong Bank could be quickly dissipated in those very areas from which it sensibly held back in earlier decades.

The bank has at least one highly visible indicator of its confidence in the territory's future in its remarkable new $1.1 billion headquarters building.

Modelled somewhat on the Pompidou Centre and the Lloyds Building in London, it is an extravaganza by the bank which has delighted and appalled its visitors by turns. The Chairman told the architect two things, 'Build me the best bank in the world,' and 'Keep it flexible.' The power function is expressed in the banking hall into which a medium-sized English cathedral could fit. But amidst all the ultra-modern ironmongery, a few relics from the past are retained, including the two 'lucky' bronze lions at the entrance named after two former Chief Managers, Stephen and Stitt.

The tension that will surely grow in the next few years is between the Hongkong Bank and China. The Chinese in Beijing see the Hongkong Bank as a $100 billion bank operating in a territory where there is no lender of last resort. The responsibility, if anything were to go wrong, either with the bank or with Hong Kong itself, would be almost unthinkable, and it would have to be borne initially by Hong Kong but ultimately by China. If the Hongkong Bank were ever to need money, unlikely as that may seem at present, or if it were to change domicile to London or anywhere else, the consequences for the stability of Hong Kong – and therefore for China – would be extremely serious. If obligations cannot be met in Hong Kong after 1997, the creditworthiness of China would be affected as much as that of Hong Kong itself. Some Chinese Communist finance officials regard the Hongkong Bank as potentially overambitious and worryingly out of touch with China and with the factors governing Hong Kong's future.

Premier Li Peng told William Purves recently that China wanted the Hongkong Bank to maintain its pre-eminent role, including the note issue, after 1997. The bank comment is that while it might be growing out of Hong Kong and becoming too big to be merely a Hong Kong bank, it would never turn its back on Hong Kong. But it seems genuinely at a loss to know whether it should aim in future to become a British international bank arising from a Chinese base, or whether it should become genuinely global. It could diversify globally, emphasising its British connection and serving the increasingly affluent Hong Kong emigrants in North America and Australia. That would be one direction, a kind of extended Anglo-Chinese role. But there is the haunting possibility that in another ten years or more China could have become the most attractive country in the world for economic expansion, and Hong Kong would certainly be in a privileged position to meet the needs of that expansion. Should the bank go back to China again, after its rude expulsion of the 1950s? The bank is not to be envied the task of charting a path through all this new ground opened up by its own unforeseen success.

Across the road, as it were, lies the Bank of China, the foreign exchange bank of the People's Republic, which represents Beijing's interests in the Hong Kong 'crocodile swamp'. It too has a new building, designed by the American–Chinese architect I. M. Pei, equally controversial but very much higher than the Hongkong Bank's. It is a straight up-and-down building, a tower of diminishing pyramids based on the bamboo plant, slender but strong. It also is highly flexible, but very much cheaper than its rival. It is a clean and magnificent lunge at the sky, but Hongkongers find it disconcerting and the *feng shui* is said to be bad.

The Bank of China has been painfully finding its way in the past twelve years among the complexities of modern finance, beginning to lead-manage syndicated loans and arrange for its own stockbrokers to trade in the share market. It has some thirteen 'sister' banks which are also controlled from Beijing (in Chinese, they are called *brother* banks). Some of them have recently been taken under the full control of the Bank of China, and two of them are actually incorporated in China – the Bank of Communications (Shanghai) and the Kwangtung Provincial Bank (Guangzhou). That leaves four acting autonomously in Hong Kong, each specialising in several aspects of Hong Kong's financial opportunities.

The new arrival is CITIC (China International Trade and Investment Corporation). This institution bought a local bank after its collapse and then resold it to the People's Bank of China, and has been active in the property as well as the investment market. The Managing Director is Larry Yung whose grandfather was the great Shanghai industrial magnate before 1949. The grandfather's fortune is said to be still accumulating interest in Beijing banks, and a Chinese Finance Minister once quipped that his balances were bigger than the national budget. These are the financial institutions through which China would implement whatever financial policies it may devise for Hong Kong: at present they have a smaller place in the market than the Hongkong Bank, but as 1997 comes nearer that may change.

Of all the foreign banks there is one that is informally accorded 'local' status because of its long association with Hong Kong and its concern for local economic development: the Standard Chartered Bank. It has fallen on difficult times recently, because when the Chartered Bank merged its Asian strength with the African network of the Standard Bank it was pulled down by the latter's bad debts. In Hong Kong itself the Chartered has been on an equal footing with the Hongkong Bank in many respects, has often been ahead of it, and has done as much if not more than its rival to grease the wheels of industry (especially textiles) and commerce. Technically, it is a London-registered bank but many satisfied Hong Kong customers might not know that.

The Stock Exchange is the weak point in Hong Kong's image as a financial centre, having been traditionally dominated by local Chinese stockbrokers (represented by Ronald Li) interested in short-term takings. Ronald Li, to his credit, forced the four separate exchanges together in 1986 to present a much more respectable face to the world. Even then, only a tiny fraction of the capital needed and raised by Hong Kong enterprises came out of the Exchange.

Efforts to regulate the securities business have usually failed to produce the results expected. For one thing, the Chinese strongly oppose the publication of what they earn and will use aliases to conceal such income even from their own family. Nominee companies are popular and pressure from Westerners to have a greater disclosure requirement is resisted. On Black Monday, in October 1987, the Stock Exchange Committee closed the Exchange for four days, complaining that foreign brokers were delaying settlement and refusing the cheques of small local brokers. 'Maybe because their skin is white, they think they can have half the seats on the council.' Actually, about one-third of Hong Kong shares are owned outside Hong Kong, in Japan, Britain, the US, Taiwan, China, etc.

Ronald Li is the third richest man in Hong Kong, with a personal fortune of $1.6 billion, and now he is now on trial for stock market irregularities. The son of a wealthy shipowner, he studied at the University of Pennsylvania, and on returning to Hong Kong he sold off all the family ships and put the money into shares and into the mortgage and money-lending business. He ran the Stock Exchange like a dictator, in the Chinese family business style. His listings committee used to fix new issue prices below the market level to ensure profits for small investors. Yet Li raised the profile of the Exchange and helped to popularise share trading, creating the most liquid market outside Japan. He was the champion of the individual member who often traded cheaply for himself, his family and his friends, more than acting as a stockbroker for the public. When the Futures Exchange broke down with thousands of defaults, Li urged the government to close it in order to protect local brokers at the expense of international institutions. Why should 'we Hong Kong patriots' lose a lot of money to the benefit of 'a bunch of New York Jews?' Yet foreign brokers by that time were doing 70 per cent of the business.

Criticism of the 1987 fiasco led to a shake-up. An official report of investigation said that Hong Kong could become 'the pre-eminent capital market in Southeast Asia' by progressive internationalisation of its security markets. But was there enough will to catch the buccaneers? And would Western-style regulation frighten off local investors who had the liquidity which the market needed? In the end, a new governing council was instituted including not only Western brokers but also the Bank of China. A new Chief Executive, Francis Yuen, was appointed to run the Exchange in a more professional and less entrepreneurial style. Not everybody agreed on the relentless modernisation and Westernisation now in train. An American fund manager commented that he was willing to live with the risks of the old system 'for the benefit of a free-wheeling open market which allows participation by locals. Regulation should focus on the flow of information.'

The biggest stockbroker was Fung King Hey, who founded the company called Sun Hung Kai. Fung was the first broker to market shares to the man in the street – taxi drivers and hawkers. He was bailed out in the early 1980s by French and American investors, and his banking arm was bought by Bahrain Arabs.

The property business is a very big business indeed in Hong Kong, and like other businesses it is a story of established British companies being outshone by new local Chinese talent. The big name was, and still is, Hong Kong Land, which has traditionally been associated with Jardine, Matheson. In the past two decades, this company has gone through astonishing twists and turns, involving rivalries within Jardine, different kinds of senior management, and varying capacities to predict market changes. Under Trevor Bedford, the company bought Exchange Square in the early 1980s, one of the most elegant complexes on the Central skyline. Yet Hong Kong Land became almost bankrupt soon afterwards, and had to sell Hong Kong Electric (to Li Kashing). As a result of this, Mandarin Hotel and Dairy Farm, the food business, were taken out of Hong Kong Land, its residential land outside Central Hong Kong was sold to Alan Bond, and most of the remaining sites in the 'land bank' were sold to such new companies as Sun Hung Kai. Hong Kong Land survived and by virtue of its strength in the Central district it remains one of the big property companies (a few years earlier it had a market capitalisation equal to the largest property companies in Britain).

Among the Chinese property kings, Henry Fok Ying Tung reigns supreme. He won the sole agency for Chinese sand just as the Hong Kong building boom began in the 1950s, and he was the first to overcome a problem that beset all the developers at that time. Because of the shortage of space and the density of people, almost everybody had to live in apartments, but there were legal problems about shared ownership of buildings. Fok succeeded in working out an arrangement whereby a prospective apartment purchaser could secure his ownership by paying half the price in advance even before the building was constructed. It was like the ingenuity of Y. K. Pao in getting the payment for ship charter even before the ship was built. In 1954 the first condominium apartment block was built by Henry Fok at the junction of Public Square Street and Canton Street in Yaumatei, setting a precedent for a mushrooming of badly needed middle-class housing. Yet when Fok had first tendered for lighters in the harbour a few years earlier and needed to deposit a cheque made out to the government, he lost his chance because he had no bank account. His son Timothy serves on the Chinese Olympic Committee, helped Taiwan to participate in the Asian Games in China, married Miss Hong Kong of 1978, and belongs to the Guangdong Province People's Consultative Conference.

The New World Property Group is a newcomer, built up by Cheng Yu-tung, who was one of those to buy up buildings during the 1967 collapse of the property market. He afterwards developed the Tsimshatsui waterfront including the Regent and New World Hotels, as well as buying out the

Ramada Hotel chain for $540 million. In the old days they used to ask, 'Are you married or do you live in Kowloon?' But today property development is competitive and profitable on both sides of the harbour, except that Kowloon still suffers from a height limitation because of the proximity of the airport flightpath.

The service sector of the Hong Kong economy is the one with the big future, whether Hong Kong develops as a service centre for China, with that country's huge needs for modern professional inputs, or whether it retains the wider characteristics of a regional Asia–Pacific base. In every profession one could name, there is a demand in East Asia for the latest thinking and *au courant* practitioners, and for many of those trail-blazers from the West Hong Kong is the most practicable headquarters.

Chapter 16
A Little *Laissez-faire*

Laissez-faire has become the ideological battle cry of Hong Kong. The territory was governed, it used to be said in the 1960s, 'by the gospel of Adam Smith as expounded by his disciple John James Cowperthwaite'. It is not often that a man matches both the time and the place in which he serves. John Cowperthwaite came to Hong Kong in 1945 as a young cadet officer who had soaked up some liberal Adam Smith economics at St Andrew's University. He arrived three months after the Japanese surrender, expecting a derelict city with a siege economy. The port was supposed to be closed while the ruins of war were repaired, yet maritime trade was already flourishing and that was, he admits, the first lesson he learned from Hong Kong practice. As the economic intellectual in the government, Cowperthwaite supervised a policy of non-intervention which won many followers. It meant that the government would hold back as much as possible from interfering in business and in the economy. If a steel rolling plant was in trouble, it would not be bailed out. If a bank ran into problems, let it crash. Cowperthwaite believed that in a perfect society, public money should not even be wasted on compiling industrial production statistics.

His disciple, Alvin Rabushka, proclaimed that nowhere else in the world could one find a lower tax rate, a smaller government, a better fiscal policy and currrency arrangement, or a free-er Chinese community. Hong Kong won the Milton Friedman seal of approval when the great economist told the world, 'To see how the free market really works, Hong Kong is the place to go.' Governor Sir David Trench wrote a letter to *The Economist*, in 1968, in support of his unyielding Financial Secretary, to say that 'attempts to manipulate the economy artificially would in most cases probably result only in weakening it in the long run'.

Cowperthwaite's successor as Financial Secretary, Sir Philip Haddon-Cave, was sufficiently equivocal about his master's philosophy to redefine it as

171

'positive non-interventionism'. But he argued that Hong Kong had no alter-native, because of its dependence on external transactions, to letting the economic fall-out lie where it landed. Intervention could not alter the cost/price structure of exports and imports to the short-term benefit of Hong Kong incomes. He defined his new version of *laissez-faire* in the words, 'We consciously refrain from substituting a bureaucratic decision-making process for the process of market determination.'

What that meant for Hong Kong's post-war businessmen was being allowed to do what they wanted, except for some basic social obligations and the payment of a very modest tax. Hong Kong was, the American–Chinese Paul Cheng declared, 'the only place in the world where individuals can have an idea in the morning, register a company by noon, and start making money in the afternoon'. Even his communist colleague, Wang Guangying of Everbright, conceded that Hong Kong was 'the best place to do busi-ness in'.

So successful was the policy that it was urged on other countries. When the Japanese government appointed the Maekawa Commission to make recommendations about the future of Japan's economy, it cited the open-ness of Hong Kong as a model for Japan to follow in the years to come. As the Seibu Department Store slogan ran in Tokyo, 'Be like Hong Kong in the year 2001'. A Japanese banker, Shijuro Ogata, enthused about the 'rare combina-tion of East and West – the marvel of harmony of neo-Confucianism from the East, and *laissez-faire* from the West'. Alas, in practice, Japanese businessmen were found to be slightly ill at ease in the freedom of Hong Kong, feeling safer in Singapore where they were told clearly what they were expected to do. *Laissez-faire* turned out to be an individualist's religion. In Britain, on those rare occasions when the affairs of this distant colony surfaced above the horizon, there was sometimes a tribute of the kind paid by Victor Goodhew, the Conservative MP, in the 1970s: 'If only we could manage our economy as Hong Kong does, we should not be having debates about crises as often as we do in the House.'

Laissez-faire certainly produced results for Hong Kong, 'the world's most successful economy', as *The Guardian* headline put it in 1981. By that time Hong Kong had already produced one of the biggest banks in the world by market value, the two biggest shipowners, and four out of the five largest property companies.

Where else are private companies ready to build a $3.2 billion airport com-plex, a cross-harbour tunnel or an underground railway system at no expense to the taxpayer? Hong Kong is a model of how to keep the government's finger out of the pie, hold taxes down and yet provide excellent services. The Post Office makes a profit, and the utility companies – electricity, gas, telecommunications – are all private and profitable. The circumstances of other places may not allow of such a thoroughgoing system, but it is sad that the outside world does not give more credit to Hong Kong for the success with which it manages its affairs.

In the umbrella-less fresh air of the Hong Kong market, enterprise flourishes more vigorously than it would in a protected greenhouse. The person who epitomised this more than anyone else was Jock Inglis, a businessman who in the early post-war years booked a permanent table in the Peninsula Hotel lobby (the first on the right of the entrance), put his nameplate out and conducted all kinds of transactions there. When he had to go out, he left a half-empty drink on the table so that other people would leave it free. He knew everybody, and everything, and visitors would check with him to hear the latest gossip before making their calls. Strictly speaking, his agency was for welding rods, but he had tips for shares and horses, being an inveterate gambler, as well as for all kinds of other business. Inglis made himself a millionaire from the Peninsula lobby.

Yet Cowperthwaite was virtually the only true *laissez-faire*-ist in the government, the only one who remained totally unmoved by accusations of Hong Kong's being a 'Shangri-la of unfettered entrepreneurial aggression'. There were colleagues of his who believed that *laissez-faire* led to an unacceptable polarisation of Hong Kong society, making it a place where sharks swam freely and small fish were gobbled up. The Cowperthwaite ideology was most neatly pricked by a *Far Eastern Economic Review* writer who said that the question was not so much *laissez-faire* but *laissez*-whom *faire*-what?

Since Cowperthwaite retired, the issue of *laissez-faire* has been more frequently put as one of balance between intervention and non-intervention. One of his successors in the 1980s described Hong Kong financial markets as 'more like a swamp of crocodiles than the inside of a Swedish dairy'.

Wages have been largely unregulated. A British minister once asked a senior Hong Kong government officer why Hong Kong deliberately allowed immigration to keep wages down. The official agreed that such was the effect of immigration but asked whether London would prefer the people in question to be shot (he nearly got the sack). Now labour is short, the Post Office is spending over $5 million a year on overtime, and the Hongkong Bank's shortage of tellers is easily measured in the queues of customers. So a limited and selective immigration is latterly allowed.

A typical outsider's comment is that wages are respectable but that hours and conditions of work are appalling. There is a built-in workaholism which derives from the social culture which the Chinese have inherited, strengthened by the refugee mentality. 'We worked seven days a week,' said Elisabeth Wong, a civil servant working on the budget, 'and took our Christmas holidays at Easter.' One woman visitor from Beijing was so stunned that she went home early, commenting, 'it was too hectic, people have to work so hard'.

Laissez-faire means that there is no uneconomic padding of industry. In times of recession it is in the Chinese character to share the available work, and for everybody to reduce hours and wages. There is also a built-in family social security. When people say that Hongkongers are worked too hard, I think back to twenty years ago, when Leung Chun-ying, the property surveyor and politician, spent much of his time with his mother and two small sisters assembling plastic flowers at home in order to supplement their father's income (and pay for the young man's three years study at Bristol Polytechnic). Should people be stopped from voluntary self-improvement to satisfy the consciences of the already-affluent?

After the war people worked hard in Hong Kong to get settled: since there are no legal or pyschological bars against it, the habit of hard work persisted long after the need. Now there is a new trend in sight, with the Marriott Hotel's decision in 1989 to operate a five-day week for its staff, to the fury of the other hotels. With full employment and high wages, people can go more readily to the employer of their choice, and if they prefer short hours to long hours and moderate pay to high pay, the Marriott example will have many followers. But it is hardly the situation any more in Hong Kong that large numbers of people work long hours only because greedy and selfish employers tell them to. The greed, if it is greed, lies on both sides of the table.

In its defence the Hong Kong government can remind critics that it has ratified and enforced more International Labour Organisation conventions than any other country in East Asia. One area of weakness is safety (especially in construction work) and workmen's compensation, where the British press has always been able to highlight cases of inhumane or callous treatment. Many small and relatively primitive enterprises flourish under *laissez-faire*.

The biggest theoretical hole in the Cowperthwaite doctrine came over power prices in the 1960s. When complaints were made about the high tariffs of Kadoorie's China Light and Power Co., the government, rather than nationalise the company or rationalise it through merger, decided on a scheme of control restricting its return on assets to only 15 per cent, and giving the government a veto over tariff increases. As a result of this, electricity prices fell and similar schemes were applied to the other power company, Hong Kong Electric, and to the telecommunications and bus companies. The system does introduce a new distortion by giving the company an incentive to increase its assets unnecessarily as a means of enlarging profits.

It was a cardinal principle of Cowperthwaite's *laissez-faire* that taxation should be held down, for reasons anticipating Thatcherism. Those who questioned why taxation could not be raised modestly in order to support higher welfare spending were isolated critics until the 1980s, when it began to be said that the government was more prepared to break the taboo on tax increases, partly to 'clean up the unacceptable face of capitalism' before 1997, but also because the co-existence of private affluence and private squalor was increasingly distasteful. Hong Kong's public debt in 1988 was less than $21 a head, about 200 times smaller than Britain's – another case of more thorough practice of Thatcherism than in the UK itself.

Meanwhile, despite *laissez-faire*, the government pays out about $130 million a year for the support of industrial development, setting land aside for high-tech companies, planning a third industrial estate, creating the new university of science and technology, etc., and this will increase in future. *Laissez-faire* is more honoured in the observance than the breach, but not by a huge margin.

Spending on the social services is now about $1 1/2 billion a year, or $2,700 per head. Medical and education services are offered virtually free, constituting the best social services in continental Asia. As a proportion of Gross Domestic Product, social security and social welfare services spending stands at about 0.8 per cent, which is fairly typical of the Far East where the family takes some responsibility.

In 1953, a disastrous fire blazed through the townlet of refugee shacks at Shek Kip Mei, making 35,000 people homeless. No permanent provision had been made for these refugees from China since they arrived four years earlier, in the hope that they would all go home again soon. That fire was a turning point. A government resettlement department rapidly redeveloped the area into Hong Kong's first housing estate. Ever since then the government has tried, without success, to catch up with the backlog of homeless. Today, those early estates are criticised for their austerity, but they were a great improvement on what had gone before and each generation of estate is better. The squatter huts have never yet disappeared, and even today some people live in bedspaces, verandahs, cocklofts, rooftops, shops, garages, staircases, boats, streets, basements, stalls and caves. After decades of government resettlement blocks, over a million people have been housed in them, and yet there are still refugee-squatters on the waiting list.

The result of this astonishing public housing record, so ill-fitting with *laissez-faire*, is that today almost half of the Hong Kong population live in public housing (a higher ratio than in any other Asian country), paying an average of only 7 per cent of their income as rent. Twenty years ago civil servants celebrated the first recruit to the high-flying administrative service to come from the public housing estates. Today, half of the recruits can claim that origin.

Children get nine years' free education, compulsory up to the age of 15. The pressure of examinations which causes frequent teenage suicides is more worrying than any weakness in providing education. Finally, it is worth remembering that infant mortality in Hong Kong is only 7.4 per thousand, one of the lowest ratios in the world, and that life expectancy at 77 is longer than in Britain or the United States. These figures are partly to be explained by Hong Kong's being almost fully urban, but they are still most creditable.

Bishop Ronald Hall excoriated Hong Kong all the same, as an idolatrous city, worshipping money, and lacking any inner core of morality or social justice. The polarities are obvious. There are people like Cheung Ming, who

175

immigrated from China after his parents, both peasant farmers, died. He spent most of his time in Hong Kong working at unpleasant physical jobs (carrying sand for $1 a day or ditch-digging for the power companies). When he had work, he usually got a mat-space to go with it, sharing a room with thirty others. Now he is 70 and past such labour. He slept for a time in the streets or on park benches, and only after an accidental injury did he find social welfare officials willing to get him a room to live in and pay him $100 per month on which to survive. Hongkongers like to boast that there are more Rolls-Royces in their city than rickshaws, and if you leave one parked in the street it will be patted in wistful envy rather than spitefully scratched. Ostentatious vulgarity is acceptable in Hong Kong society, provided there are opportunities for those at the bottom to climb the ladder.

Mobility is the redeeming feature of the social scene. Many of today's professionals had a thin start to life. Augustus Kam Chui, who became the first Secretary for Recreation and Culture in the Hong Kong government, could not afford to take up his university place in the 1940s when he was 16. He joined the Education Department as a non-graduate, and struggled up the hard way, taking his degree at 25 through private study. 'I have walked past families,' he remembered, 'so poor that just a table and chair stood on the floor, nothing hung on the walls.'

Cheung Man-yee of Radiotelevision Hong Kong articulated this feeling:

> For the past forty years this place has been a miracle, and we have been so lucky to be exposed to the best of both worlds. Compared with any other Chinese people this century – those in China, Taiwan, Singapore or ethnic Chinese in other cities – the Hong Kong Chinese have a great system for personal freedom. They have a great social mobility and infrastructure that provides you with the best. And nobody in Hong Kong can say that he or she has not been given the opportunity. We have been very lucky, all of us.

Laissez-faire has allowed the millionaire companies to flourish, but it has also thrown down ladders for ordinary people who are not entrepreneurs or businessmen to climb into the world of middle-class professionalism – ladders built by the money which *laissez-faire* allows to travel so fast and unencumbered through the society. Hong Kong was, *The Economist* observed, China's first middle-class city. Even the beggars have their compensations, throwing a restaurant party for their 'king', or playing the stock market (a judge once increased his fine on a beggar up for obstruction when he found him listening in court to a transistor radio for the latest stock market report).

Perhaps the worst thing of all is the stress and noise of a city far too tightly packed for human comfort. The density was recently calculated at 8,500 persons per acre, or about thirty times worse than inner London or

Liverpool. Some hotels rent out rooms by the hour for couples who long for a little quiet privacy away from their children. In Mongkok, which is five times more densely populated than Calcutta, the cage-men are to be found, paying $6.50 per month for 6-feet-by-2-feet-by-3-feet cages, sharing a bathroom and lavatory with twenty others. 'I used to live under a staircase,' one old man commented, 'so living in a cage was better for me.' This is where investigative journalists from outside can score, like John Pilger, who found his 'typical Hong Kong family' of six living 'like neat and resourceful rats' in a cupboard with three shelves; or Kevin Rafferty, who pointed out the contrast between a world record price for a luxury hotel site on the one hand, and pigsties being divided for human habitation, sixteen rooms to a sty for $3,400 each, on the other. Inside this shabby housing, of course, may be found consumer durable luxuries like colour TV, stereo and air conditioning – and outside there can be neatly parked Jaguars, Toyotas and Datsuns. These days there is more money around, but housing is not always the chosen priority.

It is more than twelve years since Hong Kong was named the noisiest city in the world. In one of the new schools started by Elsie Tu in Kowloon City, teaching had to be suspended whenever a plane passed over to land at the nearby Kaitak Airport. 'It is stress city, it runs largely on greed,' said Dr William Green, a local psychiatrist. It is a city where there are only sixty psychiatrists, it should be added, vastly fewer per head than Western countries – but then it is said that the Chinese stoically ignore such afflictions until the crisis point is reached. All the same, it is not comfortable to have 1,700 suicide attempts in a year, almost half of them successful. 'Hong Kong is like a ferris wheel going too fast,' a local businessman complained, and although he probably had the circulation of investors' money in mind, it could equally well be an image for society as a whole.

Crime is getting worse, especially drug-related crime. The most reputable people – newspaper publishers, boy scout leaders – stand revealed as drug-runners. They usually get to Taiwan before they are caught, and the enormous daily spending on drugs in the streets goes on. It was once stated as a fact that every third man in Hong Kong belonged to a triad, or criminal gang. Clashes between rival gangs, such as that fought with knives and sharpened water pipes between the 14K and the Tanyee gangs over the protection racket in Wanchai a few years ago, are becoming more frequent. The dragonhead or leader of the Sun Yee On, the biggest triad, had a job as a solicitor's clerk when he was arrested for blackmail and gaoled for seven years. Now the news is all about foreign affiliations – with the Mott Street gangs in Manhattan, with the *yakuza* in Japan. The fights recur, but now in Amsterdam as well as Hong Kong.

It is said that fifty gangs control Hong Kong, and that ten of them are loosely federated into the 14K. They take protection money from more than

177

three-quarters of the cinemas, restaurants, bars and clubs, typically about $1,100 a month. Some in the entertainment industry call the extortion TAT – Triad Added Tax. Now some of these headaches have been exported, through personalities such as ex-Police Sergeant Eddie Chan Tsuchiu, who emigrated from Hong Kong to the US in the 1970s with his loot, having run for some time the Ong Leong Tong triad.

But the increasing enjoyment of higher wages and better living standards is just as important to discern. A man's textile mill earnings may be a little below his British counterpart's but his taxation is very much lower, and he does not need a car as much, being in a compact city well-served by public transport. With subsidised housing, it should be no surprise to find him spending more on restaurants and on his children's education, and if there is still something over, on foreign travel and on clothes and consumer durables.

Hong Kong began its discussions with the Organisation for Economic Cooperation and Development in Paris in 1989, after the American Congress had found Hong Kong to be enjoying a higher income per head than such OECD members as Greece, Spain and Portugal, and eligible, therefore, to be considered for membership of this rich nations' club. When William Purves of the Hongkong Bank mentioned a recent figure of Hong Kong's Gross Domestic Product per head, he added in parentheses that it was substantially higher 'than in my native land' – meaning Scotland.

The last Financial Secretary calculated in 1983 that, 'The disposable income of a bus driver here is higher than his counterpart's in London.' Actually, it was found by *Fortune* magazine in 1989 that the Hong Kong bus driver's earnings after tax were not far behind London, but that was for working 3,018 hours in a year, very much more than in London. A department manager earned more than he would in London, but for half as many hours again. More meaningful perhaps to the Hong Kong bus driver is the fact that his earnings, however you calculate them, are considerably higher than anywhere in China or in any other city on the Asian mainland. That is something he enjoys, both the knowledge of it and the substance.

Like the beggar in the courtroom, most people in Hong Kong are conscious of the tangible wealth all around them, and know that some of it, with luck and skill, could come into their hands. The waitresses at the Mandarin Hotel will tell you the latest gold price, and the room maids may well offer a comment on the day's share movements on the stock market. Hong Kong's religion, an American sociologist wrote, is 'moneytheism'. One of the conspicuous buildings in Central Hong Kong has reflective gold-coloured glass all round it; the Cantonese nickname it 'Hakka's tooth', because the Hakkas allegedly show off their wealth by smiling to reveal their gold fillings. It seems that some curious workers did actually drill a hole to see if the panes were filled with gold dust. It is a strange feeling for a Westerner to be in a city which is so rich, but where those riches are brandished shamelessly yet joyously to the world – and still polarised. The middle class has filled up steadily since the 1960s, but the few faces from the poverty-stricken past can still be seen on every street.

There is no shortage of conspicuous consumption. Law Ting-pong, the textile tycoon, recently paid $560,000 for the car number plate with the single number 'eight', which in Cantonese sounds just like the word 'prosperity'. At 75, Law was perhaps entitled to his extravagance. 'I was prepared to pay anything for it.'

Not everybody is selfish or family-oriented in their generosity. T. T. Tsui is a Hong Kong businessman who collects art. He once went to the Victoria and Albert Museum in London but found the gallery he wanted to see was shut. Luckily for the gallery, a staff member opened it for him. Stimulated by what he saw, Tsui sought the museum's advice, and eventually gave it $1.6 million to open a new gallery of Chinese art and design. There have been many instances of philanthropy on this scale and even higher – like Sir Run Run Shaw's $16 million donation to Oxford University.

One more aspect of Hong Kong's financial success is the flowering of architecture, art and culture. Certainly, the skyscrapers which have been put up in recent years have a reasonable number of architectural masterpieces among them. It is no longer necessary for Hongkongers to feel that they live in a philistine city lacking in elegance. Almost 2 million people go to plays, concerts and similar presentations, including the Hong Kong Arts Festival and Festival of Asian Arts, every year. The younger generation in Hong Kong is proving particularly appreciative of the world-class musicians, artists, actors and film-makers whom they can see almost daily in one of the many new cultural centres.

Laissez-faire was never quite what its guru, Sir John Cowperthwaite, presented it as. It was not a rigid universal formula for government withdrawal from everything to do with the economy. It was a broad principle of truth from which departures should be few and separately justified as necessary. The main point was to allow entrepreneurs to make their own decisions about the best use of money and resources, subject only to very broad considerations of public policy, and to allow them to be a major channel for money to flow through the economy and through the hands of people (their employees, customers, bankers, suppliers, etc.) instead of forcing some of it through government hands to support an unproductive bureaucracy which would feed upon itself and need ever more funds for new wasteful projects and programmes.

In a Chinese society, with built-in family social security, and in the circumstances of Hong Kong transience, it is a formula that worked very well indeed. Gradually, the middle class has swollen and Hong Kong has become a sophisticated, independent and prosperous community, certainly compared with others in the East Asian region. For this, British colonial rule can take the credit. And yet within the narrow circle of colonial decision-makers, even at the top, there were some who disagreed with *laissez-faire*, many faint-hearts who were stung by Bishop Hall's reproaches and would have preferred more welfare spending and industrial regulation. Only one man, Cowperthwaite, consistently stood out against such sentimentalism, and he may fairly be judged the intellectual father of the modern Hong Kong economy.

Chapter 17

Hongs in New Hands

There is much interest nowadays in the capture by the Hong Kong Chinese of the business supremacy formerly held by British companies like Jardine Matheson. Yet the more interesting question might be, why did it take them so long? Or, alternatively, how did the British merchants, indissolubly linked with anachronistic colonialism, go on making so much money during the post-war decades? The Chinese were always more numerous and their shortage of capital at the beginning was soon overcome. But they were not impelled by anti-colonial political motives, and were happy to take up the new business opportunities that continually arose without toppling the British from their perch.

Only in the past ten years have some ambitious, clever and capital-rich Chinese businessmen begun to take serious nibbles at these little British empires, and even, in a couple of cases, to take them over entirely. This is one end of the process of Chinese take-over, the other being the gradual buying-in of thousands of small Hong Kong Chinese investors to become substantial (even majority) equity holders in such quoted companies as Jardines or the Hongkong Bank. That enables them to leave the usually successful management at arm's length while getting a welcome share of the profits.

Another new factor in the 1980s was the entry of the People's Republic of China, either through its own companies like the Bank of China, China Resources, CITIC, etc., or in collaboration with leading Hong Kong companies of the kind that produced the new airline, Dragonair. Some Westerners fear that China will not be able to control this expansion, and may come to take over too much foreign business. The same thing happened in Shanghai in the 1950s. But the Chinese government has said that it will not acquire more than a tenth of the Hong Kong market capitalisation, and the *taipan* of Swire reported: 'China has gone out of its way to assure us that it

181

is absolutely essential that British companies remain a substantial part of Hong Kong.'

Jardine Matheson, which likes to be called the princely *hong*, is certainly the most stylish and aristocratic – and yet erratic – of the four major *hongs* (a Cantonese word meaning 'trading house'). It has a very long history, but the milestone for the modern period is 1961 when the Keswicks, who had worked for the Jardine family, bought the controlling equity of the last Jardine and have been the substantial owners of the company ever since. It also went public at that time. The Keswicks are among the seventy richest families in Britain, with wealth estimated at $160 million. They are Scottish, like the firm's founders, and the senior executives usually hail from the same corner of southwest Scotland.

Like many of the British traders in China, Jardine came to Hong Kong in 1949 after the communist victory in ruffled mood, making no secret of provincial Hong Kong's intrinsic inferiority to Shanghai or other big Chinese cities. Jardine's anger over the expropriation of its assets in China was tempered by gratification at the apparently warm personal relationships which Sir John Keswick had been able to forge with the communist leaders, from Premier Zhou Enlai downward. The losses almost led the firm to bankruptcy in 1950, but Sir John's entrée enabled it to be the only *hong* able to send its own Chinese executives to Beijing for negotiations. The succeeding generation of Keswicks reacted with a certain indifference to China, 'a great place to lose money in', as one of his nephews would say. When that nephew, Henry Keswick, was asked by MPs about his view of China in 1989, he referred to its 'Marxist–Leninist thuggish government'.

It was often suspected that the Chinese Communists themselves resented the Jardine airs and assumptions, and the company's capacity to perpetuate these was illustrated by a party in 1989 for a departing colleague. Twenty-five young public school Jardine men flew to Shanghai for the weekend and sat down in dinner jackets and dickie bows to a Chinese banquet in the old-fashioned Peace Hotel, moving the tables afterwards so that they could dance and jive – and one of them pursued a post-prandial striptease down to his lurid boxer shorts. Jardine, which had never been whole-hearted in its new ventures in China, and was always complaining about the obstructions, pulled out all its twenty-five expatriates working in China after the Tiananmen Square massacre and stopped all new expansion there.

When Henry Keswick took charge twenty years ago, he diversified the company's business activities away from China to Australia and other new areas, bought property and trading companies in South Africa, Hawaii and England and started the extremely successful merchant banking arm, Jardine Fleming. Then he returned to London to take over *The Spectator* and try for a parliamentary seat. His successor was less flamboyant and worked very hard, but allowed the company and its subsidiaries to expand too rashly.

Then the first blow was struck by the Hong Kong Chinese tycoons, when the shipowner Sir Y.K. Pao produced, within a matter of hours, $320 million to take his holdings in the Jardine company, Hong Kong and Kowloon Wharf Company, to 49 per cent, from which position he was able, in 1979, to lead it with its rich potential property from the Jardine stable to his own colours. Never before had there been such a contest at the highest level, and the unprecedented feature of it was that Pao got financial backing from the Hongkong Bank. An upstart who had come from nowhere in the preceeding twenty years was now able not only to challenge the princely *hong* but to defeat it, and set the seal on a second career in property.

Jardine whipped itself into a frenzy to protect itself and its 'other half', Hong Kong Land, from further raids. Jardine bought up Hong Kong Land shares to strengthen its control, and Hong Kong Land bought into Jardine, to make an interlocking edifice. Although Pao and another eager potential buyer, Li Kashing, at one time controlled more than a quarter of the Jardine equity, the crisis passed with the Keswicks still in command.

Then it was the turn of Simon Keswick, Henry's younger brother. In spite of its being said that he had inherited the looks of the family, while Henry got the brains, Simon showed himself good at recruiting new talent, and over a decade he wiped the firm's slate clean of debt and brought it up to record earnings. He sold off some of Henry's less desirable acquisitions and brought in a New York merchant banker, Brian Powers, to create a new corporate structure, allowing Jardine to control its subsidiaries while protecting all of them from take-overs. In the course of this the holding company was domiciled in Bermuda, which caused uproar among the traditionalists. It was 'like the Pope abandoning the Vatican City', one commentator wrote, 'or the Queen emigrating to Australia'.

The Keswicks defended it by the uncertainty about Hong Kong's legal position in international law under Chinese sovereignty after 1997. Simon had gone to the Xinhua office in Hong Kong twice to elicit details about the structure that would prevail, and came away unenlightened. If Jardine was to protect its ability to make very large long-term contracts, joint ventures and financial arrangements worldwide, it needed to be in a domicile which was not communist, and as a British-managed company it wanted to stay under British jurisdiction. These rationales were ridiculed at the time, but so many other companies followed Jardine's example later, including several with Chinese connections, like Sir Y.K. Pao's Lane Crawford department store, that the move was in retrospect accepted.

The property crash of 1980 knocked Jardine badly, but a few years later its market capitalisation of over $5 billion made it the top company in Hong Kong, ranking among the top forty in Europe. It employs 88,000 people in more than twenty countries. At one point it indicated that it would build up its assets outside Hong Kong to more than half, but the profits are so big from the local half that it soon retracted. 'We will not sell down assets here,' said Simon, 'to buy abroad.'

Simon is charmingly free in his admission of past mistakes; the company had 'overreached' itself and made 'unwise' investments. At one point he said of Jardine's handling of Hong Kong Land, 'We are catastrophically bad traders.'

Now the succession looks again like going to the family. A recent arrival in the Hong Kong headquarters is David Keswick, son of Chippendale Keswick (known as 'Chips'), the brother of Henry and Simon. He will inherit a corporate name that stirs up strong emotions and has a turbulent history, but has not by any means bowed out of the Hong Kong story.

An endearing trait of Jardine executives is their weakness for novelists. They played host to Ian Fleming in 1960 on his first visit to Hong Kong, which he described as 'the most vivid and the most exciting city I have ever seen'. As for Alexander Clavell's *Noble House*, the Jardine line is not to take it seriously, although Simon Keswick and the lifetime secretary Elaine Ho are rather recognisable in its pages, but to accept it as excellent publicity for the firm.

The Swire group, which has been Jardine's main rival throughout, is much more homespun and low key. It is run ultimately from London, and the management in Hong Kong is appointed from London, though given its head thereafter. The Swires own almost half of the voting equity of the Hong Kong-quoted company Swire-Pacific. They regret the floating of Swire Properties, which they feel pressurises them towards short-term growth instead of the long-term development they would prefer.

Some of the chief executives in Hong Kong have been almost Victorian figures, strong on benevolence and patient application to projects, and with a surprising turn of morality. John Bremridge, for example, declared, 'It would be grossly immoral to remove all that money we are going to make from our property development,' especially with a profit of 21,000 times its original value! Perhaps Swire's most dramatic success was with Cathay Pacific Airways, where it supplied capital and business management to the enthusiastic aviator-founders, and made it into one of the world's great airlines.

Like Jardine, Swire was active in China before, and one little incident shows what immense consequences those old connections can have today. One of the pre-war customers of Swire's shipping line in Shanghai was Rong Yiren, then a young businessman. For thirty years after the communist victory there was no contact. But Rong retained his independent capitalist businessman status all that time, suddenly blossoming in the 1980s with an international role under Deng Xiaoping who made Rong chief executive of the new company CITIC (China International Trade and Investment Corporation). CITIC set up in Hong Kong and made a substantial investment in Cathay

Pacific Airways. Why invest in the British-owned company whose monopoly in Hong Kong aviation several Hong Kong Chinese businessmen and Communist Chinese companies were trying to break with a new airline, Dragonair, supposedly having the blessing of Beijing? The answer, of course, lay in that pre-war connection with Swire.

Swire's steady, sensible style also triumphed in the career of Lydia Dunn, Hong Kong's only 'Dame' – and now Baroness. From a trading family, she rose to the highest level in Swire and was allowed by them to pursue a political career as well, becoming the leader of first the Legislative Council and then the Executive Council of the government. She wept twice on public occasions of great emotion (over the nationality question, for instance), and yet is cool and effective in debate and conveys sincerity.

By luck, in the case of Jardine, and good judgement in the case of Swire, these two long-standing trading houses have survived, though Jardine has lost some of its subsidiaries along the way. The other two major British *hongs* were not so fortunate. One was established in Hong Kong only in 1946 by one of the toughest characters on the China coast in the second quarter of the twentieth century, George Marden. Marden came out to China with the British Army before the First World War, and stayed to help run the Chinese Maritime Customs Service. He left that to start a Customs School and ship-to-shore lighterage business in Shanghai. One of his pupils at the school was V. K. Song, and they went into business together as G. E. Marden and Company. From that in turn sprouted the shipping line which later became Eastern Asia Navigation.

After the Pacific War, Marden settled in Hong Kong, pulled the rug from under his partner V. K. Song by refusing to hand the company over to him (eventually buying him out) and formed a strong association with Y. K. Pao, who had the same Shanghai background and shared by then his interest in shipping. In the 1960s George's son John Marden, a less decisive version of his father, took over. But Hong Kong is a pool of sharks, and just as George had squeezed his old Shanghai partner out, so his son John was outwitted by Y. K. Pao, who gradually insinuated himself in the Marden companies and eventually took them over. It is Pao who now sits on a high floor in Wheelock House.

There was another haemorrhage at Wheelock Marden when Colonel Douglas Clague, the wartime hero, bought into one of Marden's small subsidiaries called John D. Hutchison. Clague was a natural wheeler-dealer, and in the early post-war years, he seemed to sweep the board, always taking on new and successful lines of business, always absorbing other companies into a vast new local empire. Hong Kong, it was said, changed under his feet. He was everywhere at once, and made the decisions in the end for more than 300 companies, including the Textile Corporation, which he acquired from Marden, and the Hong Kong and Whampoa Dock Company. His association with Marden was friendly for a long time, but he eventually broke off and became a *taipan* in his own right. A chain smoker, a compulsive overtrader, very dependent on credit, he amazed everybody with his self-confidence. A colleague remembered going with him to London to negotiate for official financing of the cross-harbour tunnel, of which he was the strongest advocate. Clague asked for $30 million, and when the British offered only half of that, Clague stood up and said, 'Well, let us not waste each other's time,' thus forcing a higher offer. What the British did not know was that Clague already had a French offer of more than $30 million in his pocket.

The tunnel was completed in 1972, transforming the life of the city which had hitherto lived almost as two separate communities. Clague was the first to walk all the way through, from Hong Kong to Kowloon. But then his troubles began, with the business recession of 1974. He could not make his income meet his commitments and his investments in Indonesia went sour. The bankers had to take charge, and the Hongkong Bank put money in for new shares in order to have equity control of such an important trading company on which many other businesses depended, after which the bank unkindly showed Clague the door, and brought in an Australian whizz kid to turn the company round with better financial management. Within a few years Hutchison was healthy again, the biggest *hong* after Jardine's. Whereupon the bank, in 1979, sold its controlling share to another businessman whose ability and earlier success were beyond question, and he was not British but Chinese – Li Kashing.

Li was born in Guangdong Province in 1928 and first came to Hong Kong in 1939 for secondary education. He was, in effect, a penniless immigrant, dependent on his father – and when the father died, the young Li had to abandon his studies and work as a salesman for a plastics factory. Within three years he was the manager, and within five years he was able to start his own tiny plastic comb and soap-holder factory with a capital of $120. It was called Cheung Kong, meaning 'Long River', and it remains his flagship company to this day. This was just before the worldwide plastic flowers craze which enabled Li to expand his factory many times over, so that eventually it became the biggest plastics factory in the world.

By 1958 plastic flowers had made Li Kashing a millionaire, and he bought his first industrial property. He invented the brilliant scheme of getting a property owner like Marden, or a small Chinese property company, to contribute land for development by Li at a generous fixed price in return for half of the profit. Since property was constantly rising in value in Hong Kong, this meant that Li could get half of the increase in the value of a property without owning it and he was able to pre-sell the development in order to hedge his risk. Li handled the marketing, construction and finance of the development, with the assistance of British professional aides who continued to advise him in later years. In the 1970s he made a second fortune out of this.

In the recession of the 1970s, Li Kashing, still liquid, bought the Hilton Hotel and many other properties. He bought up shares in blue chip companies in Hong Kong and offloaded them to others like Pao at a profit, seeming always to know when to buy and when to sell, when to go for control and when to concede to others – 'when to trot', as one commentator put it, 'when to gallop, and when to switch horses'. He even bought 10 per cent of Jardine and sold it at a profit to Hong Kong Land, Jardine's associate, when Jardine was constructing its costly defence against take-over. 'His brilliance,' it was said, 'was to realise that property can be traded as just another commodity.'

In 1979, Li Kashing was ready for something big, and the Hongkong Bank served it up to him on a plate in the form of a 22 per cent stake in Hutchison, enough to control it in practice, for $82 million.

How would a Chinese tycoon lacking any formal business training manage one of the giant, formerly British, trading houses? Li behaved very rationally. He sacked several Hutchison executives whose performance had been equivocal, kept the good ones, and put in a new *taipan*, a former Jardine employee called Simon Murray. Hutchison became the only *hong* to be Western-structured but with an oriental layer on top – 'Anglo in operating structure and management philosophy', as Murray defined it recently, 'and Chinese in rewards and strategic direction'. Yet Li himself is somewhat secretive and non-accountable. 'With 20 per cent he thinks he owns a company,' people say, and 'his employees must keep demonstrating their loyalty.'

His personal reputation is nevertheless several grades higher than most of his rivals'. 'Other cowboys will cut your throat,' people in the market say, 'but not Li.' He was censured for culpable insider-dealing in 1984, on a technicality where he had not known of his subordinates' action and not profited from it. He felt badly enough about it to fly in three British QCs to clear his name, and was angry when their efforts failed. But his image in Hong Kong was not hurt. In personal terms he is almost a recluse, still living in the same house that he occupied twenty years ago, wearing a plain watch for its utility rather than for show. There is an engrained vulnerability and modesty about him, and he remains a very private man. His integrity is recognised and welcomed in a city which does not see much of that commodity, and he himself says that 'honesty is power'.

The key to his success is his logical mind and his self-control. He is quick to recognise a good investment, but he has the control to stop paying too much for it, to know when to stop bidding. Many Chinese presume that he must have some kind of sixth sense, that he is born lucky, but the real explanation for his financial exploits is a more mundane one: long evening hours of detailed homework to marshal all the relevant information.

So Li Kashing – Li the Cash, they call him – found himself seated on the Hongkong Bank board in control of the enormous and rich empire that

Clague had created. But he did not stop there. In 1985, he acquired Hong Kong Electric, an important piece of the Jardine conglomerate, and then he started to go international, trying to build up a stake in Pearson, the British publishing group, and in Cluff Oil. He acquired more than half of Husky Oil of Calgary and developed some other Canadian interests to go with it. Hutchison had always been a Hong Kong-oriented company, and Li's goal was to build up the assets outside Hong Kong to a level of about 40 per cent of the total. Recently, he has acquired a stake of almost 5 per cent in Cable and Wireless, the British telecommunications group. The original retailing company John D. Hutchinson and its sister Hutchinson-Boag Engineering were sold to the UK group Inchcape in 1990 for $93 million.

In terms of stock market values, Hutchison became larger than its rivals, bigger even than Jardine and Hong Kong Land put together and larger than the Hongkong Bank. Li Kashing says that he does not wish his stake in Hong Kong to exceed 10 per cent of the market, though it has risen above that from time to time. The companies in his group have a profit after tax in the most recent year of $1 billion. Little is revealed about his personal wealth, which has been estimated at between $1.5 billion and 2 billion. His two sons, Victor and Richard, are Canadian-based, although they have responsibilities with the group on both sides of the Pacific.

The question which is always asked in Hong Kong about a new Chinese tycoon is his attitude to that incalculable force behind the border, China. Merely by being a hero in the Chinese assault on the British hold over the Hong Kong economy, Li Kashing cannot avoid having a good relation with China. He sat on the Basic Law Drafting Committee and is usually open to the Chinese press. His philanthropy has been largely directed to China. His donations for Chinese universities have been put at $94 million, especially benefiting his native Shantou University. He has been received by Li Peng and Deng Xiaoping on several occasions, and Deng's words to him were, 'Your help is solid.'

When Beijing leaders tell British *taipans* that their presence in Hong Kong, now and in the future, is welcomed, they are not merely being diplomatic. One of their nightmares would be a Hong Kong in which capitalist Chinese businessmen have undisputed sway. The British business presence not only ensures a connection with the Western economic world, but also gives China another option in its Hong Kong dealings. They may even consider the Hongkong Bank a trifle rash in dishing out equity to Chinese businessmen. The present division of the *hongs*, two Chinese and two British, may be the pattern for the next period of time. There is no obvious threat now to Jardine after the loss of Wharf and Hong Kong Electric, and Swire has never seemed to be in danger. A healthy interaction is now likely.

Within that broad framework, it is worth considering whether the Chinese-ownership Western-management formula, symbolised by Sohmen as one of the two right-hand men to Pao, and Murray as Li Kashing's chief manager, will spread. It can also work the other way around, given Lydia Dunn's strategic role at Swire, though Jardine shows no interest in local Chinese advancement. Might there eventually be a *hong* in which racial origin of executives literally does not matter? That, of course, will be much affected by the impact of Chinese sovereignty in 1997.

PART IV

The Future Hong Kong

Chapter 18

Britain Agrees to Hand Over

As the 1970s drew to an end, Hongkongers saw themselves as living next door to a mostly distanced and inactive China which had not seriously threatened Hong Kong's *status quo* for thirty years. They perceived themselves as inhabiting an effectively autonomous Chinese city-state, parading under the unexpectedly helpful guise of a British colony. Some felt self-conscious about the colonial status, though William Fung, a Princeton and Harvard graduate, explained that, 'you only feel ashamed if you have lots of Western ideals about democracy and nation'.

A chill therefore descended when the British revealed that they were sounding China out about Hong Kong's future, and the chill dropped to freezing point when the British Foreign Secretary, Sir Geoffrey Howe, told the people of Hong Kong for the first time in April 1984 that British rule would come to an end in 1997. The possibility of change in status had always existed, of course. When the Chinese Emperor was overthrown in 1912, the enthusiastic revolutionaries of Guangzhou wanted to recover Hong Kong as well, and the provincial government agreed that it would be good to expel the British – 'although our government might lose a small amount of revenue'. Sun Yat Sen supported the plan, but the revolutionaries soon found other claims on their attention.

A more serious threat was faced by the British during the Pacific War, when Winston Churchill struggled to gain his allies' recognition of their anachronistic title to Hong Kong. The Chinese had no military clout but called on the Americans and Russians to press for an end to British colonialism, a goal to which the two superpowers were emotionally committed. Churchill had to promise President Roosevelt to discuss the future of Hong Kong with China after the war was over.

The British divided on the question with Churchill leading the 'over my dead body' school, but several senior officials and politicians believing it wiser to give Hong Kong back for the sake of better relations with China. At that time, the British had more investments in China than in Hong Kong. 'It does not seem likely,' one diplomat minuted, 'that any Chinese government will be prepared to renew the (New Territories) lease. Without these territories, Hong Kong would be untenable and it is therefore probable that before 1997 the UK government of the day will have to consider the status of Hong Kong.' Lie low and say nothing was the contrary advice from Churchill's corner.

When the war ended, the British benefited from the arrival in the White House of Harry Truman, who was disillusioned with Roosevelt's hero, Jiang Jieshi. Against Jiang's protests, Truman ordered the Japanese Army in Hong Kong to surrender to the British rather than to a Chinese commander: Roosevelt would have done the opposite. The British got their Royal Navy to Hong Kong in double time, and were thus enabled to re-establish their control in 1945, although China's Seventh Route Army entered the New Territories soon afterwards and occupied Kowloon Tong for several months before it could be persuaded to leave again.

There followed three years during which the British fended off both sides in China's civil war, observing a neutrality different from America's open endorsement of the Guomindang. Qiao Guanhua, the Communists' representative in Hong Kong, expressed China's appreciation of this neutrality, and of Hong Kong's tolerant attitude to the Communist Party, adding that China under communist rule would not use force to recover Hong Kong. Jiang, by contrast, called on Prime Minister Clement Attlee to retrocede Hong Kong so that the communist agents there could be liquidated.

When the British asked their allies if they would help in the event of China's attacking Hong Kong, only New Zealand stood up to be counted. The Americans and others turned a deaf ear. In any case, Whitehall had reluctantly concluded that Hong Kong was militarily indefensible. The British therefore took the line that they would not suppress the Communists.

As the likelihood of a communist victory grew, Britain took heart from the fact that Mao Zedong, unlike Jiang, had never asked the British to return the New Territories or even discuss the matter. It was concluded that the Communists needed Hong Kong for their trade and as a centre for political work among the overseas Chinese in Southeast Asia. When the Americans pressed yet again for a compromise solution of declaring Hong Kong to be an international free port, the British Cabinet rejected it, doubting if China would agree to a joint administration and fearing that the Russians would use the facility to build up their Pacific fleet. The British Foreign Office toyed with the idea of putting Hong Kong under UN trusteeship, but that carried the implication of eventual self-government, which would involve a plebiscite – and the people of Hong Kong 'would not dare to vote against a return to China'. All these arguments were to be heard again in the decades to follow.

On 15 October 1949, the Guomindang frontier troops sailed away, and two days later the Red Army arrived at the Shenzhen River bordering Hong Kong, having marched with unexpected speed across South China. Its lines were stretched, and it may well have reasoned that a breach of the border could provoke a defence of the colony not only by Britain but by its American ally as well – which might in turn jeopardise the communist control of the adjacent part of the mainland. It did not cross into Hong Kong.

Instead, China gradually made clear that it accepted the *status quo* in Hong Kong. Representatives of the railway administrations of the two sides met to discuss how to restore passenger traffic, and through trains started to run early in 1950. China was then drawn into the Korean War and had no time for the Hong Kong issue, but came to depend on Chinese merchants there for vital supplies in defiance of the United Nations embargo on trade with China. Hong Kong was becoming more useful to the Chinese who began to make huge amounts of money there. China was the major supplier of foodstuffs and basic consumer goods to the much enlarged population of Hong Kong. The Hong Kong Chinese may have voted with their feet against commmunism, but their stomachs definitely preferred Chinese rice, meat and vegetables. As the Hong Kong economy advanced, its spending power increased – to China's benefit.

China had virtually no need for anything made in Hong Kong, so these exports for consumption were unrequited, yielding a large inflow of Hong Kong dollars – which were freely convertible into US dollars and other hard currencies. On top of all that, Hong Kong became the main funnel for remittances of money by dutiful overseas Chinese to their families left behind in China. By the 1960s, China was earning around $700 million a year from Hong Kong, which was more than a third of the convertible foreign exchange China earned from all sources. You do not lightly throw away a source of such valuable currency, of the order that could equip an army or a navy or bring in a whole series of heavy industrial plant. So China found herself unexpectedly caught in a constraint of her own with regard to Hong Kong. As Peng Zhen, one of the inner core of the Chinese Communist leadership, had conceded as early as 1951, it would benefit the Chinese economy to maintain the status of Hong Kong.

The other side of the picture was that China provided a buffer for Hong Kong against international recession, by keeping its food prices steady regardless of sterling devaluations and other international currency crises. Chinese business journals talked about Guangdong subsidising 'the highly wasteful consumer-oriented Hong Kong economy', attributing Hong Kong's success in part to the sacrifices of many mainland Chinese. But it was, of course, a voluntary policy on China's part, advertising its own perception of the value to itself of Hong Kong's stability.

In 1955, Premier Zhou Enlai passed through Kaitak Airport on his way home to Beijing from the Bandung conference in Indonesia. The Governor,

Sir Alexander Grantham, did not go to meet him, it being an unofficial visit, but he wrote a letter which was handed to Zhou at the airport, to which Zhou replied, and later in the year Grantham paid an unofficial visit to Beijing, the first to be made by a Hong Kong Governor to Communist China. After conversations with Zhou Enlai and other senior officials, Grantham was able to return with the unofficial message that China accepted the British presence and would not undermine it, that Hong Kong was a problem left over by history which could be resolved at leisure, and that China accepted the *status quo* – as long as Britain kept order, and did not allow Hong Kong to become either self-governing (because that would rule out rejoining China) or a Guomindang base. To these 'conditions' was later added an injunction against allowing the Russians to build up a presence there. This was the basic British–Chinese understanding about Hong Kong which was to last into the 1990s. Under this formula a whole generation of Hongkongers was to grow up in blissful ignorance of the real nature of Hong Kong's situation. When opinion polls began to be taken much later, they showed that one Hongkonger in three did not even know which parts of Hong Kong might cease to be governed by Britain after 1997 under the existing treaties.

There were irritants, certainly. The status of the Chinese Communist representatives in Hong Kong was always a bone of contention, and the Walled City of Kowloon became another. This was a part of the urban complex where administrative control was ambiguous under the various nineteenth century Sino-British agreements The British left it alone and did not apply full administrative control, as a result of which some residents sought the protection of the Chinese government, which declared that it was Chinese territory. Only in the 1980s did Beijing agree to the demolition of this appalling slum complex. It was in the Walled City that Jackie Pullinger pioneered her reform of drug addicts (one of whom she took with her to Buckingham Palace when she received her MBE).

More worrying to the British were the surges of refugees from China. In the immediate post-war years many of the 1 million who had been expelled by the Japanese returned because the Chinese economy could not support them. Then, in 1949–50, the number of new entrants soared to a peak of 20,000 a week. Entry was then restricted to those with mainland exit permits, the others being regarded as illegal entrants to be sent back to China. A new rush came in 1962 when the communist government forced many of its town-dwellers to go back to live in the countryside. Tens of thousands chose the trek to Hong Kong instead. For six weeks the Chinese border guards abandoned their controls and this really scared the British. 'All they had to do,' a senior British official said, 'was to send a mass of people over and flood Hong Kong. They could have done it at any time. They could stop the food supplies, they could stop the water supplies. They have so many means of swamping us and finishing it off, if they wanted. Whereas sending troops would have created international repercussions . . .' A lower-ranking official put it more pithily: 'All they have to do is to send in 2 million of the buggers . . . and we can kiss it all goodbye.'

But they did not. The next crisis was the Cultural Revolution, when China kissed goodbye to socialist law and order. When this nationwide campaign spilled over into Hong Kong in 1967, it caused rioting and violent protest involving more than 800 dead or injured, and presented the first public challenge to British authority since the war. Labour grievances, against a shipping line, two taxi companies, a textile mill, cement plant and plastic flower factory, gave the Hong Kong Communists their excuse for action. When police tried to disperse a crowd of picketers at two Kowloon factories (one British and the other Chinese), a violent confrontation ensued which led to riots by young people who were not obviously proletarian.

The industrial disputes were genuine. But political overtones were soon added. The Post Office began to get mail from Guangzhou, where the Red Guards ruled, addressed to 'Get Out Imperialists City', instead of the name Hong Kong. A Guangzhou newspaper called British imperialism an 'old paper cat', not even to be dignified with the name of tiger. All this was deeply unsettling to the Hong Kong Chinese: was Mao about to take them over or not? 'If the Communists do come here,' a tram worker told a local magazine, 'the British will offer me no protection; they will not take me to London, so it is wiser to follow the communist way at present.' He spoke for the vast silent majority.

Derek Davies, a local editor, took issue with the Communists' claim that Britain was milking Hong Kong for its own benefit, and succeeded in convincing some of his adversaries that Britain actually made remarkably little out of Hong Kong, which in money terms was more important to China than to the UK. Further proof that the real animus of these disorders was not against British rule as such was seen in the fact that the most vicious attacks were on the Hong Kong Chinese police, who had acid, jars of urine and petrol bombs thrown at them, with the cry, 'Aren't you Chinese too?' Bank of China loudspeakers blared the same message to the policemen in the streets below: 'The British will not be here much longer, and do you think they will take you with them when you leave?' (a question still being asked in the 1990s). Hong Kong remembered uneasily the exposure of Assistant Police Superintendent John Tsang as a spy for China in 1961. It was found out after he returned from an élite one-year course at Cambridge University, that he had been passing information to the Chinese authorities for twenty years. China made him a professor of English and Vice-Chairman of the Guangdong People's Congress after his deportation.

Actually, the Hong Kong Communists were split. Those leading the Chinese finance and trade companies in Hong Kong tried at all costs to keep the Cultural Revolution out, following the lead of the party boss in South China at that time, Tao Chu. When Tao Chu eventually fell victim to the Red Guards and his gradualist line was discredited, some of his followers in Hong Kong felt obliged to take a strongly revolutionary stance in order to protect their jobs and positions. Meanwhile, another group of more politically extreme leaders – trade union officials, film stars, teachers – had all along been ready to overthrow the British, if that were possible. Eventually, Mao vetoed Jiang Qing's plans to reintegrate Hong Kong, ruling that its strategic importance required that it be left alone for the time being. Gradually, Beijing brought the Cultural Revolution down into lower gear, leaving the brash activists who had shaken their fists at the Hong Kong Governor looking silly. The old 'conditions' for continued British rule were restated: no suppression of the Communist Party, no military use of Hong Kong (China was especially worried about American warships entering the harbour), and no policies hostile to China. Finally, in 1971, the last Maoist slogan was pulled down from the Bank of China building. The chapter was closed.

The Cultural Revolution was the only occasion for control of the party's Hong Kong–Macao Work Committee, which has supreme authority over the Communists in Hong Kong, to pass from Beijing to Guangzhou. This body has the status of a provincial Communist Party, an indicator of the importance which China's leaders attach to Hong Kong, with the brief to coordinate the communist presence and policies in Hong Kong – but it may even gather military intelligence and negotiate arms deals with third countries.

The emotions stirred up by these events in many intelligent and idealistic young Hongkongers were not so easily damped down. Interviewed in prison a year later, some who had participated in the violence showed the scars of their colonial life. 'Hong Kong's existence is an insult to racial pride and respect . . . The *gwailos* hold the reins of economic and political power, and they use it to further the interests of their own country.' The education system was 'aimed at depriving people of their racial self-respect. It plans to convince the next generation that they are not Chinese, that they do not love their own country.'

One of the prisoners, a sixth form scientist in a good missionary school, put the matter more personally:

> I used to think of the many white collar workers who go to work every day, marry, play *mah jong*, and gamble on horses and greyhounds. What is the point of passing a lifetime like this? When I was in forms one and two, I turned to religion, but this did not hold me. I have always been aware of the injustices in Hong Kong society. I recall one incident vividly which made a deep impression on me. One day after school, I saw a policeman overturn a hawker's tomatoes and then stamp on them deliberately. Then look at our youth: they are going the decadent way, following The Beatles. Compare this with the good morality in China.

What finally made this young man join the rebellion in 1967 was the 'unreasonable beatings' of demonstrators by the police. He was arrested and goaled for putting up inflammatory posters in his school.

After these excitements had died away, the Chinese consistently sought to regularise the *status quo*. China joined the United Nations, and in 1972 had to take a position on Hong Kong at the UN committee on decolonisation which wanted to discuss what was happening in Hong Kong. The Chinese said firmly that it was an internal matter, that Hong Kong was Chinese territory temporarily administered by Britain, and that the question should be removed from the UN agenda – which it was.

In 1976, Mao died and the British hoped that his successors would display a less emotional and more rational attitude to the Hong Kong question, enabling both sides to agree in good time on what should happen after the end of the New Territories lease in 1997, instead of leaving it to the last minute. The British probably raised the question with the ineffectual Hua Guofeng, who was the interim leader before the rise of Deng Xiaoping. They put it about that the ideal solution would be to combine outward signs of Chinese sovereignty with unfettered *de facto* British administration, and it was recalled that a similar agreement had been made before the war about the British concession in Hankow, while another for Weihaiwei had been similarly disposed of. This was a period when all kinds of balloons were floated. The idea of renewing the lease after 1997 had often been discussed: Jeremy Bray, the Labour MP with Hong Kong ties, had publicly proposed it as early as 1963 at the House of Commons. In the 1970s, many others followed but when Stanley Ho privately canvassed the Chinese about new fifty-year leases for Hong Kong, the New Territories and Macao, he got no reply.

If it was a question of some kind of informal internationalisation, along the lines of Danzig or Tangiers in the past, then some kind of internal self-government might become necessary. The Cultural Revolution crystallised people's ideas about what had happened to Hong Kong: it was no longer a mere colonial anachronism, but a vehicle for a community of Chinese outside the People's Republic to demonstrate their talents in a non-political atmosphere. So how to preserve that? Investors were getting anxious about the uncertainty after 1997, and so were prospective mortgagers of New Territories houses. It was openly predicted that the Governor, now Sir Murray Maclehose, might engage in shuttle diplomacy to reach agreement with the Chinese. From their side, the Chinese began to drop hints that the lease might be extended, possibly 'under a slightly altered flag of convenience', and David Bonavia of *The Times* reported the Chinese as giving 'clear assurances' that Hong Kong would 'be allowed to remain under British rule beyond . . . 1997'.

Deng Xiaoping, that prince of pragmatism, consolidated his power in China in 1978, and one of the earliest acts of his regime was to create, opposite Hong Kong, a new Special Economic Zone at Shenzhen, with the purpose of building within the People's Republic an industrial and commercial centre as successful as Hong Kong – and initially dependent upon Hong Kong. It was as near to free enterprise capitalism as the People's Republic dared to go at that time, wanting the fruits of capitalism without sullying the modified socialist system followed in the rest of China.

It was even suggested by Shenzhen officials that the border could eventually be abolished, and both sides rely on the second border control which the Chinese themselves built between Shenzhen and the rest of Guangdong province – twelve feet of illuminated barbed wire running from coast to coast, to keep the Chinese out of Shenzhen (and also out of Hong Kong?). Customs checks could be removed to this new border, it was suggested, allowing Shenzhen to become a duty free area. Hong Kong Chinese businessmen welcomed the idea of a duty free belt on both sides of the present border, but the prospect of giving up the present border controls was not attractive to the Hong Kong authorities. The whole discussion raised the question, which side would absorb the other? China appeared to expect Shenzhen to absorb Hong Kong in the long run, but Hongkongers dreamed of eventually absorbing Shenzhen and perhaps even larger parts of China. The economist Tim Congdon mischievously suggested that China ask for British sovereignty to be extended from Hong Kong to the whole of China in order to cultivate successful capitalism.

At the beginning of the 1980s Shenzhen was a sleepy little town of 20,000 inhabitants. By the end of the decade it had more than 600,000 and boasted China's tallest building. It had become the largest trading territory in China and among the top five for agricultural or industrial production. It generated more than three-quarters of China's foreign exchange and its people enjoyed a net income per head one-third higher than the national average. It was able to attract a disproportionate number of returned students from the West to work there, including a graduate of Oxford.

Beijing decreed that Hong Kong's economic laws and regulations should be systematically introduced in Shenzhen, which some saw as the beginning of an official 'Hong Kong-isation' all along the Chinese coast where other special zones were being created. But it was not without its troubles. It rapidly became the centre of China's black market for currency and labour disputes became frequent, even though most enterprises were foreign-owned. Employers were said to have no respect for the trade unions, to falsify their accounts, to speculate, misappropriate and embezzle, and to make illegal imports of cars and video recorders.

Such complaints were used by the conservatives in Beijing as ammunition against the reformers. Deng Xiaoping was reduced to saying of Shenzhen in 1985, 'We hope it will succeed, but if it fails we can draw lessons from it.' Inside Shenzhen is the Shekou Industrial District, a 'zone within a zone' where industry is concentrated, mostly managed by a Hong Kong-based but China-owned company under reformist influence. Its chairman was under investigation in the later part of 1989 for involvement with the democracy movement. What started at the beginning of the decade as China's white hope for economic development thus turned into a potential victim of political divisions within the party leadership.

Shenzhen's initial dependence on Hong Kong was a development in the continuing responsibility of the latter for important inputs into the Chinese economy. In the 1980s Hong Kong was taking about a quarter of China's exports, and official and unofficial estimates of China's annual earnings from Hong Kong from all sources averaged at $6–7 billion. Hong Kong has proved habit-forming for China. It was, as Qiao Zonghuai, of the Xinhua office in Hong Kong said, 'very necessary to China . . . an enormous market for Chinese products'. Then there is the investment which Chinese companies make into China: the Bank of China group in Hong Kong was investing some $600 million a year in China in the mid-1980s. Some of the commercial contracts already made between Hong Kong and China are to continue beyond 1997, the supply of electricity from the China Light and Power Company to Guangdong province being one example. China also benefits from the huge charitable donations made by leading Hong Kong Chinese businessmen to universities, schools, hospitals, libraries, sports facilities and research institutes in China. Henry Fok sent a $1 million cheque to the International Olympic Committee towards the Olympic Museum in the name of the Chinese National Olympic Committee, and there are dozens more examples of China obtaining the use of foreign exchange through a Hong Kong connection. Sir Y.K. Pao, Li Kashing and Sir Run Run Shaw are the biggest donors, but there are many others.

How important are these earnings for China? Their loss would not ruin the prospects of China's modernisation, according to Y.C. Jao of Hong Kong University, but would constitute a 'disastrous setback'. What was said about the earlier position in the 1950s and 1960s can be restated, that China would survive the loss of these earnings, but would find its purchasing options on the world market so reduced that it would have to be a very big political gain indeed to outweigh it. Lucien Pye, the American sinologist, calculated that China would earn more foreign exchange by incorporating Hong Kong into its own economy, but that was on the false assumption that Hong Kong's exports to third countries like the US and EC under quota are transferable: neither the US nor the EC nor many other countries would switch consumer goods quotas from Hong Kong suppliers to People's Republic of China suppliers (i.e. the same Hong Kong suppliers under a different sovereignty), merely because Hong Kong was legally subsumed into China. The habit of not treating Communist Chinese goods liberally is ingrained in the Western consciousness, as the controversy in the US in 1990 over China trade privileges showed. It may be that in the future China will enjoy sufficient goodwill in the world to merit favourable trade treatment, but that day is certainly a long way off and will not occur before 1997.

From 1958 water was added to the regular shopping list. During the drought of 1963 Premier Zhou allowed Hong Kong-chartered tankers into the Pearl River every day to draw fresh water, and joint studies were made for water supplies from the East River which were implemented soon afterwards, China reversing the stream to the Shenzhen reservoir. Hong Kong became sufficiently nervous of its growing dependence on mainland water in the 1970s to get Asian Development Bank finance to build the world's largest desalting plant in the New Territories, but within a few years it was no longer used, becoming Hong Kong's biggest white elephant. Once China cooperated in straightening the Shenzhen River and agreed to supply two-thirds of Hong Kong's water needs in 1989, desalination became an expensive luxury – though it may regain its attraction if Hong Kong's needs and Guangdong's conservation measures increase in future. Meanwhile, water is another easy export earner for China.

By the late 1970s, there was little land left to develop in the ceded part of Hong Kong, so the main remaining source was the leased New Territories. The banks were ready to extend mortgages beyond 1997, but the accountants doubted if investment in land or property could be written off over the whole lease, if that included a period after 1997. By now it was understood by everyone in Hong Kong that the two parts, the ceded and leased territories, could not become split again and remain viable. If the New Territories were to revert to Chinese rule, Hong Kong Island and the tip of the Kowloon Peninsula would be left without the resources to support their population – totally at the mercy of China's goodwill. Professor Peter Harris of Hong Kong University said it would be like 'leaving the house and living in the toolshed'.

At the end of 1978, the Chinese Foreign Trade Minister paid an official visit to Hong Kong and in the course of lunching at Government House he invited Sir Murray Maclehose to visit Beijing. The Governor grasped the opportunity of solving the urgent practical problem of the industrial and commercial subleases in the New Territories. He duly went to China from 24 March to 4 April 1979 and opened a Pandora's box of misunderstanding, forced hands and allegations of bad faith.

If, the Hong Kong government had speculated, it gave subleases beyond 1997, as it would have liked to do for practical business reasons, would China turn a blind eye? Was China's acquiescence necessary? Could the problem be solved without talking to China at all? These matters were exhaustively discussed among British and Hong Kong government officials, who concluded that it would be more dangerous to act without reference to China, thus running the risk of a political backlash damaging to Hong Kong, than to attempt to bring the Chinese into an act which they would in any case have to enter at some time or other. When the British decided to broach the subject, the final question was, could they talk only about subleases and leave the bigger long-term issue on one side? Here again the consensus was that they should not. The pressure from the American lawyers advising American corporations on substantial investment projects in Hong Kong was a big factor in all this.

So Maclehose popped the question to Deng Xiaoping, then at the beginning of his period of power, in an interview lasting less than an hour, and the extent of misunderstanding is still unclear despite the fact that the question had been fully discussed by subordinate officials on both sides beforehand. The trouble was that British lawyers, who are not the most flexible and imaginative of their profession, warned Maclehose and his superiors in London that subleases beyond 1997 would require an extension of the British Order in Council, under which the Hong Kong government derives its powers from the Queen, and it was hard for the British to do such a formal thing without getting a Chinese say-so.

Deng Xiaoping is not known to have responded to this particular question, but about the subleases he said, 'Tell your investors to put their hearts at ease.' What he said about the overall lease was very general, to the effect that it would not be renewed after 1997: China would take Hong Kong back, but no date or timetable was mentioned.

When Maclehose returned to Hong Kong, he heavily stressed the need to protect confidentiality, retailing only the single sentence of Deng's about putting 'hearts at ease'. The immediate result was to send Hong Kong confidence through the roof because of the superficial implication that Deng had not asked for Hong Kong back in 1997, since that was not mentioned by Maclehose. Property values went into a boom. But a few years later the suspicion surfaced, with a strongly held rumour that Deng had told Maclehose that China would press to recover sovereignty in 1997, that Maclehose had deliberately withheld this from the Hong Kong public, and that he had done so in order to allow the UK government to put legislation in place which would keep out Hong Kong British passport holders who would flock to Britain when the take-over plan eventually became known.

The rumour was absurd, for two reasons. In the first place, the allegedly withheld message of Deng was nothing more than the official Chinese position at the time, about which there was no secret. It left open the possibility of subsequent Sino-British negotiations which Maclehose would not have wished to bedevil by press remarks. Secondly, the administrative rules denying Hong Kong Chinese the right to live in Britain had been introduced already in 1979, and the Nationality Act of 1981 which spelt out the details of Hongkongers' exclusion from the UK traces back to earlier legislation and in particular a Green Paper of the Labour government in 1977. It can hardly be argued that Maclehose was covering up for something which had already been decided and publicised by the British government. All the same, he did come home empty-handed in the sense that no solution of either the sublease or the Order in Council questions had been provided.

Margaret Thatcher once said, ingenuously, that if the New Territories had been ceded outright like Hong Kong island, the present colony of Hong Kong would long ago have been made independent. To create an independent state on the edge of the vast brooding People's Republic of China would, in the light of the recent history of that country, be not only foolhardy but irresponsible: the result would almost certainly be a violent take-over in the course of which the former colonial subjects would suffer gravely. When the Hong Kong Observers, a responsible group of Hong Kong intellectuals, put out one of the earliest political manifestos, in 1982, they said, 'Our plea is for a voice in shaping our future, for autonomy. It is *not* a call for independence. We recognise that Hong Kong can never be an independent city-state. We ask for autonomy within China.'

But Mrs Thatcher was right to identify the lease as the source of great ambiguity and difficulties. Long before Maclehose tentatively suggested giving post-1997 subleases, some expatriate high-fliers in the government had proposed that China Resources, which is owned by China in Hong Kong, but has much autonomy in business matters, be given a long lease of land in the New Territories for oil storage operations (this was in the aftermath of the OPEC oil price crises) lasting well into the twenty-first century. For a Chinese company to be the pioneer in what might then be a gradual accumulation of such extensions would give everybody confidence, indicating the unofficial acquiescence of the Chinese authorities. It would not prevent China from asking for a return of the New Territories at any time, but it would be a tangible signal to the business community that the Chinese government envisaged the *status quo* in Hong Kong continuing. Unfortunately this imaginative scheme was torpedoed by the Hong Kong government's Political Adviser, who is paid to minimise Hong Kong's offending or provoking China.

Maclehose had not been able to carry all his Cabinet with him on his Chinese adventure. Some of them resented the way in which Britain foisted Foreign Office diplomats on them as Governors who instinctively put Britain's relations with China before Hong Kong interests, seeing Hong Kong as an embarrassing anachronism which tended to spoil those relations with China and cause Britain's trade and diplomacy with China to lag behind those of other Western nations. The viability and integrity of Hong Kong's society and economy were sometimes not fully recognised in Whitehall, and many Hong Kong officials felt that Maclehose exhibited these traits in full measure. Even his superhuman efforts to modernise Hong Kong and clean it up were attributed by critics to a desire that China should have a better opinion of the British. In this instance, these government critics felt that Maclehose had acted too early with Deng Xiaoping, and had been too direct in taking up the sublease question with China. In the Chinese way of doing things, go-betweens would have better explained the purpose, put it in the most acceptable way, and got tentative reactions without commitment so that both sides could save face.

The sleeping dog theory, or *wu-wei* (meaning inaction) strategy, had many adherents in Hong Kong. If Britain had not pressed China, this argument went, the Chinese would have let it slide, and Britain might well have been able to carry on unchallenged after 1997 without even a new Order in Council or treaty. But once an answer was requested, the Chinese were put in a position where they had to press their claim, even though unprepared, and had to take into consideration the effect of their answer on the similar problems they had with other Chinese territory as yet unincorporated into the People's Republic, i.e. Taiwan and the disputed Soviet border territories. Ambiguity was therefore of the essence, in this view. But the official British mainstream counter-argued that while ambiguity may be effective for postponing difficult solutions to difficult problems, it was not what American investment lawyers needed. Even for the Hong Kong Chinese, one open endorsement from China would be worth ten or twenty tacit acquiescences. And did Hong Kong really relish, it was added, a scenario of domestic reforms – political, economic, social – proceeding piecemeal and even petering out if the 1997 deadline were to draw near without any agreement?

This was the background to the idea which now took shape in Hong Kong, to try to achieve a retention of British administration by surrendering sovereignty to China – not primarily out of chauvinism or for considerations of British prestige, although some of that was no doubt mixed in, but because the difference in the legal–administrative–political–business systems in Hong Kong and China respectively was so enormous that Hong Kong would necessarily go into a downward spiral if Chinese trained in communism attempted suddenly to replace the British. That would reflect badly on China, although the main losers would be the Hongkongers. This formula was certainly what the Hong Kong people would have preferred, allowing the Chinese to gain dignity in the eyes of the world, while the British stayed to run the administration. It was now that the precedents of pre-war Guomindang diplomacy were invoked, for example regarding Weihaiwei, and also the Macao example.

Macao had been run by Portugal for 400 years without a treaty as a 'Chinese territory temporarily under Portuguese administration', and perhaps that formula would do for Hong Kong. By early 1982 it looked as if both governments were inching towards the idea of a treaty embodying something like the 'Macao solution', with Chinese sovereignty acknowledged and the UK invited to administer Hong Kong for the foreseeable future – but China seemed to need time to prepare its own cadres for this, time to re-educate them, and it was made very clear that there would have to be total confidentiality of negotiation to allow the Chinese to keep face. To put it shortly, Britain would repudiate the unequal treaties and win a lease of the whole territory. One difficulty with this strategy was the understandable reluctance of Hong Kong Chinese to come out openly and shout for a continuation of British administration, however much they might want it in their hearts. Communist newspapers called those few who did back the idea 'slaves of foreigners'.

China's goal was to restore Chinese sovereignty over the whole of Hong Kong in 1997. In fact sovereignty had little meaning for the British in Hong Kong. They ruled there all the time on Chinese sufferance. Post-war Hong Kong had become effectively autonomous even from Britain itself, which derived little material benefit from its possession.

The stage was set for the new dialogue when a Chinese leader predicted in October 1979, that satisfactory negotiations over Hong Kong would take place, adding 'we will take into consideration the interest of the investors there'. That was the first time the Chinese government had conceded publicly that it would negotiate with Britain about Hong Kong, that it would take into account the interests of other parties, and implicitly that it recognised the legality of British authority – all three statements being unprecedented. There was even a hint of the way China might couch its concession of administration, when Qiao Zhonghuai observed that 'withdrawal of the British administration would hurt British dignity'. This might have missed the real point, but it was an unprecedented recognition of the other side of the case and an obvious suggestion that one bit of face-saving deserves another.

Also unprecedented was the flurry of consultations which the Chinese authorities now held with various interest groups among the Hong Kong Chinese. From early 1982 onwards there were frequent shuttles of Hong Kong businessmen, trade unionists, intellectuals, newsmen, etc., to Guangzhou and Beijing. At these meetings numerous ideas were advanced from the Hong Kong side, for a joint China–UK ruling council with alternating governors, for Hong Kong to be run as a Sino-British joint venture on a fifty-fifty basis employing British 'technicians', or for Hong Kong to be an 'independent special zone' in China. The former scheme was put forward by R. C. Lee, one of the sons of the property magnate Lee Hysan: he had been a fellow student at Oxford with an influential People's Republic official and was one of the few Hong Kong Chinese apparently trusted by both sides. On the Beijing side stood Liao Chengzhi, who also claimed the respect of Chinese on both sides. Tragically, since these men might have been able to carry through crucial lobbying during the ultimate Sino-British negotiations, both died just before they started.

When the agenda had been fixed by officials, Margaret Thatcher went to Beijing in September 1982 to agree formally to begin talks 'with the common aim of maintaining the stability and prosperity of Hong Kong'. The British were rather pleased that the Chinese version of the communiqué referred to China's 'recovery' of sovereignty, the first official recognition perhaps that there was something to recover, i.e. an indirect recognition of the unequal treaties.

It was not a happy visit for Mrs Thatcher, who had just been hit by the Falklands crisis and was not in the mood to have another jewel snatched from the imperial crown. She harped on Britain's moral responsibility to the

Hong Kong Chinese, ignoring the implication that China had none: the Hong Kong students declared this to be a 'pretext to rule Hong Kong forever'. And she unwisely lectured the Chinese in public on their attitude to the unequal treaties. 'Those who do not honour one treaty will not honour another,' she warned. She had probably noticed that the Chinese who complained most passionately about the unequal treaties being an affront to China's national pride went on enjoying life in Hong Kong regardless. But was she reminded that the Chinese official who had ceded Hong Kong in the first place, in 1841, had been recalled to Beijing and ordered to be cut into small pieces for the fowls of the air to eat? One Hong Kong Chinese explained: 'No Chinese dare accept . . . the validity of these treaties. They were signed by the Emperor during the Opium Wars and are a matter of shame.'

In spite of Thatcher's gaucherie, the Chinese enthusiastically laid the ground for the negotiations with a spate of rumours about a twenty-five-year transit period, rule by a committee of Hongkongers chosen by Beijing, with British officials continuing in their posts but Chinese being promoted to vacancies, negotiations about administrative transfer but not over sovereignty which was indisputable – and finally, in a characteristically Chinese touch, the promise that China would buy a large quantity of second-hand machinery from the UK as a reward for good behaviour.

When Xu Jiatun, the new head of the Xinhua office in Hong Kong, and China's unofficial 'ambassador', arrived on the train from the Chinese border in 1983, with the elegant former pastor Li Chuwen from Shanghai in attendance as his deputy, China's effort to win Hong Kong opinion over to the Chinese side in the talks with Britain took a serious turn. The first thing Xu did was to expel the so-called East River Gang which had dominated the Xinhua leadership in Hong Kong for decades, people who had earned glory in the 1940s in the anti-Japan guerrilla units north of Hong Kong, but whose contribution to the debate of the 1980s was negligible. They were mostly promoted sideways or given early retirement, and Xinhua became much more sophisticated. Its staff courted Hong Kong intellectuals and writers, sending them rare fruits from the Chinese interior, with handwritten messages. 'Many of us didn't know what to do,' a university lecturer explained after receiving such a gift, 'we couldn't send the fruit back, so we accepted it.' They understood the message, of course – to be kinder to the Communists in their writings.

The communist cadres in Hong Kong fell mostly into three categories: the older mainland officers who spoke no Cantonese; the so-called 'cradle communists' who supported Xinhua because they had gone to communist schools in Hong Kong or had communist parents or employers, and tended to lack strong individual commitment; and finally the trade union and ex-guerrilla veterans from the 1940s who were very tough, and despised any display of softness. Xu had to do his best with this unpromising material.

Behind the soft words, Xinhua's expanded office built a network of communist cadres, intended, according to a defector who fled to Taipei, to rule Hong Kong after 1997. Xu himself said that the party's role after 1997 would be to 'assist' the new government in Hong Kong. During the 1980s Xinhua set up district offices shadowing the Hong Kong government ones and built up local followings to select individuals to stand in District Board elections against the non-communist incumbents. They were not very successful in the elections of the later 1980s, but it was assumed that the Communists were feeling their way and preparing the ground in a longer term strategy.

The substance of the Sino-British negotiations which went on from 1982 until the end of 1984 was the question of sovereignty and administration, but many other issues affected the bargaining. For China one of these was the question of Taiwan, which had evaded the Chinese reunification net for more than thirty years but which Deng Xiaoping wanted to regain in order to go down in history as the great reunifier. One way of reassuring Taiwan opinion that life in the People's Republic would not be all that bad, and that autonomy would mean something, would be to implement a convincing autonomy for Hong Kong, and this was a powerful impulse bringing the Chinese and the British together, for different reasons, in support of an autonomous Hong Kong under Chinese sovereignty.

The fact that the Guomindang monopoly of political power in Taiwan was broken at the beginning of the 1980s, with new indigenous Taiwanese parties and leaders coming forward with very little sense of residual links with China, made this all the more urgent from Beijing's point of view. When the Sino-British agreement was eventually reached, the Chinese Foreign Minister remarked that it would 'have a far reaching effect on China's reunification with Taiwan'.

A basic question for the British side was whether China would place economic considerations before political ones in disposing of the Hong Kong question. Hong Kong optimists claimed that China's foreign exchange and other economic inputs from Hong Kong would always persuade any Chinese leadership not to kill the goose that laid these golden eggs, and they referred back to the supply of food and water that continued during the Cultural Revolution as a proof of this. The pessimists argued differently, pointing out that Deng Xiaoping had broken off ties with the Soviet Union, in 1958, at the cost of valuable economic aid and technical assistance, and that the action against the students in Tiananmen Square, in 1989, positively invited Western economic sanctions at a time when Western trade and investment was vital for China's modernisation plans.

This debate was at cross purposes: whether an economic sacrifice is worth making obviously depends, for any government, on the magnitude of the political gain to be bought. China might in a tight corner sacrifice an arm to save its life, but would try hard to survive without the loss of any limb. If

Hong Kong became a base for hostile forces intending to undo the Chinese government and replace it by another, the economists in Beijing pleading for the retention of the foreign exchange earnings from Hong Kong might find themselves in a minority. But it would have to be something as big as that, surely, for these golden eggs to be forgone. In fact, China made it very clear throughout the 1980s that the Hong Kong economic input was important. The Guangdong province governor Xi Zhongxun declared in 1980 that China would 'not tolerate' any threat to Hong Kong's economic stability. Naturally, when the British used this known desire by China as an argument to support a continuing British role after 1997, the left wing press in Hong Kong sought to rebut it along the lines that patriotism required Hong Kong's reunification in China as a higher goal, and that national dignity would not allow a British role beyond 1997, as part of the tactics of negotiation.

Cultural differences manifested themselves in the negotiations, as they do in any Sino-Western encounter. The sinologists within the British team urged their colleagues not to press China in public for concessions, because this brought in questions of 'face' and focused attention on the form rather than the substance of the differences. The British actually found that the quiet informal suggestions which they made in private sessions with the Chinese were sometimes presented later as Chinese proposals, which was a much more fruitful way of getting results. China was in a difficulty, of course, in not being fully briefed on how Hong Kong worked under its British administration, and what exactly its position was in international law and commerce. It was as humiliating for them to have to ask the British for the answers, as it was for them to approach the Hong Kong Chinese. But they did both, and were rapidly educated into the situation of this capitalist enclave.

The Chinese started with the principle of 'one country, two systems', an umbrella slogan which legitimised the coexistence of socialism and capitalism within the People's Republic. Article 31 of the new Chinese constitution which Deng's government introduced allowed for Special Administrative Regions, under which Hong Kong could have virtual self-government on the basis of Chinese sovereignty and continuing capitalism. Hong Kong, Liao Chengzhi had told Hong Kong industrialists in 1982, would be ruled autonomously by its own people, with its own system and lifestyle unchanged, and China would not send a single soldier or official. Xu Jiatun committed China to retaining Hong Kong's capitalist system and autonomy for fifty years, and Deng himself later indicated that it could be 100 years.

The British concern in the negotiations was to retain an administrative presence beyond 1997, in order to ensure that the system which had made Hong Kong so prosperous and so profitable to China would not be sabotaged by the sudden intrusion of untrained hands on sensitive tillers. Britain would still be needed, it was argued, as an insulator between communism and capitalism, especially in the fields of law, finance, economy and administration. The British trump card was seen by some as the threat to withdraw from Hong Kong, or to let the place run down before 1997. Britain could give back gold or dross. But that was never a serious strategy for the British team. As the Hong Kong Observers said, 'our future is too valuable to be used as a pawn'.

It took a long time for the two sides to table their voluminous position papers and come to grips with each other's arguments. The British showed no sign of wanting to recognise Chinese sovereignty, demanding instead that the *status quo* be regularised for a longer term. But eventually the British agreed to leave the sovereignty question aside in order to discuss the practical questions of the post-1997 regime. When a second round of talks began in July 1983 China pledged that it would interfere with Hong Kong only on questions of defence or foreign relations, that Hong Kong could elect its own Chief Executive and that no socialist reforms would be implemented against local wishes. Finally, worn down by Chinese pressure, the British said that if they agreed to revoke the unequal treaties, conceding both sovereignty and administration to China, what undertaking about post-1997 would China offer in return? The Chinese eagerly responded, and the British concentrated on trying to embody Chinese promises in international law.

When Sir Geoffrey Howe formally told Hong Kong that British rule would end in 1997, the left wing press said that 'we cannot refrain from expressing admiration for the present British leaders – though some indignant Hongkonger shouted to Howe: 'You fight for the Falklands, and you deliver us up to the communists like trussed hens.' So the final agreement came whereby Hong Kong would be a Special Administrative Region with a high degree of autonomy administered by Hongkongers, with its socio-economic system and lifestyle unchanged and its laws basically unchanged, and managing its own external economic relations as a free port and international financial centre – with due regard to the economic interests in Hong Kong of the British and other foreigners.

What held things up was not so much the substance of the agreement but the method of expressing it. The British wanted a legally binding pact, incorporated into the Basic Law which China intended to draft and promulgate for Hong Kong after 1997. But the Chinese preferred parallel declarations, a habit to which Henry Kissinger had introduced them. The Chinese also proposed a Joint Liaison Group in the interim period, apparently to monitor the money supply in case Britain left the shop empty (there was considerable suspicion over the disposition of Hong Kong's currency reserves in London). In the end, the British agreed to a Joint Liaison Group with a limited brief, and China undertook to present the details of Hong Kong's autonomy as binding annexes to the agreement. Hong Kong did not like the Joint Liaison Group, which was, as one newspaper commented, like inviting the undertaker in before the patient expires. But it proved its worth afterwards.

Many Hongkongers felt that Britain had been too timid in these negotiations and could have called China's bluff more often. The same was almost certainly said by domestic critics on the communist side. Some Hong Kong opinion leaders believed that the British had been swayed by the prospect of trade deals. 'Look how easily the British have given in,' Emily Lau, a leading journalist complained. 'It is disgraceful . . . The British think that the real relationship is UK–China, and that if they can get big contracts with the mainland, then Hong Kong doesn't matter. But they are stupid. They cringe and they kowtow and the Chinese laugh at them.' Martin Lee, the liberal lawyer, talked of Britain's sacrificing Hong Kong 'for a few good contracts'. There had once been an MP in Westminster in the 1950s, Emrys Hughes, who said, why not swap Hong Kong for a trade agreement? But mysteriously, the 1980s contracts, whether for second-hand machinery or anything else, never materialised, and Britain's exports to China remained disappointing by comparison with all her competitors.

The jibe made about Sir David Wilson, appointed as Governor in 1987, that instead of training beforehand in various British cities in the problems of municipal administration, all he really needed was a week or two at Harrods in the gift-wrapping department, was inept. Hong Kong had become so used to the artificial freedom of being a physical part of China and yet being able to criticise China, that the idea of intelligent diplomacy aiming to build up a constructive Chinese commitment to support Hong Kong was too new.

The Sino-British agreement was signed in Beijing's Great Hall of the People at the end of 1984, with at least two Hong Kong multimillionaires present, and was celebrated by a banquet of pigeons' eggs, stewed abalone, fried prawn balls and crab apple – while the band played *Greensleeves* and *Barbara Allen*. The British, judged *The Washington Post*, were 'playing a conscientious end-game within the limits of their power'.

An American sinologist described Hong Kong as having been 'mouse-trapped'. But the trap, if trap it was, had always been there, and the spring had been steadily weakening over the decades. In any realistic and honest analysis of twentieth-century and twenty-first-century ideals, Hong Kong has to be Chinese. But it should not have to give up its highly successful international capitalist system on that account, and that is what the British believed they had ensured.

Chapter 19

After Tiananmen Square

Hong Kong in 1984 was, as a local politician put it, like the man on the flying trapeze who has to clasp a new pair of hands. If anything went wrong, 'it is we who will drop dead', and thirteen years of waiting were bound to breed morbid fears. At the time, the Sino-British agreement was generally welcomed as the best deal Hong Kong could have got, but once the euphoria had dissipated it was found that only one Hongkonger in five trusted China to live up to its attractive promises. There were fundamental doubts over China's ability to leave Hong Kong alone to pursue its capitalist system. The well-educated, partially Westernised middle and professional class worried about the likelihood of a resinifying process after 1997, which would reabsorb them into the Chinese culture they had expended much energy in shedding. Under Chinese sovereignty, Chinese values would inevitably return to tilt the balance away from Western modes and back to the pre-modern Chinese tradition. To suggest to such cultural voyagers that constructing a Western life on Chinese soil in contemptuous disregard of the modernisation problems of the other 99 per cent of Chinese people was artificial and unviable, did not relieve their anxiety.

In 1986, the Hong Kong Chinese were able to see for themselves how they might fare under Chinese justice. A Hong Kong businessman trying to export steel products was tried for bribery. The mainland official who accepted the bribe was imprisoned for life. The Hong Kong merchant had his travel document seized, which people in Hong Kong could not understand. The Chinese authorities invited Hong Kong reporters to the trial, and it was shown on Hong Kong television. 'Here, the public is used to seeing judge here, the accused here, and the lawyer over there,' one of these Hong Kong reports said, 'but in China it is like a round table conference. With the lawyer sternly pointing a finger at him, the defendant was making some kind of plea to the judge. Hong Kong people thought it was ridiculous, mistaking the lawyer for the judge and vice versa. They just can't understand why a lawyer was paid to pass a criminal sentence on the defendant. We thought it was a joke.'

It was gradually realised that to talk of Hong Kong passing from one undemocratic autocracy to another was superficial. The British Parliament provided a distant safeguard for the civil rights of Hongkongers, in that executive power was exercised only by virtue of the link with Britain – and that provided a near-guarantee that the dictatorial powers theoretically enjoyed by the government would not be exercised. While not democratic itself, Hong Kong enjoyed a certain 'democracy by proxy' through the UK. After 1997, however, Hong Kong would no longer have the assurance of democratic Western standards of government which the link of authority to Britain provided. If Hong Kong was a benevolent dictatorship, it was the benevolence which made it succeed, and that could not be expected in the future from a Chinese government lacking such traditions.

In the early days after the Sino-British agreement, the Chinese freely repeated the slogan, *gangren zhigang* – 'Hongkongers rule Hong Kong'. Later in the 1980s, the phrase dropped from Beijing usage, having presumably aroused too many expectations. Deng Xiaoping had declared that Hong Kong should be governed by patriots. When he refused to recognise the Executive Council leaders who went to see him in Beijing, receiving them only in their individual capacities, he was making an understandable political point about the nature of the British authority which had appointed them. In the relatively benevolent atmosphere of 1984, Deng conceded that some anti-communist elements would be tolerated in the Hong Kong leadership. 'After all, the Communist Party won't be toppled by critical bombast.' But most of Hong Kong's leaders should be political moderates.

A little later he defined his 'patriotism'. Dismissing Western-style democracy by complaining that 'one-man, one-vote' would not guarantee Hong Kong's rule by 'socialist patriots', Deng defined a patriot as having 'respect for his own nation, earnest and sincere support for the motherland's resumption of its sovereignty over Hong Kong and restraint from harming the stability and prosperity of Hong Kong. So long as they meet these requirements, they are patriots, no matter whether they believe in capitalism, or feudalism or even the slave-owning society.' Some visitors reported that Deng allowed the possibility of a triad member being patriotic.

More light was shed on this concept of patriotism whenever the Chinese railed against the British colonial system for allowing 'local scoundrels pandering to foreign interests' to rule Hong Kong – language harking back to Bishop Hall's denunciation of the 'Sik-nin Chau clique'. Xu Jiatun specifically reproved Lydia Dunn, Sir Sze-yuen Chung and other appointed Exco and Legco members for lack of patriotism. So much so, that China could not trust Britain to hold fair elections, and the first government of the Special

Administrative Region after 1997 would for that reason have to be chosen by consultation rather than by election. All these Chinese statements seemed to rule out the possibility of Hong Kong's natural leaders, until now brought forward within the British patronage system, taking power under Chinese sovereignty. Yet the others are untried and inexperienced. It was something of a relief when it was later stated by the Chinese that the first Chief Executive might best come from the Hong Kong Civil Service. That would at least produce someone capable and familiar with Hong Kong's problems and earlier attempts to solve them.

The Joint Liaison Group was remarkably successful, despite initial British reservations, providing a venue where British and Chinese officials could meet regularly and privately to tie up the loose threads left over from the 1984 agreement. They quickly settled such questions as the continuing membership of Hong Kong as a Special Administrative Region in more than twenty international organisations, from UNCTAD to GATT; the establishment of a shipping registry; the regulation of civil service pensions; and the renegotiation of air service agreements. The sharing of the income from land sales in the interim period was agreed, and the 600 treaties which Britain over the years had entered into on Hong Kong's behalf were examined and a way of dealing with them agreed. 'It's a mutual learning process,' one of the Hong Kong Chinese participants commented. 'We learn their preoccupations and worries, they learn how this funny little place works.' Hongkongers were perturbed all the same when the Chinese side raised difficulties over Hong Kong Chinese officials participating in the talks, and Britain even gave one of them a UK passport to ensure his contribution of expertise on the matters being discussed. But this was a gesture against Britain, rather than against the Hong Kong Chinese as such.

Between 1985 and 1990 the Basic Law to govern Hong Kong after 1997 was drawn up and promulgated by the Chinese government. Some fifty-nine experts appointed by China, almost two-fifths of them Hongkongers, held frequent meetings over this period to draft the document, helped by a Consultative Committee in Hong Kong with 180 members. The latter had no power, but was the most representative assembly which had ever been seen in Hong Kong, including millionaires as well as students, pro-Guomindang figures as well as Xinhua officials. In its turn, it invited sixteen advisers to help it make constructive comments to the drafting committee, and these advisers included not only former senior Hong Kong government officers like Sir Jack Chater, and the 'unpatriotic' Exco leaders, Lydia Dunn and Sir Sze-yuen Chung, but also leaders of the British, American, Japanese and French business communities. When the American Chamber of Commerce in Hong Kong was later invited to send a delegation to Beijing and present a position paper about the Basic Law, it chose to concentrate on the need to have more senior government jobs open to non-Chinese after 1997, to retain the city's international authenticity.

The Chinese leaders praised the drafting committee for composing 'China's Number One Reunification Symphony', an admission that the Taiwan angle should be at the front of the drafters' minds. But a clash of values came before any matters of substance could be addressed, when Dorothy Liu Yiuchu, a pro-Chinese but idiosyncratically obstinate Hong Kong lawyer, took objection to the phrase 'democratic consultation' which had been used in the guidelines about selecting the officers of the Consultative Committee. It so obviously meant that the Communists were going to run the committee in their own way. As a result of her outburst the phrase was dropped. But when the time came for the officers of the Consultative Committee to be elected, the discussion was interrupted by the entry of a few senior members of the drafting committee, including Sir Y.K. Pao, who made nominations for the various offices and then had those nominations adopted by acclamation, through the customary Chinese practice whereby the speaker claps what he himself has said, and everybody else claps in agreement. It is a way of formalising what the Chinese normally arrange by private consultation beforehand.

Actually, the list of officers was eminently acceptable, just what an ideal election would have produced. But Martin Lee for one questioned the method by which these persons had been put in office, and so another election was held on more Western lines – with the identical result, so that everybody was happy. Xu Jiatun, however, was said to have remarked to one of the critics that 'consultation, after all, is one form of election', and everybody in Hong Kong knew that they would have to work hard and exercise keen vigilance if Hong Kong were not to fall victim to the autocracy which these Chinese traditions can allow.

Battle was fought over who should interpret or adjudicate the Basic Law. Martin Lee and others argued for residual powers to be retained in Hong Kong which the Chinese said was not appropriate. But the Hong Kong lawyers wanted the Sino-British arrangements to be protected by efficient legal or constitutional guarantees justiciable in Hong Kong, rather than allow them merely to depend on policy statements by the Chinese government. One of the British legal experts brought in to give an opinion on this conceded that it was natural for a Chinese lawyer to suppose that 'there can be no legal remedies against the state', but that would undermine the provisions for autonomy. The Chinese drafters of the Basic Law thus found themselves in the dilemma that they either had to question the Chinese constitution, or else to emasculate the Sino-British agreement and erode Hong Kong confidence. The residual and adjudicatory powers remained in Beijing.

Another difficult problem was that of human rights. There was a fierce controversy in *The Times* of London between Bernard Levin and his critics over whether the human rights set out in the Basic Law rested ultimately on the Chinese constitution or on international convenants. The United Nations covenant on civil and political rights had been signed by Britain but not by China. Indeed, Britain had been hauled over the coals by the Human Rights Committee of the United Nations on the Hong Kong question and was reprimanded by the delegate of Mauritius in the terms, 'you don't return it as an empty apartment. There are people in it' (never mind that they or their forebears were almost all not there when Britain took possession, or that they have all been free to go home to China at any time!).

Finally, there were the difficult questions of political structure. Hongkongers could not get their act together on this, and when Louis Cha, the publisher, proposed that a referendum be held after 1997 to decide whether universal suffrage was wanted by the Hong Kong people, students who believed he had betrayed democracy burned his newspaper. In the end, the Drafting Committee went for his conservative model, with a majority directly elected legislature not envisaged until after 2007.

The drafting took five years, yet some of the Beijing drafters never set foot in Hong Kong, and thoughtful Hongkongers began to speculate what sort of image China had of their city. The official picture given to their people by the Chinese authorities was mostly negative until the 1980s. 'All ugly ideas and decadent life of the capitalist society spread their influences here every minute through various channels,' the Cantonese newspaper *Nanfang Jihpao* stated in 1984, commenting on the people's commune just across the creek from Hong Kong's New Territories. Chinese militia on border duty described Hong Kong as a world where 'there was a stench of wine and meat inside the red doors: the bones of the frozen dead alongside the roadsides'.

Under Deng Xiaoping the tone became more friendly. A book published in China, in 1987, described Hong Kong as 'a bright pearl set in the Orient'. The Peninsula Hotel was praised for displaying 'western efficiency, eastern warmth' – but in other parts of the city there were bunkbeds for the elderly, utter filth in the Walled City, crime and corruption evident, and sad exploited Filipina maids in Statue Square. The book also noted that writers in Hong Kong had to struggle by themselves without state subsidy. 'But since Hong Kong people are in a position to read all manner of good books, printed locally . . . we can hardly accept the frequent retort that Hong Kong is a cultural desert, can we?'

The informal influences at work are also positive. In some shops in China selling greetings cards there are coloured photographs of the skyscrapers alongside Hong Kong harbour. Noticing such cards in Tianjin, a city as far from Hong Kong as Algiers is from London, I asked the Chinese lecturer who was with me, and who was not supplied by the party authorities, why people would buy them. 'Because they show what Chinese people can achieve,' he instantly replied. The Chinese who get the most intimate picture of Hong Kong life are those in Guangdong province who can receive TV broadcasts from Hong Kong. The key information thus derived about the number of cars, the standard of dress and household equipment, and general living standards is relayed by grapevine across the provinces.

The Chinese media are now more interested than they were in Hong Kong. In the 1980s, a Hong Kong column was begun in the *Guangming Daily* and also in the *Shanghai Literary News*. A monthly digest of Hong Kong media became at one time a bestseller, distributing 3 million copies in China. For the most part Chinese are surprised at the polarisation of rich and poor, which they have not experienced in their own country since before most of them were born, but impressed by the way everything works. Wang Jixian, who came from Beijing at the age of 31 to do a master's degree in geography at Hong Kong University, said that what he most admires is 'the freedom to complain'.

But there can also be envy, and even contempt. When Hong Kong, incredibly, beat China in the run-up to the World Cup in 1985, there were riots, in the course of which one Hong Kong footballer was cut by a flying bottle. When tempers are aroused in those circumstances, Chinese who know nothing about Hong Kong instinctively revert to the old reproach that its inhabitants are 'slaves of foreigners', emasculated by subjection to foreign rule and infected by Western decadence. Some Westerners themselves perpetuate negative ideas of Hong Kong, as Jan Morris does when she describes it as a 'permanent parasite' on China's skin. (Delivering $6 billion a year to the parent organism is hardly the role of a parasite, and a more accurate biological term might be symbiont, which both gives and takes).

In the 1980s, an unprecedented number of Chinese from the People's Republic visited Hong Kong to study its institutions and system – planning, management, road traffic, the civil service, housing, industrial estates – the list is endless. 'They find Hong Kong curious,' said a Hongkonger involved in hosting some of these visitors, 'the way we operate and think, the way it is not controlled, the way government does not intervene in any walk of life.' A leftist Hong Kong journal declared, 'China regards the colony not as a hostile enclave but as a settlement of compatriots to be wooed and cared for, as a corollary for taking their money.'

Indeed, after the agreement with Britain, China had a new challenge, to explain to its own people why it was necessary to grant Hong Kong so many privileges not enjoyed by the rest of the Chinese population. 'To retain a small capitalist enclave,' China's Foreign Minister declared, 'will be beneficial to socialism and the rest of the country', but that is not self-evident and some propaganda and education is necessary. There was a certain anxiety in the tone of Xu Jiatun when he replied to a question on this in 1985, to the effect that the vast majority of Chinese would support Hong Kong's special rights *after the matter was explained to them*. When Sir Sze-yuen Chung asked the Chinese

218

Prime Minister how Hongkongers could be sure that China would keep its word after 1997, the Premier testily replied: 'Our problem was not whether or not to honour our commitments, but how to respond to the 1 billion people in our country and tell them that they don't get these rights.'

Gordon Wu, the developer and champion investor in South China, likes to argue that capitalism is not all that different from socialism, in the sense that part of every capitalist enterprise 'belongs to the state . . . by way of taxes'. He portrays Hong Kong's tax system, for all its low rates, as 'a sort of socialism. A small per cent of something meaningful is better than 100 per cent of nothing.' This is perhaps a way of getting it across to the Chinese that Hong Kong is not entirely out of their world but something ultimately compatible and even assimilable.

The Sino-British honeymoon lasted barely a year. By the end of 1985 Xu Jiatun was publicly accusing Britain of deviating from the agreement, banging his spectacles angrily on the table at a press conference to denounce the British plans for elections to Legco. Every argument against democracy was trotted out by the communist side. Democratic politicians had to make promises which were expensive to keep and added to government spending, inflation and taxes. 'We do not wish to reduce the profits to foreign investors,' the Communists said ingenuously.

The Chinese were particularly angry at the point made by many Hong-kongers (and Westerners too) that direct elections were needed in order to resist anticipated pressure from Beijing. Democracy would indeed come to Hong Kong one day, the Communists agreed, but it would take many decades to build up the level of education and sophistication required. 'Even then it is still doubtful if full democracy necessarily brings really strong and efficient government.' Louis Cha, a calm and realistic voice throughout this period, suggested that 'the way to keep China out is by being useful to Beijing'. The Communists took up the refrain of convergence, a concept to allow the 'railway lines' which Britain was building up to 1997 to meet the ones which China was planning to lay thereafter. This led to the 'through train' idea of allowing China to monitor the Legco elections of 1995 and the selection of a Chief Executive in the following year under the provisions of the Basic Law, and thus avoid a sudden and total change of personnel at the top in 1997.

The People's Liberation Army got into the fight because Deng publicly rebuked those of his lieutenants, including a former Defence Minister and Foreign Minister, who had repeated the promise that China would not send troops into Hong Kong. In 1984, Deng described this as 'rubbish' and 'nonsense', probably reflecting pressure from the army. Hong Kong was part of Chinese territory, so 'why can't we send troops there?', he asked plaintively. This became a big issue later, when Hongkongers were able to observe how the Red Army behaved in Tiananmen Square and Tibet, but the best view seemed to be that the Chinese Army merely wanted a small part of the perks in Hong Kong, including use of the relatively luxurious facilities which the British would vacate. Everybody realised that it would be counter-productive to send in a large number of troops, and the figure of around 4,000 mentioned by Deng was not much more than half the current British strength.

Then came Tiananmen Square. When China's student democratic movement erupted in Beijing in May–June 1989, the effect on Hong Kong was immediate and profound. Concern for the students, and alarm over the consequences of their repression for China and Hong Kong, brought former opponents together – in joint statements, on the same platforms, and even, in the end, in the same organisations. Some twenty-seven Legco members of various persuasions jointly appealed to China's leaders to respect free expression and not resort to violence. As the communist leaders' put-down of the students became more and more brutal, many of their followers in Hong Kong deserted, including their paid officials.

The first casualty was Cheng Kainam, leader of the Hong Kong Federation of Education Workers, formerly one of the most reliable supporters of Beijing. He joined the popular protest calling for the resignation of Premier Li Peng, followed by some Xinhua employees. The pro-Beijing newspaper *Wen Wei Po* expressed its feelings in a four-character headline, 'Painful Heart and Aching Head'. Its editor was dismissed: he had supported Mao Zedong right through the Cultural Revolution of the 1960s. Even staff of the Bank of China accused Li Peng of 'distorting facts and going against the people's wishes'.

The Basic Law committees lost four leading members by resignation, including the Bishop of Hong Kong and the sturdily independent Louis Cha, and another four by temporary withdrawal. Cha noted that none of the personal freedoms, human rights, and rule of law enjoyed by Hong Kong existed in China, making the students' role in China 'a struggle for these precious things which we have always enjoyed here'.

For three successive Sundays Hongkongers took to the streets in orderly marches and rallies to voice their disgust with Li Peng's crackdown on students and imposition of martial law. The first attracted over half a million, the second about one and a half million, and the third almost a million, quite unprecedented figures in a small population proverbially averse to politics. A new grouping was formed under the name of the All Hong Kong Alliance in Support of the Chinese Patriotic Pro-democracy Movement. This called for the People's Liberation Army not to fight against Chinese civilians and to withdraw from Tiananmen Square, leaving the struggle for democracy to be peacefully waged, while the National People's Congress should overrule martial law and recognise the patriotic student movement. Anita Mui, a popular singer, led the crowd (in defiance of typhoon Brenda which was then imminent) in singing 'Brave Chinese'.

Hongkongers donated $3¹/4 million to the Chinese students' cause. Three thousand bus conductors and drivers gave a full day's takings, and T-shirts with appropriate slogans were sold by a firm 30 per cent owned by a mainland corporation, for the benefit of the student fund. School and university exams were postponed. The Governor of Hong Kong praised the discipline of the crowds. They had, he said, expressed their concern 'with great intensity of feeling but also with a sense of responsibility'.

Shareholders saw the value of their stocks plunge badly. The principal share index dropped by 11 per cent on the day after the first Hong Kong rally, and some of the richest men in the territory took a wry pride in belonging to the exclusive club of five who lost more than a billion Hong Kong dollars each in the stock market free-fall (Li Kashing, Cheng Yu-tung, Sir Y. K. Pao, Lord Kadoorie, and the Swires). They all knew, of course, the volatility of the Hong Kong market and were all in a good position to stand tight until market values picked up, as eventually they did.

Chinese Communist intransigence was lingeringly captured on Hong Kong TV screens for weeks on end, and Hong Kong's conservative politicians began to change their views and priorities. Stephen Cheong said, 'I am now inclined to support speedier democratic changes.' More than fifty Hong Kong delegates picked by China to sit on one of the important regular political conferences in Guangdong province demanded that martial law be declared unconstitutional.

Many joint statements were put out, with hundreds of prominent signatures, though some said afterwards that it was a misunderstanding, they had not signed at all. Li Kashing, who had earlier enjoyed several tête-á-têtes with Premier Li Peng, was quoted as agreeing in principle with the students' demands and admiring their patriotism. At the second rally on 28 May Eric Hotung, a descendant of the legendary Sir Robert Hotung, told the crowd that they had 'seen with the greatest clarity, how indifferent the leaders in Beijing are capable of being towards the legitimate aspirations of their own people'.

This time, Hong Kong students and activists translated their feelings and words into action by going to Beijing to help. Stationing themselves in four colourful tents at one side of Tiananmen Square, a score of Hong Kong undergraduates brought food, bedding and medical supplies, or the money to buy them on the market, to distribute among the Chinese demonstrators. 'Most of the food and drink you see on the square,' said Wong Tin-sing, the Chinese University of Hong Kong graduate who acted as treasurer, 'now comes from us.' They were soon alerted to the élitism and provincial rivalries of their Chinese colleagues. 'At first, we did not know they were so corrupt,' one remarked. The Chinese student leaders expected good food and a continuous supply of foreign cigarettes even when students from provincial universities supporting the demonstration had nothing to eat.

221

One of the couriers, Lee Cheuk-Yan, a Hong Kong University graduate and leader of the clothmakers' trade union as well as of the Christian Industrial Committee, was arrested in China after helping to carry some of the cash raised in Hong Kong for the Beijing students. He returned to Hong Kong a few days later after signing a confession of having violated martial law, and after handing over to the authorities more than $250,000 which had been intended for the students. 'I received some very unkind treatment,' he told reporters in a measured statement. 'I fear for my own future, although I think China will reconcile itself to the pro-democracy movement before the 1997 hand-over.' (Hongkongers had not forgotten the twenty-odd earlier cases, including Liu Shanqing of the China Democratic Resource Centre in Hong Kong, who spent the 1980s in a Guangzhou gaol for helping dissident intellectuals.)

Then people began to withdraw deposits from the Bank of China and the other communist banks. Pamphlets circulated saying that every fifth bullet killing the students on Tiananmen Square had been bought with Hong Kong deposit money. Angry customers switched their cash into the British banks, but under the standing arrangements for bank runs, the latter in turn drafted cash to meet the higher demand at the Chinese banks, putting in train a wasteful circle of cash flows.

The final giant rally was on the fateful day of 4 June itself, when the army fired its guns into the Tiananmen Square crowd. Martin Lee, the leading liberal politician, wore a black headband. Others dressed in the traditional mourning colours of black and white. A former senior British official in the Hong Kong government told the rally that talks should not be continued on Hong Kong's future until there was a 'decent' government in Beijing. Joseph Cheng, one of Hong Kong's leading political scientists, lamented that 'all our hopes for democracy are now dashed'. They sang the song 'I am Chinese' with a particular tremolo on the line: 'No matter where I was born, no matter where I am, I die a Chinese soul'. Some on the rally even sang, 'Rise up, ye who will be no longer slaves', which is the Chinese Communist national anthem, and for the first time they used the emotive phrase previously monopolised by the Communists, *tung bao* – 'Defend our compatriots'. Louis Cha, the publisher and novelist who had worked so hard for agreement with China, cried 'with anguish and rage' at the news of the Tiananmen Square massacre.

It was impossible not to feel the new sense of identity, something like patriotism, that emerged for the first time in these Hong Kong rallies, where leftists and rightists, conservatives and liberals, Christians and atheists marched side by side. Posters proclaimed 'China needs you', with the letter H portrayed by two upraised wrists joined by manacles. A caricature of Li Peng with a noose around his neck and the slogan 'Hang Li Peng now' was widely circulated. Banners with blood-red characters called for Li Peng's downfall. A replica of the giant statue of the Goddess of Democracy which the Beijing students had built in Tiananmen Square and was then destroyed by the Chinese authorities was built in Hong Kong's Victoria Park.

Tiananmen exerted a powerful unifying influence over Hong Kong politics. The unofficial members of Exco and Legco agreed on a programme for introducing direct elections, because, as Lydia Dunn remarked, it could no longer be said that Hongkongers were immature and not interested in politics. Liberals and conservatives joined forces in a new group called Hong Kong People Saving Hong Kong. For the first time such leaders as Allen Lee and Martin Lee united, burying their differences, on a manifesto of getting the right to settle in Britain, accelerated democracy and a bill of rights.

The British, for once, were on the sidelines of this very Chinese crisis. 'The British,' a student leader stated, 'will not ultimately protect Hong Kong. This is a Chinese matter, a Chinese struggle. We have to forget about Britain and fight the tyrants in China.' The Chinese, for their part, soon conveyed their anger at Hong Kong's reaction. Ji Pengfei, the former Foreign Minister now heading Beijing's Hong Kong Affairs Bureau, castigated the Hong Kong students in the words: 'A few people have done something on the mainland that is not allowed under the Chinese constitution. They have . . . encouraged the unlawful student movement.' In Guangdong, citizens were told to remove the TV antennae which allowed them to see Hong Kong programmes. Hong Kong newspapers were banned in the Shenzhen Special Economic Zone just over the border, and more Hong Kong activists were arrested in China. The well-informed Xinhua rebel Xu Haining, who knew the inner secrets of China's senior men in Hong Kong, had flown to Britain, but returned to China after crude threats were made against his mother there. The old China had not yet died.

The despairing unity of 4 June did not last very long. Vincent Lo, the young industrialist newly ventured into politics and one of the least emotional figures on the local scene, warned that Beijing would now see Hong Kong as a counter-revolutionary base, as a consequence of which the goodwill of recent years would give way to hostility. Before June was out two leading moderates, Allen Lee and Stephen Cheong, pulled out of the Hong Kong People Saving Hong Kong campaign because in advertisements it identified a change of government in China as the best safeguard of Hong Kong's future. 'We must not be seen to be interfering unduly in China's internal affairs,' Cheong explained.

A Gallup poll taken on the two days following the massacre showed 48 per cent of Hongkongers against the retrocession to China, but a significant 32 per cent still felt that the agreement for it should stand. Gordon Wu, the ebullient Princeton engineer, tried to salvage some optimism. 'I know both camps in Beijing,' he stated, 'and both sides say they want the open door policy to continue. They can't afford to change it.' But his cheerful confidence was not shared by most Hongkongers. As the repression continued in China during the rest of 1989 and into 1990, they threw off their armbands and went back to work, but with heavy hearts at the prospect of joining the kind of China they had seen on their television screens during those bloodcurdling first few days of June.

The episode caused turmoil in the communist ranks, too. Differences among them had been noticed before 1989 over the degree of flexibility to be allowed in the Basic Law. But after Tiananmen Square several unions reported their members demoralised and shattered by the events in Beijing, and journalists were particularly shocked. Unfortunately, the traditional reaction of cadres in the field when their leaders, patrons and protectors in the centre are disgraced, is to go to great pains to prove their loyalty to the newly ascendant faction: in this case it means that the communist representatives in Hong Kong are now being tougher than necessary, in order to convince Beijing of their trustworthiness and save their jobs (which means, of course, that Beijing policy may be coming over as worse than it really means to be). These communist representatives are also under the strain of human problems. They are usually without their families in Hong Kong, although if they are lucky they might be able to arrange for wives and children to come to Shenzhen. They have to conceal their envy, therefore, when they visit counterpart British officials' homes to find *their* children handing round the biscuits to the visitor.

The immediate instinct of some Hongkongers after Tiananmen was to demand a renegotiation of the Sino-British agreement. But then they realised that with a less liberal administration in Beijing the terms would not be as good, even assuming that China was willing to renegotiate. Without the Sino-British agreement, there would still be a reversion to China, in 1997, at least of the New Territories and therefore almost certainly of Hong Kong as well, but unaccompanied by any Chinese commitments to maintain the system there. For all these reasons it was recognised that it would be better to stick to the agreement. That did not prevent a number of alternatives being suggested by inventive Hongkongers. One was for a Taiwan administration, assuming that China and Taiwan were likely to come together during the 1990s in some kind of economic union. Another was the old standby of UN trusteeship. Martin Lee threw the idea of federation into the ring, something which would give Hong Kong theoretical equality with China. And then the usual propositions were made to renew the lease for ten, twenty or fifty years, and Helmut Sohmen of the Sir Y.K. Pao group suggested an annual rent of $1.5 billion.

The issue which did not go away was the one about Hong Kong's interfering in Chinese politics. 'We practise our socialism,' said the Secretary General of the Chinese Communist Party severely, 'and you may practise your capitalism. The well water does not interfere with the river water.' Chinese leaders reiterated that it was impermissible for Hongkongers to bring the capitalist system and capitalist lifestyle into the mainland. The Hong Kong Alliance for Democratic China was therefore savaged by the *People's Daily* as 'counter-revolutionary' and 'subversive'. To which its leaders in Hong Kong retorted that their aims were peaceful, and that they sought by rational means to bring about a democratic multi-party system in China – but not to overthrow the Communist Party, if only it were willing to coexist peacefully with others.

There were historical precedents for the debate. Just over a hundred years earlier, Ho Kai, the leading Chinese in Hong Kong, had written in the *China Mail* that China needed equitable rule, right government and a reformed administration. It was people, he said, who make a country prosperous, not the Emperor, and civil service exams should include science, not just literature. Was that interference? Sun Yat Sen's activities in the 1900s were certainly interference, as the British quickly appreciated, and dealt with accordingly.

On the Hong Kong side, the legitimacy of helping the students in China was repeatedly asserted. 'We are supporting our own people,' said one democrat, 'to fight for freedom and democracy,' and he did not care whether China was angry or not. The Federation of Education Workers was the first to get cold feet, deeming it unwise, whatever the provocation, to make Hong Kong a base for the Chinese opposition. It would be more effective, it suggested, to influence Chinese teachers more discreetly. The education workers' leader, Cheng Kainam, urged Hong Kong to do more and shout less in dealing with China, to build Hong Kong before promoting political beliefs in China, to be certain of its bargaining position before participating in Chinese affairs.

'Hong Kong people are also Chinese citizens,' said Xu Simin, another publisher with first-hand experience of China. 'How can their concern over national affairs be interference?' If the Communists demanded an end to such interference it would renege on the 'one country, two systems' concept. So one comes back to the interpretation of this highly ambiguous phrase. Does it mean that two systems may operate free from mutual interference in two separate parts of the country? Or does it mean that two systems may compete for acceptance over the whole country? Or does it not matter, provided that the Communist Party plays a leading role?

The naivety of calling for the downfall of a government which is about to give you autonomy was pointed out by Maria Tam, though many were not prepared to listen. Leung Chun-ying said that the massacre had made Hongkongers feel that they belonged to China, that they could no longer keep silent, that they wanted to influence China in the right direction – but 'people here will have to consider whether they want to be Hong Kong people or Chinese people'.

Martin Lee suggested Western countries should channel their funds to China via Hong Kong, in order to ensure that China would not take action against Hong Kong. This was elaborated by a Hongkonger teaching in Glasgow who proposed a very large subsidised loan to China by a British consortium, to be made conditional on China's abiding by the Sino-British agreement. China's foreign assets could be used as security, and Hong Kong could subsidise the loan with low interest. Such ideas gravely exaggerated the bargaining power of lenders to China, quite apart from misreading Chinese psychology. The *People's Daily* accused Martin Lee, though not by name, of attempting to overthrow the Chinese government.

The comment that truly reflected the wishes of every single Hongkonger came from Allen Lee, who pleaded for China to 'get used to us – to accept that this is a free society and that anyone who wishes to express their opinion one way or another can do so'. China accepted this of foreign countries, but could it accept it of a Chinese community living in its midst?

Every aspect of the Hong Kong–China relationship was poisoned, at least temporarily, by Tiananmen Square. The swimming champion, Yang Yang, overstayed in Hong Kong at the end of 1989 and would normally have been deported, but he pleaded that his pro-democracy activities would lead to his imprisonment, and in the end he was allowed to go to the USA. The Chinese were so angry that for two weeks they refused to receive the illegal immigrants normally repatriated by the British side. This was the worst breach since 1962 in the frontier control on which Hong Kong's stability depended. In the intervening years China had kept to its side of the border bargain, although in 1972 it issued so many exit permits for Indonesian and Malaysian Chinese wishing to leave China that the Hong Kong government stepped up its repatriation of illegal immigrants except for those who succeeded in 'touching base' in the urban area.

At the end of the Cultural Revolution there had been another surge, this time of 35,000 former Red Guards, into Hong Kong, and a few years later China again liberalised its emigration rules. When the number of illegal immigrants 'touching base' reached 160,000 in 1979, the Hong Kong government considered a new Berlin-type wall, but settled for ending the 'touch base' concession, requiring all Hong Kong residents to carry identity cards and expelling anyone found without one. Refugees continued to climb wire fences, swim rivers and keep out of the way of patrols, in order to reach the city of gold. Even if a year later they were living in a tiny packing case shack on a Kwuntong hillside, a couple might then be earning princely wages by the standards of China. By the later 1980s those slipping into Hong Kong overland had to negotiate a 16-foot fence topped by two tightly packed rolls of barbed wire containing an alarm system, and if they survived that they had to dodge buried geophones, tracker dogs, helicopters and Gurkha soldiers. One refugee became almost professional, escaping five times from China and being returned four times: another veteran who was picked up in the sea by a Royal Navy patrol asked for a British sublieutenant by name!

In 1982, a new agreement was made between the British and Chinese to allow 27,500 holders of one-way exit permits into Hong Kong every year.

The waiting list of those wanting to settle in Hong Kong under this pact soon ran to hundreds of thousands, many of them having families in Hong Kong, with a waiting time of up to ten years. That encouraged corruption. In 1984, a communist official in Shenzhen was arrested for procuring Hong Kong visas at $500 a time. Once a rumour spread that Hong Kong was declaring an amnesty for immigrants, and thousands flooded to the border in frenzy in the hope of getting across. Huang Ruixing, a village youth who had left school at 12, told a reporter as he waited for the gates to open: 'Hong Kong will be a paradise for me, I can change my life if I succeed in sneaking in.' The steel fence between Shenzhen and Guangdong province is not well manned, and Hongkongers worry over the possibility of serious recession in Guangdong which would make people desperate to come to Hong Kong and weaken the resolve of those guarding the frontier. China would presumably not regard an eruption of Chinese into Hong Kong after 1997 as seriously as an eruption into British-ruled Hong Kong, with all the international implications. So the two-week suspension of receiving back illegal immigrants in 1989 did not augur well.

Yet Hong Kong is helping Guangdong to keep recession at bay by its investments there, and one important new factor in the whole equation in the 1980s was Hong Kong's growing economic integration with Guangdong. As long ago as the early 1960s the 'Hong Kong MP' at Westminster, Jeremy Bray, had proposed joint economic development between Hong Kong and the adjoining province of Guangdong. In the 1970s, Lord Kadoorie put teeth into the idea by negotiating an agreement to supply offpeak electricity to Guangdong, which is chronically short of power. This was followed a few years later by the agreement for a nuclear power station at Daya Bay, for which Hong Kong provided finance and Western technology, while its power company, Lord Kadoorie's China Light and Power, undertook to buy electricity back from the plant after commissioning, thus guaranteeing a steady inflow of foreign exchange for China to meet its repayment commitments. Kadoorie foresaw the growth of a great metropolitan area stretching from Hong Kong to Guangzhou in the twenty-first century.

Hong Kong Telecommunications, another pioneer in cross-frontier collaboration, put out a video called *The Vanishing Border*. Two Hongkongers in three now visit China every year, and the annual level of Chinese visitors to Hong Kong had reached about half a million before Tiananmen Square. Slightly worrying to the Hong Kong government is the fact that between a fifth and a quarter of the coin and note issue circulates outside Hong Kong, mostly in South China, though a small amount in the Philippines also. It is a compliment which brings responsibilities. Hong Kong banks lend large sums to customers on the mainland, totalling about $3 billion before Tiananmen. Some 80 per cent of the investment into Guangdong province in the 1980s came from Hong Kong. It was not a loss to Hong

Kong, which saw simultaneous investment by its manufacturing industry into labour-saving machinery. It was more a case of moving jobs to where the labour is, instead of bringing labour in to where the jobs are, and that was the better option for Hong Kong development. The Chinese claimed for their part that in seeking to copy Hong Kong on their side of the border they would not 'steal the ricebowls' from their Hong Kong compatriots, but rather 'add a few nice dishes to the dinner table'.

The Pearl River Delta, of which Guangzhou is the focus, is the jewel in the crown of Chinese modernisation. It has so outshone the Shanghai region and the northern industrial areas of China around Beijing and what used to be called Manchuria that jealousy is detectable – though that is not good for Hong Kong, since the political decisions affecting Hong Kong will come from Beijing for the foreseeable future. The key to the Guangdong success lies partly in its intrinsic agricultural wealth, but also in the links which it has enjoyed for a long time with the outside world through emigrants, not only to Hong Kong but beyond, to the United States. There are some Pearl River Delta towns where half the population have relations in America.

That has more recently been buttressed by the patronage of Guangdongers who have made it in Hong Kong. 'That's my native county,' said Clifford Pang, the owner of Lafe Computer Magnetics in Hong Kong. 'My ancestors have been living there for a few hundred years.' This Hong Kong industrialist began to invest in his native region of Panyu in 1984, wisely avoiding friction by recruiting local people to be trained in Hong Kong rather than sending supervisory staff from Hong Kong. Another prodigal son to return to the Delta is Chao Kwok, admired there because his mouth is full of gold fillings: in his home town of Chang Ping, he has built a three-storey building and a retirement home, and is processing goods for incorporation in Hong Kong manufactures. There are countless other examples of these blood ties being rediscovered, to the advantage of both sides.

The Hong Kong investors point out the uniqueness of the role they are playing. 'Chinese companies find it very difficult to deal directly with Westerners,' said Billy Yung, the world's biggest manufacturer of electric fans, who recently moved his entire production line to China. 'Westerners get frustrated so easily, but we can communicate well with the Chinese and at the same time we know the West.' 'Ambassador' Xu Jiatun confirmed the point. 'Hong Kong people are also Chinese. Their thinking is readily adjustable. They are educated in the Western way and it is easier for them to do business with the West. Ideologically, and in terms of their wide-ranging contacts, Hong Kong people are very suitable for this work.'

Indeed, some Hong Kong leaders view this development in an even wider context. Paul Cheng sees Hong Kong emerging as 'the financial and service centre of southern China, a vast new region stretching south from the Yangzi River, embracing Hainan and including Taiwan, the home to nearly 300 million industrious people' (so that, if independent, it would rank as the world's third largest nation!). That may be for the later twenty-first century. In the meanwhile, the Pearl River Delta will not lose its place as the engine of Chinese economic development. Shanghai might seem to be a rival, but when Xu took a group of Hong Kong entrepreneurs on a tour of Shanghai and its hinterland, they agreed that it had a stronger industrial and technological base than the Pearl Delta, but found it crippingly weak in infrastructure, particularly telephones, communications and highways.

There are now more than 2 million Guangdongers who work directly or indirectly for Hong Kong manufacturers. They are not regarded as perfect workers, lacking some of the discipline and the capacity for sheer hard work for which Hong Kong was famous in earlier decades. The President of the Hong Kong Medical Association took a Hong Kong medical demonstration team to China in 1989 and found that its opposite numbers there were used to a late start and a short day, so that keeping up with the Hong Kong group's activities left them 'exhausted and dumbfounded'. But these old habits will change, no doubt.

Meanwhile Hong Kong is exporting very large amounts of semi-manu-factures for China to process and return for final assembly, packaging and marketing in Hong Kong. Even the Tiananmen Square massacre did not substantially interfere with this new intermanufacturing relationship, though it may well have slowed down future growth. But then the phenomenon was already causing concern in terms of the availability of labour, the overde-velopment of Guangdong compared with neighbouring provinces and the saturation of many delta towns with Hong Kong investments. Presumably the emphasis will turn now to the quality more than the quantity of investment, and future collaborations will spread further inland.

As Hong Kong buys into China, so China buys into Hong Kong. When China bought the New Territories Tuen Mun Wharf company, in 1981, for just over $50 million, a tingle of excitement ran round the boardrooms because of the inference that China did not intend to resume control of the New Territories in 1997, otherwise why would it spend all that money? Now, ten years later, Chinese investment is taken for granted and not dissected for political messages. China's accumulated investment in Hong Kong by the end of the 1980s decade was $10 billion, more than either the Americans or the Japanese (or, come to that, the British). There were more than 500 companies in which China had an official interest, and another 2,000 acting as agents of some kind. CITIC acquired a stake for China in Cathay Pacific Airways, the second cross-harbour tunnel, the Hung Hom reclamation project, the Hong Kong Telephone Co. and the Ka Wah Bank. Companies linked with China may own as much as 15 per cent of the equity traded on the stock exchange, although Chinese spokesmen have occasionally reaffirmed their policy of not going above 10 per cent of the market. The paper profits which China earned on its investments in Hong Kong in only eighteen months in 1986–7 almost reached the value of China's official foreign reserves.

Chinese companies, which are often the trading or financial arms of provincial or municipal governments in China, use Hong Kong not only as a place for investment but also as a base from which to invest in foreign countries. Yue Ziu, which is the city of Guangzhou's company, bought a toymaker and acquired financial and property stakes in Hong Kong, but it then put money into joint venture hotels and property development in Thailand, other large investments into Singapore, France, Canada and the United States, and invested in more than fifty projects in China itself. From almost total neglect, China jumped in one decade to the utilisation of the institutions and system of Hong Kong to the fullest extent in international investment terms.

Nowadays, Hongkongers refer deprecatingly to some Chinese companies in Hong Kong which are not genuine businesses but covers for various kinds of illicit activity, including that by the families of 'high-ups'. The Chinese government itself tries to clean up these operations from time to time, but it is hard to dislodge the truly highly connected, and the sickness has a habit of coming back as soon as the doctors have gone home. Bring Fast Limited was opened in Hong Kong in 1985 as a subsidiary of the Kanghua Development Corporation, which is controlled by Deng Xiaoping's son, Deng Pufeng – disabled since he was made to jump from a high window during the Cultural Revolution. Kanghua's chairman was an old schoolfriend of Pufeng's, and one of the directors was the daughter of a former Chinese Foreign Minister who had served under Deng Xiaoping. No outsider can cleanse the conduct of China's international economy, when even the Chinese people themselves have been unable to do so and do not look likely to succeed in the near future. What worries Hong Kong is the possibility of high-level personalities in Beijing exerting political pressure, in their relatives' or friends' defence, on the technical management of Hong Kong as an international trading and financial centre. It has not happened yet but it could happen in the future.

The most interesting character to stroll in from China in the early 1980s with a wallet full of money and the backing of the biggest names in Beijing was the genial Wang Guangying. Wang was famous because his sister had married Liu Shaoqi, the President of China until his fall in the Cultural Revolution. Born the son of a northern warlord minister in 1919, Wang had been educated in Beijing as a Catholic and taught chemistry in Tianjin. His family tie with Liu Shaoqi protected him in the 1950s, but he too fell in the Cultural Revolution and was imprisoned for ten years. 'I am not a member of the Communist Party,' he once said, 'and that is the truth. But I am a genuine patriot. I was imprisoned three times, by the Japanese militarist police, by the Guomindang, and by the Gang of Four in the Cultural Revolution.' Soon after the reformist policies of Deng Xiaoping came in, Wang recommended the government to develop horizontal organisations in Hong Kong like the Japanese *zaibatsu*: the Prime Minister told him to go ahead and start one.

Wang arrived in Hong Kong in 1983 with permission to spend $50 million. He registered his company Everbright, was visited by Henry Kissinger and began to throw his weight around. 'I am here,' he said, 'to give oxygen to Hong Kong.' He quickly got into many different industries, many different kinds of property deals, financing a sugar refinery on the mainland and assisting with microcomputer factories in China and the urban rail system for Beijing. But he was not superhuman. A joint venture with Li Kashing for apartment blocks and another with Henry Fok and Stanley Ho for a resort complex in Macao were both cancelled, and like everybody else Everbright lost in the market crash of October 1987. He cheerfully commented, that 'when we invest in China we have to pay over our own money. But in Hong Kong the cash is borrowed from the bank.' By the end of the 1980s he was venturing into Thailand with another property deal.

When the conservatives defeated the reformers in China in 1989 Wang's star paled, but his corporation has indeed become a giant multipurpose enterprise and remains, no doubt, very useful to China, though his business acumen is doubted by old hands in Hong Kong.

On the Hong Kong side, the outstanding personality among investors in China is Gordon Wu, the Princeton-trained engineer who is painting the map of Guangdong province blue with development projects. He borrowed from Sir Y.K. Pao the idea of getting the production of something paid for by leasing it in advance. In Pao's case it was ships, but Gordon Wu, who bounces with energy like a self-propelling rubber ball, applied it to power stations.

His first project across the border was the China Hotel in Guangzhou. It needed electricity.

I needed 150,000 kilowatt hours a day, and I asked the city authorities, how much electricity do you have? It was embarrassing for them and me to find out that I would consume roughly 2 per cent of it. I said that was dangerous, because there might be other demands leading to a black-out. I mean, I can't expect my paying guests to walk up nineteen floors with their suitcases. I said, look, no black-outs. And the next thing is a new plant. So I struck a deal with them. I told them, I really don't know anything about power stations, but never mind, you need the electricity so I will supply it, because I can contact the people who can build it.

They said, we would like to build power stations but we don't have the money. So I asked them, can the general public afford the price they are paying at the moment for electricity? They said, yes, so I said, you got yourself a deal. I will ring up the bankers and put up the equity, and I'll ring up the technical boys, the civil engineers and so on, and get the Japanese consultant, and put the act together. Then we just keep on selling them kilowatt hours, and after ten years, when they've bought enough of it, then we give them the time free. This way, we told them, you don't have to worry about who is going to finance the power station, or how you run it, all that is our problem – and they like the concept.

The difference between this formula and Pao's shipbuilding recipe is that at the end of the power agreement, Gordon Wu hands over the plant as a gift to the Chinese, whereas Pao keeps his ships.

Wu, a third generation Hongkonger, is openly proselytising about China. 'Let's work together,' is his message to the Chinese, 'and we'll lead you into the promised land.' It is a game where both sides win, because Hong Kong 'must have a hinterland before it can work'.

Tiananmen Square wiped some of the ebullience (and *embonpoint*) off Wu's face: he had, after all, relied at crucial moments in his Guangdong development projects on the support of the now disgraced reformist leader Zhao Ziyang, and could not now expect the same treatment. But changes of personality are a known and constant risk in dealings with China, and no conceivable change in Beijing could sever the organic link developed in the 1980s between the Pearl River Delta and Hong Kong. Nor could any political decisions about the future implementation of China's commitments to Hong Kong conceivably take place without reference to this largely spontaneous, natural and mutually beneficial economic relationship with Guangdong.

The right turn in China's socio-economic policy that began to be made in the last few months of 1988, and was later embroiled in the politics of student protest and the events of Tiananmen Square, put a damper on Hong Kong's hopes for generous treatment and a sympathetic shepherding from British colonialism into a new international capitalist role under Chinese sovereignty. So many Hong Kong hopes had rested on the continuance and fortifying of the Chinese reform movement that the very sight of its televised suppression on Tiananmen Square incited many Hongkongers to try to save it by physical intervention, thus making things even more difficult for Hong Kong. The mild euphoria of the Sino-British agreement in 1984 was replaced by a black despair about the possibility of ever being able to live with China at all.

Chapter 20

Emigrating to the Colonies

With such uncertainty hanging over their future, it is hardly surprising that so many Hong Kong professionals and businessmen left for the subcolonies already established by Hong Kong people in the lands previously settled by the British – Australia, Canada, the United States and Britain itself. It began to look like a mini-diaspora of Hong Kong Chinese along the same paths already pioneered in the great Anglo-Saxon migration – a sort of reverse colonialism. The echo was conscious. When a Sydney immigration officer asked a young Hong Kong would-be immigrant whether he had a criminal record, the Hongkonger cheerfully replied: 'Do we still need that?'

Today there are at least half a million Hong Kong Chinese living in those four countries, probably more. They own Toronto's Harbour Castle Hilton, the Calgary Holiday Inn, one of San Francisco's largest hotels (its Hong Kong Chinese owner sports a gold Mercedes to go with it), a golf course in Vancouver, the largest shopping centre in British Columbia and one of the three shopping centres in Toronto's Scarboro suburb. They include a greengrocery millionaire in New Zealand and the owner of a Sydney clothing chain who wears a black T-shirt with the slogan 'Chinese Do It Better'. They own chains of up-market restaurants around the world, most of Vancouver's skyscrapers, and more than 120 businesses in Flushing, in New York. In Toronto, where there are five separate Chinatowns, Hong Kong buyers have become the main customers for new luxury flats. A Canadian estate agent took one Hong Kong Chinese matron out looking at houses: when they had passed twenty of them, and she would not get out of the car, he thought he had wasted his time. 'That's enough,' she suddenly said, 'I'll take them all.'

They form one-fifth of the Vancouver population, they have endowed a Canadian university with a $10 million performing arts centre, and they have produced a Lieutenant-Governor of British Columbia, a Civil Rights

Commissioner in the United States and an Adelaide teenager who was pronounced the most mathematically gifted child of his age in the world. They have also produced acclaimed authors and actors (Timothy Mo and David Yip).

Success brings its own rewards. 'I have a Japanese wife,' said Thomas Yuen, a computer executive in Los Angeles who is not yet 40, 'drive a German car and eat Chinese food. What else can I ask for?' But even those wandering Hongkongers whom success has eluded swallow their regrets for the sake of a much better environment for their children. 'We took a risk,' said a jeweller in Australia, 'and we were prepared to do without much, so our boys will prosper in the future.' The former waiter who emigrated to England, worked seven days a week and came to own his own restaurant, and whose sons took engineering and mathematics degrees and became professionals, has thousands of counterparts across the Hong Kong emigrant community.

Hongkongers have been emigrating for more than a century – as long as Hong Kong has been seen as the 'stepping-stone' for Chinese to the outside world. People have been continually entering Hong Kong from China as Chinese immigrants, and after some time many of them or their descendants have left Hong Kong as Hong Kong emigrants. What has happened since 1984 is a build-up in the figures to record levels. Emigration has almost become an industry, with specialist companies and advisers. A magazine was started in 1988 called *The Emigrant*, to give news and information about emigration to prospective departers: it proved so persuasive that many of its staff were found to be preparing to leave Hong Kong. Lo Takshing started a new company called Hong Kong Freedom of Movement and Rights of Abode Limited in 1983 to offer non-commercial, independent and reliable advice to those uncertain about their national status and plans to move.

There were many reasons for people to leave. The education of children came very high on the list. Many professionals were already sending their children to these Anglo-Saxon countries for English-language education, so it was not such a wrench to consider joining them 'over there'. The education system in Hong Kong was proving inadequate for the numbers involved, and there were fears about falling standards of English in schools.

The prospect of '1997' was the major cause for the departures. The agreement which the British and Chinese had made about Hong Kong was, in the words of T.L. Tsim, Director of the Chinese Univesity Press in Hong Kong, 'an act of faith – but if you have a choice, then why accept it?' China had always believed in central control and regarded democracy and human rights as Western inventions. 'I am a seasoned risk-taker, but what are our chances – 0.5 per cent? Five million for Hong Kong, one billion against . . . It is against the Chinese character to own something and not run it. Just look at Chinese entrepreneurs.' Such views were widely shared among the Western-educated professional men and women of Hong Kong. It was in a very broad sense a 'brain drain', since the people involved had almost all had higher education in order to gain their professional qualifications, and even the less formally trained businessmen–entrepreneurs played crucial roles in the Hong Kong economy. The departers were mostly middle aged, or parents of young children. Younger adults were not so caught up in the rush to avoid 1997, perhaps feeling a little less settled in their ways, and definitely attracted by the prospect of more promotion as their seniors left.

In fact the outlook for emigration was limited because the receiving countries restrict immigration. The United States, Canada and Australia liberalised their immigration rules and quotas in the late 1980s, but there is still a fixed limit to the number of Hongkongers who can hope to settle in those countries each year. Besides, each prospective country of settlement had particular preferences of occupation. Canada wanted opticians, paramedics, physiotherapists, morticians and private detectives; Australia sought air traffic controllers and meteorologists; the British recruited for nurses. One can imagine the havoc when a large international airline like Qantas recruited 150 aircraft engineers from Hong Kong, and Hong Kong lost overnight more than a third of its skilled staff in this sector.

Hong Kong professionals are driven to desperate measures to get round the restrictions and ensure a new life free from communism. One woman who was eight months pregnant flew to Canada with a false doctor's certificate stating that the child was not due for another four months: a month later she had the child, which was thus born a Canadian citizen, enabling both mother and father and their other children to come to join it. 'In Hong Kong,' Frank Ching commented, 'when people ask you where you are going to have your baby, they don't mean which hospital. They mean which country.' Passports have always been on sale in Hong Kong. In the early post-war years you could buy a passport of a European country for $300, or a British birth certificate for $100. Nowadays, they would be prohibitive and the risk of detection much greater. Without going so far, however, the cost of a fully legal resettlement abroad has been put at about $200,000.

Emigrating is no picnic. 'There will not be a fourth time,' said Lee Chao-hwa, a furniture-maker who had left his home in China three times, twice to escape the Japanese, and finally fleeing to Hong Kong from the Communists. 'The sights and sounds and smells of the panic stay with you forever. Families are broken up, the work of a lifetime is destroyed and things are never really the same again. No, I will not be a refugee again, nor will my children.' He and his family are now in Canada. Hong Kong executives naturally expect to continue running their businesses, and making money from them, while they are going through the citizenship or naturalisation process. One in America complained:

I have to stay there nine months each year for five consecutive years before I can get US citizenship. As my factory is in Hong Kong, this means each year I can only spend three months running the factory, then I have to leave everything in the charge of my secretary and fly to the US with my wife and stay there till the next winter. It is so troublesome that I am now considering if I should give up.

A Hong Kong doctor sent his wife to Australia promising to meet her in Sydney every weekend. He bought fifty return tickets so that he could save his marriage while keeping his Hong Kong clinic going. No affairs, they agreed, 'but you may fall in love' she warned, 'with an air hostess'. The doctor's friends advised him to save his money, give up being a doctor and become a Qantas air steward instead. Some Hongkongers came back to their jobs and homes in Hong Kong, leaving Canadian lawyers to maintain a fictitious address to preserve their right of entry, but that of course was risky. They began to talk of 'widow streets' in Sydney and Vancouver, where the wives and children of Hong Kong professionals whiled away their time clocking up residence qualifications, to allow their husbands to qualify for the passport which would enable them all to live in Hong Kong – in the security of knowing that they could leave for Australia or Canada at a moment's notice and not be trapped.

An unintended consequence is the alienation of children divided not only from their family but from their native culture. 'We are dismantling an established system for coping with people,' said a despairing civil servant. Some parents send 9 or 11 year olds to one of these countries without fully appreciating that they will almost certainly return having lost a speaking knowledge of Chinese, or the ability to write Chinese, or both. This will have immense consequences for family unity and cohesion. If for any reason such children returned to Hong Kong and the family were to stay there, they would be particularly handicapped by such a language deficiency – more so after 1997 than before. If, on the other hand, the family eventually settled in the other country, then the children's fluency in English would be an asset. Such insurance policies have to be taken out early before the final outcome can be seen, and it is the children who pay the price of any misjudgement.

Since 1984 there have been scores of films on Hong Kong screens about the problems of family stress relating to these 'passport astronauts' and divided families. The lack of confidence in the change of sovereignty in 1997 has social consequences which are almost as damaging as the economic ones, and may prove to be more so. Even if the poor Hongkonger settles down in his new Anglo-Saxon milieu, he becomes liable to severe bouts of homesickness. 'I remember a midnight winter in the Boston snow,' recalled Donald Tsang of the Hong Kong government, 'when I woke up, and my wife too, and we both said 'I'd do anything for a bowl of *won ton* noodles, and we talked all night about how we missed the dirt, the noise, the people, schoolmates, the excitement, everything.' One of the absconding policemen who fled corruption charges and settled in Taiwan was said to be willing to pay $120,000 to go home again to Hong Kong – with immunity, of course.

With sophisticated communications and busy media, Hongkongers do not emigrate under many illusions. They know that they are likely to earn lower salaries abroad and also to experience racial prejudice. They read about the incident in Soho where English customers refused to pay a restaurant bill and punched and kicked the head waiter instead. They were then attacked by four of the Hong Kong Chinese waiters, who were gaoled for their intervention in defence of their boss. 'When a white person does something like that,' said one of the waiters sourly, 'it is all right. When I do it I am a "bloody Chink".' Another Hong Kong Chinese in Gerrard Street tried to dismiss the incident. 'Because it happens frequently, you cannot take it too seriously. We have got to the point of being pretty numb now.' (On the other hand, when a Hong Kong Chinese boy killed an English schoolmate after being bullied by him for a year, he was acquitted.) One reason sometimes given for not joining the emigration bandwagon is the conformist terror of belonging to 'a minority group'. Sometimes, a Hongkonger gets taken for another nationality and suffers for it, like Vincent Chin who was beaten to death in Detroit, in 1989, at the height of the anti-Japanese outbursts over the car trade war.

In Vancouver, where Hong Kong Chinese property buying has gone further than almost anywhere else, the backlash has arrived. The city council was asked to restrict the number of new flats given to new arrivals, older residents formed a group to promote more immigration from Europe and 'Go Back To Hong Kong' graffiti appeared. Victor Li, Li Kashing's son, said that racism was driving Hong Kong investment away from Vancouver, and T-shirts were seen flashing the word 'Hong-couver'. This is not because the Hongkongers are 'cheap labour', as they used to be only a generation ago: quite the contrary. 'Never before,' said Brian Sung of the Canadian Broadcasting Corporation, 'has an immigrant group descended that has the perception they have of being wealthier, better educated and more successful than the host population.'

The issue of nationality, right of abode and passports has become highly charged in Hong Kong, and can strain Chinese–British friendships of long standing there almost to breaking point. But the starting point is a simple proposition. Hongkongers (defined as those born in Hong Kong or those resident there for seven years) have in the past, still are and will for the next seven years be British in nationality. After the end of June 1997, they will necessarily become Chinese by nationality. Their right of abode has been, is now and will be Hong Kong throughout, from the beginning of British rule until far beyond 1997. The more complicated question is whether the right of abode in Hong Kong carries with it a right of abode in the UK. That is because roughly half of the 6 million Hongkongers either hold or are entitled to hold British passports, as British subjects, and these 3 million contain a large proportion of the professionally qualified who are seeking urgently to obtain foreign citizenship.

When Lord Palmerston informed the world a century and a half ago that a British subject would be protected by the British government regardless of his ethnic origins or place of residence, following the splendid Latin rallying cry, *Civis Romanus sum*, Britons wallowed in the superiority of their system and the richness of the gifts they had brought to the world. Such imperial self-delusions were harmless before the aeroplane started to bring colonial subjects to live in Britain at a rapid rate and in large numbers, and it was only then that the British realised their mistake. The 1962 Commonwealth Immigration Act began the process of denying the right of abode in the UK to the Hong Kong-born Chinese, among others. Hongkongers hardly noticed it at the time, since few of them wanted to live in the UK anyway. After 1984, however, in the face of '1997' they strenuously lobbied to reopen their option.

Sir Y.K. Kan, the legislator, noted that the British Parliament had given citizenship to the Gibraltarians, but now denied it to Hongkongers because, 'unlike the people of Gibraltar, the people of Hong Kong are non-white'. Margaret Thatcher indeed defended the new policy by drawing attention to the fact that Hong Kong's 3.2 million potential holders of British passports would, if they came to live in Britain, treble the entire post-war arrivals of new Commonwealth immigrants, meaning, as a *New Statesman* writer put it more bluntly, two new yellow faces alongside every old black one. There was recognition that Hong Kong Chinese were better potential citizens, would need less looking after and would contribute more to the British economy, but they were applying too late: the number of culturally different immigrants which British society was willing to absorb had already been filled from the Caribbean, Africa and South Asia. To take it higher, especially to treble it, would be inviting an enormous backlash that MPs could sense from their constituency opinion, dramatically articulated by Norman Tebbit in 1990. Such a backlash would hit not only Britain and its white population, but also its existing black and Chinese population.

It was understandable, nevertheless, that Hongkongers felt rejected. Martin Lee said that the 1962 Act had 'deprived' Hongkongers of 'their birthright of entering and residing in the UK'. The barrister, Winston Poon, savaged the British decision as 'an act of apartheid'. There were embarrassing incidents, as when Lydia Dunn queued up to show her passport at the 'British Nationals' gate at Gatwick Airport and was told to go to the 'Others' queue. She described the new British policy as 'morally indefensible'. Another extraordinary gaffe occurred when a group of Hong Kong Chinese immigration officers training in Britain went to see the UK immigration service headquarters at Croydon. They were told to join the very long queue of hopeful would-be immigrants because the British reception officials refused to believe that the Hongkongers were on an official visit.

A Hong Kong newspaper leader complained that it was the fate of Hongkongers 'to be perpetual castaways of Britain'. Britain had made a promise it could not keep and then reneged upon it in 1962, and it is no wonder that the people affected feel betrayed. This is particularly true of those who were not born in Hong Kong but became naturalised, undergoing the emotional bruising of giving up their Chinese nationality in order to swear allegiance to the Queen.

The American Congress and media mostly missed the point about all this. 'No other democracy,' said the *New York Times*, 'has ever forced its passport holders to live under communist rule.' A Congressman said it was bizarre for British passport holders to be refused abode, and another said that the British government 'ought to be ashamed of itself'. In part this highlights a difference between the attitude to immigration in an old, settled country with stable and rather fixed traditions, on the one hand, and a country itself formed by relatively recent immigration where no one ethnicity has the confidence to feel its culture should rule.

Some Hongkongers were very literal about what they had been promised. A group of young Hongkongers wrote to *The Guardian* in 1987 insisting that Britain was 'legally obliged to offer us alternative and equivalent accommodation when she turns over our present accommodation to the Chinese Communists'. There were many people of goodwill in both Britain and Hong Kong who sought to retrieve British honour, such as the Honour Hong Kong Campaign, funded by the British trading houses and the Hongkong Bank, to lobby in Westminster for passports. Many Britons agreed. The words of the late Harry Johnson, the economist, were recalled, that 'there is nothing wrong with the British economy that 100,000 Chinese would not cure'. Auberon Waugh said teasingly that all 3 million should come in, and that the British electorate should be persuaded that we need 'fewer Britons and more Chinese'. Peregrine Worsthorne advocated handing Liverpool over to the Hong Kong Chinese.

But these were either maverick or apolitical opinions. It did in the end seem a blind alley to try to persuade British politicians to do something which they knew the electorate would resent. A Manchester letter-writer in *The Daily Telegraph* claimed that the arrival of 3 million Hongkongers would 'destroy the last vestige of our tribal and cultural identity'. Gradually, the Hong Kong Chinese will resign themselves to losing their right of settlement in the UK. They came to Hong Kong in the first instance not to salute the Union Jack, but to take advantage of the opportunities which Britain had created there. Retrocession will mean that Hongkongers will become aliens in the UK and should not count on anything different.

What will happen to them, then, in 1997? The Chinese law is fundamentally racist, in the sense that all ethnic Chinese, whether born in Hong Kong or not, are regarded as Chinese nationals. This view has still not been tested against the weight of international law, but it represents the present Chinese attitude towards Hong Kong nationality questions. What will be the status, for example, of a Hongkonger returning from Canada with a Canadian passport after 1997? The Chinese law does not allow double nationality, and the Chinese who settles abroad and acquires a foreign nationality automatically loses Chinese nationality. But if a man returns from Canada to live in Hong Kong, would the Chinese authorities regard him as not 'settled' abroad and thus catch him in their nationality net? All these questions are still to be resolved, and the unreadiness of China to clarify them is one of the reasons for professional flight. Only the young in Hong Kong profess to be unworried, but they have fewer options to choose from.

When prospective emigrants began to knock against the limits of the four countries with Anglo-Saxon systems, they searched further afield. Singapore offered passports, primarily for high-tech professionals, but the numbers were very small and although people in Britain seem to think that Hongkongers and Singaporeans should happily interchange, that is not the case. The *South China Morning Post* regularly publishes lists of countries and their requirements for immigration – 'The Price of a Passport'. Belize is sometimes recommended for its rapid issue of 'economic citizenship' for a $35,000 investment. South African companies are also taking advantage of the situation to attract professionals looking for a new citizenship. But there is not much scope for Hong Kong Chinese in Southeast Asia, or in Japan where citizenship is not normally available, or in the other countries of Asia.

Outsiders often assume that when Hong Kong Chinese see the final curtain come down on British colonialism they will have at least two Chinas to choose from, namely, communist China and Taiwan. Since Taiwan is capitalist and American-backed, why not go there? But Taiwan has a very high population density, a delicate demographic balance between earlier communities of Fujianese settlers and more recently arrived mainlanders, and if the Hong Kong Cantonese population suddenly arrived, it would disrupt political stability and confuse the language problems. Taiwan is now rich, and does not need Hong Kong investment money, it is still sufficiently anti-communist to see Hongkongers with their closer connection to the mainland as security risks, and Hongkongers are mostly sophisticated city boys who view the Taiwanese as country bumpkins.

Ironically, with all these possible new homes ruled out, China itself is gradually making the lists as a possible place to live, at least if Hong Kong becomes untenable. After all, some businessmen and professionals say, China is changing fast (in the wrong direction at the moment, maybe, but that will alter again), a rich man can still manipulate the Chinese communist system to his own advantage and stay rich (that has been made clear from the experience of some of the former capitalist class in China, notably Rong Yiren, but also several others). So why not 'go home'? That is at present a very small 'chauvinist' minority view, but it may gain a few more adherents in the 1990s, especially when the aged Chinese conservatives in Beijing actually die away.

When I lived in Hong Kong in the 1960s, two of the less hide-bound Hong Kong government officials who anticipated possible Chinese interference in the future concocted a plan to start Hong Kong all over again, on a little island somewhere else far from the centres of power. Maybe that was an overromanticised *Robinson Crusoe* or *Swiss Family Robinson* syndrome, but twenty years later a group of Hongkongers advertised in *The Times* of London for Britain and the United Nations between them to find as quickly as possible 'a suitable place for building a new Hong Kong'. Admiral Bergen had by then already launched what he called Hong Kong West, intended as a replica in Grand Bahama, and Enrique Zobel of the Philippines offered support for a 'new Hong Kong' on Mactan Island.

But the site which progressed furthest as an alternative for Hong Kong was Darwin in Australia. The 200 companies from Hong Kong and Taiwan already operating in the Darwin Trade Development Zone provided some basis for this, and suggestions ranged from taking out a 99-year lease for $450 million to renting it as a new British dependent territory (in order faithfully to copy the conditions for Hong Kong's success, and take care of international status and relationships). The ministers of the Northern Territory were enthusiastic: 'They can close Victoria and New South Wales down. Darwin is the ideal place to replace Hong Kong.' Although a thriving Chinese city overlooking Indonesia would not be good for Australian diplomacy, the other conditions seemed favourable – but the scheme has not yet gained momentum.

In Europe a Northern Irish site has been proposed as one to meet Hongkongers' need for a challenge, and Douglas Mason of the Adam Smith Institute proposed that Hong Kong be resited on an underpopulated or uninhabited island or coastal area in western Scotland. Hong Kong would certainly have been Adam Smith's favourite island, but whether Rhum, Ulva, Taransay or Scalpay could ever become the favourite island of the Hong Kong Chinese is more doubtful – and would the Keswicks approve of Hong Kong moving into their backyard? The *South China Morning Post* probably treated the matter in the right tone when it reported it under the headline 'Scotch Plan on the Rocks'. Most of these ideas may seem hare-brained, but the appointed members of Legco and Exco did devote two inconclusive hours to the Scottish and Australian propositions, and there is enough wealth in

Hong Kong for the idea of buying a little island somewhere as a new home of last resort to keep recurring.

But it was obviously more important to pressurise the Anglo-Saxons to be more accommodating, and so Edward Chen suggested negotiating a 'Commonwealth solution' to Hong Kong's emigration problem, whereby many different Commonwealth countries would all pledge to take a certain number each year which would roughly add up to the total required – as special annual quotas for this particular decolonisation purpose and not to be invoked as a precedent for other cases. The UK tried to start the ball rolling in 1990 with a scheme to allow 225,000 Hongkongers (including families) the right of abode in Britain, expecting that this would allow them to stay put until they actually found their situation intolerable. The British justification for the move, both to its own furious home opinion and to the Chinese government which strongly criticised the scheme, was that these key people could go on working to make Hong Kong a success and prevent it going into a premature downward spiral by not having to worry about any need to leave until it became strictly necessary – and it was hoped, of course, that the point of intolerability would never arrive. What on the surface may have seemed a reasonable British offer in the circumstances, when looked at more closely, carries some disadvantages. The psychological commitment to Hong Kong (and to the new China which after 1997 will include Hong Kong) is reduced by the backstop of a ticket to London, and China is humiliated by the public advertisement that such a key group of her own people might prefer life in Europe to life in China. Can one really encourage a man to become committed to the community where he lives and works by giving him the assurance of being able to leave whenever he wants? The UK should not be surprised to find, assuming developments in China are reasonably favourable, that many Hong Kong Chinese tear up their British passports in 1997, voluntarily or under pressure from the new Chinese authorities.

There is another constituency of Hongkongers who do not set their sights on being able to emigrate, but who strongly desire not to be treated arbitrarily or subjected to arrest like other Chinese nationals when they visit China after 1997, without having the protection of the status of being resident in a British colony. They also worry about difficulty in travelling to other countries, which is essential for both business and holiday purposes, and in particular to third countries which discriminate against People's Republic of China passports. They know the suspicion which clouds the eye of many a consular or immigration official in Southeast Asia or Europe when he sees a Chinese passport. They fear becoming cut off from a world in which British colonial status allowed them to travel freely. These problems are quite different from right of abode and could be addressed with patience, ingenuity and goodwill without the need of British passports.

In the Stanford Research Institute's 1989 report on Hong Kong's economic prospects, Hong Kong's private sector was urged to create a 'brain gain' foundation to cultivate systematically every possible means of discouraging departers and nurturing trained replacements. The Hong Kong Freedom of Movement and Right of Abode Limited proposed that intending departers should contribute, perhaps $1,000 a year, to an investment fund for the benefit of countries granting abode, as a general incentive for the latter and also a contribution towards their immigration costs.

The companies most affected by resignations to emigrate took steps to minimise the damage. When Cathay Pacific Airways found that the majority of its data processing staff were emigrating to Australia, it set up an information systems office in Sydney in the hope of retaining them as employees 'over there', this being work that in the modern communication age can be done anywhere. Similarly, the Bank of East Asia bought a Canadian subsidiary partly to accommodate members of its staff who wanted Canadian residence in order to get a passport, and who might otherwise have resigned from the bank in order to do so. Some corporate migration schemes have now come out which keep open the option of transferring back to the original employer after the escape route is secured.

The ingenuity of Hongkongers is being applied to the problem of how to get the passport which will allow them to leave Hong Kong after 1997 if they wish to, and how to get it at the least possible cost – ideally without leaving Hong Kong at all, without breaking up their families, and without jeopardising their jobs. But it is not so easy for the 3 million people involved in this extraordinary exercise to gain foreign citizenship with such ease, in such numbers and so rapidly.

Few people expect there to be violence, either on the part of the Chinese or by Hongkongers, in June or July 1997, but the fertile minds of refugee-obsessed outsiders like Bernard Levin have already elaborated the possible scenarios which might prompt the international reception of these 3 million Hongkongers, on the assumption that they would be as morally pitiable as the German Jews, Ugandan Asians or Vietnamese boat people. That is to exaggerate the problem, to exaggerate the nature of what the Chinese government calls communism in China, and to show little concerned understanding for the problems faced by 1,100 million Chinese people in their wayward march to modernisation. A big contribution could be made to that modernisation by the Hong Kong of the twenty-first century if the capitalist system can be maintained there as successful and generally beneficial. An outsider should not perhaps prevent Hongkongers from leaving, but it is questionable behaviour to encourage them to leave and cruel to fill them with false hopes and horizons.

These 3 million Hongkongers are a lucky small minority of the Chinese people which has left the stagnant mainstream of Chinese modernisation to show decisively how free enterprise capitalism and the Western rule of law can produce demonstrable wealth and progress. If they all leave the China which after 1997 must include Hong Kong, the chances of convincing China's leaders to move in this more rational, enterprise-oriented direction will diminish. If they stay, the 1,100 million will benefit, perhaps decisively. That should be the context for judging the eagerness of liberal Western intellectuals to see in the Hong Kong emigration question another rescue operation to be launched, and entered for good conduct in the West's moral markbook. However forcefully, sometimes hysterically, some of them may appeal to the West for help in their predicament, Hongkongers do not completely discount the possibility of enjoying acceptable roles and lifestyles after 1997 (albeit a little different from today's).

In the few years before the Sino-British agreement of 1984, emigration was averaging at a manageable 20,000 people a year including wives and children. Since then it has more than doubled, and was expected to exceed 50,000 in 1990, rising further to about 60,000 in the first half of the 1990s. These figures are more in the nature of 'guesstimates' than statistics, because emigration procedures do not require a Hongkonger to say exactly where he is going or why or for how long (that is part of their 'freedom'), and so the information has to be put together from other sources as well, chiefly from the foreign consulates issuing visas. It is not always clear, anyway, whether a figure refers to the number of professionals leaving or to the number of persons in professionals' families leaving, and the difference can be as much as twelvefold. The government likes to put out figures of 'net emigration', where the returnees are deducted. Here again, it is extremely difficult to be sure about returnees, there being no way of knowing definitely whether a person entering Hong Kong is going to stay and become a resident or resume residence status, or not. Certainly a proportion of emigrants return, and the government has suggested that it is about one in six. There is continuing immigration from China – but not of professionally trained persons who could replace the Hongkongers leaving.

It is the middle class which is leaving, and that middle class is usually put at half a million, so that an annual loss of 50,000 sustained over a decade would wipe it out. That is to put the 'brain drain' problem at its worst. It confirms what some Hong Kong leaders with a very wide circle of acquaintances say, that 'I don't know a single executive-class family which is staying'. But it would be rash to overrely on such evidence: coteries tend to think alike, and it is in the Hong Kong Cantonese character to have a positive horror of being seen as socially out of step. Some of the people who now admit to wanting to go may well, when the time comes, and in the later political circumstances that arise, and after considering the disruption that would be caused to their families, quietly fail to follow through on their stated intention.

Another question needs to be asked about the middle class. If Westernised middle class is meant, then the figure of half a million is fair, but if it is defined a little more widely to include 'people on middle-class salaries' or people sufficiently well educated to reckon to be able to climb during their lifetimes into the middle class, then it is larger. About 250,000 emigrants have left Hong Kong since 1984. Has the middle class been halved by that? Not exactly, it would have to be answered. Where a work vacancy is left, everybody steps up one, whether or not the new job holders at the higher end would consider themselves or be considered as middle class. Hong Kong is a new, yuppie, flexible society in which the class differentiations are not so important.

The damaging thing is the very large proportion of professionally qualified Hongkongers who have left, are leaving and plan to leave. Surveys constantly show that very few accountants, engineers, doctors, lawyers, economists, dentists, etc., say that they will not leave Hong Kong. When the accountants were polled recently by their professional body, 80 per cent of them said they planned to emigrate. A professional is someone who has studied for anything between two and seven years to gain the qualifications needed for his work or practice, and that cannot be simply replaced from below. When a senior professional leaves, a junior professional with the same qualifications but less experience may be promoted. But who will fill the gap of the young professional from below? To some extent there may be room for people with qualifications just below the requirement, but in the long run a fully qualified person has to be found. Whether discounted or inflated, the emigration figures provide good reason for the widespread pessimism prevailing in Hong Kong, and indeed the one feeds upon the other. In this Oriental *trahison des clercs* it is the main part of the working population below the professional class which will suffer, even though a small proportion of them will get promotion, from the risk of a downward economic spiral. As David Li of the Bank of East Asia warned in 1988, referring specifically to the financial sector: 'There is a real danger that within a decade, Hong Kong will begin to lose not only business vitality, but also some of its ability to function credibly as an international financial centre.'

However, there is another side to the picture which is not often examined, either by insiders or outsiders. First of all, nobody knows the potential of Hong Kong society for self-corrective therapy. In economists' jargon the 'brain drain' becomes a question of relative opportunity. The more people leave, the more opportunities are presented for those who stay. Anyone proposing to leave now is almost certainly going to be offered a higher salary and other inducements in order to stay, and these may tilt the balance against actually leaving. This is true of skilled workers, many technicians, secretarial and other office workers, businessmen and entrepreneurs, and people working at the lower fringe of the professional world who might be able to take on a particular responsibility even if they lack the complete qualification. Hongkongers are quick to learn, and habituated to the idea of learning from the person above how to do the work. With the professionals who constitute the majority of emigrants such direct replacement from below is not normally possible, except that there is a constant stream of new graduates coming into the society from within as well as from overseas universities.

There are three universities in Hong Kong, and there are an equal number of Hong Kong students at foreign universities all round the world, especially in those 'Anglo-Saxon' countries, most of whom will have to return if only because immigration restrictions are so rigid now in those countries. They will return with their eyes open about Hong Kong's situation, in full knowledge of '1997', and will most likely make a big contribution. That is not to say that a new graduate can replace an experienced professional with the same efficiency, but it does mean that the possibility of a company having to stop operations and close down is lessened. They also have to be paid less, which perhaps sugars the pill a little for the company. A new Business School is being opened to train people to replace departing entrepreneurs.

If a young local is not forthcoming, the next thing to consider would be bringing in an expatriate professional to fill the gap. The prospect is not quite so daunting as it used to be because of the change in relative salary levels and exchange rates. 'We actually pay less,' said one satisfied Hong Kong Chinese chairman, 'for good accountants from England. We get better quality than locals.' Wages in Hong Kong have soared so high that it is no longer necessarily more expensive to bring in staff from abroad, so British firms bring in Britons and Japanese bring in Japanese, and Hong Kong Chinese companies are increasingly bringing in a wide range of expatriate Westerners. Given that American taxation is about double the Hong Kong rate, it is calculated by the American Chamber of Commerce in Hong Kong that a Hong Kong professional is actually better off in take-home terms than his American counterpart. One of the great ironies of Hong Kong's future is that there are likely to be more Western expatriate workers there in both government and business than before. 'The brain drain,' says George Cardona of the Hongkong Bank, 'has spoilt our policy of trying to appoint local people into top positions.'

Other Asian professionals are also being brought in, although they do not fit so easily into the Hong Kong structure. There used to be a simple hierarchy of Western expatriates at the top of the tree and local employees below them, with lower salaries and less generous terms and conditions. Now there are two new categories in between. First, there are the Asian expatriate professionals, perhaps from Malaysia or the Philippines, who secure the same salary as the Western expatriate but do not qualify for such perquisites as free housing (or housing allowance) and regular paid travel home. Beneath them are the Hong Kong Chinese returnees who are slightly better off than the locals but not as well rewarded as the Southeast Asian expatriate. Bitterness has been expressed about these new gradations. But what appeals to employers is the fact that somebody hired from another country is not likely to resign precipitately or need to emigrate. The returnees are preferred to locals because they already have their foreign passport and do not need to plan to leave again unless something very bad indeed happens.

Clifford Pang of Lafe Computer Magnetics was an emigrant to the United States in the 1950s who returned in 1969 to start his own construction company, only to lose everything in the crash of 1973. He recovered and went on to become one of the four biggest independent producers of computer peripherals. Albert Cheng King-hon was an emigrant of the 1960s to Vancouver, but he returned in 1983 and started the Chinese-language edition of *Playboy* and became a sponsor of the plan for a new Hong Kong in Australia. Tony Ng spent thirteen years working in North American, British and New Zealand hospitals and returned to Hong Kong on a bout of homesickness after reading Han Suyin's novel *A Many Splendoured Thing*.

It is not just a question of a few individuals. There are probably 30,000 returnees from Canada alone working and living in Hong Kong, and more than 100,000 from all four Anglo-Saxon countries. Some companies in Hong Kong are paying sign-on bonuses, amounting in some cases to a full year's salary, in order to lure these qualified Hongkongers back. These are among the reasons why, of the 80 per cent of accountants who said they would emigrate, well over half intended to return to work in Hong Kong after getting their foreign passport. As usual, the difficulty turns out to be the children. It is not easy to get them entered into Hong Kong schools.

The Hong Kong People Saving Hong Kong campaign put out advertisements stating, 'We wish to stay in Hong Kong, as it is our home, and we are proud to be Chinese'. That did not prevent it from supporting the right of abode in Britain, but young Hongkongers are more logical. The student leader Andrew To Qwan-hang rejected the appeal for settlement in Britain. 'We see Hong Kong,' he said, 'as part of China, and its people, Chinese nationals . . . There is no question that we consider Britain as our mother country . . . We should ask the UK to give us more democracy and not a passport.' A newspaper columnist, Simon S.C. Chau, wrote: 'I don't dream of anything from the communists, I just do as I should do as a Chinese. To get real happiness you have to pay the price.' His attitude was endorsed by Dr Lau Nai-keung, who said, 'Going away doesn't help anything. If you feel you are one of the billion, you know your responsibilities. I think it is time for the stay-here people to have their voice too.'

That voice is not only the voice of those 'trapped' in Hong Kong. Johnston Wong Hong-chun returned from Canada in the belief that his professional expertise in social welfare would be valuable not only in Hong Kong but also eventually in China as a whole. 'I want to say that I will not emigrate.

We only live once and we should make the best of it. I feel that serving my own people and the community will be of the greatest value of all.' The 'stay-here' people have no interest in projecting themselves to Bernard Levin or other outsiders, and their voice is not often heard in the West. It is subdued even in Hong Kong. But given the realism of the Cantonese, and the fact that five-sixths of the population, or 5 million people, cannot hope to emigrate even if they wanted to, this is bound to become a more powerful voice as the years go by.

Chapter 21

Could the Tail Wag the Dog?

'What will happen after 1997?' eager pressmen used to ask Gordon Wu, thought by many to have the most 'inside' view of the China–Hong Kong relationship.

'After 1997,' he would gravely reply, leaving a pause – 'there will be 1998!'

To some fevered Hongkongers, scared beyond reason, the reminder that time and life will not stop for the most publicised deadline in modern history is welcome. But one can do better than that. One can point to the major ingredients in the recipe for Hong Kong success and work out what is most likely to happen to each one – is it likely to survive or not, and to what degree? The situation in the run-up to 1997 is itself very difficult to predict, but that is mainly because of the political situation in Beijing and the self-fulfilling anxieties of the brain drain. There is nothing badly wrong with the economy in itself. Over the past forty-five years it has invariably been able to adapt, sometimes dramatically, to changing external circumstances.

Starting with its traditional trade entrepôt role in the late 1940s, Hong Kong became a leading exporter of manufactures, first of textiles and then of electronics and a wide variety of goods, in the 1950s and 1960s. In the 1970s it found a new vocation as a regional financial centre, and then in the 1980s began to return to its old entrepôt role for a new 'open door' China. These developments are accretions, not substitutions, and the economy has become increasingly rich and complicated, with manufacturing, financial and business services and the entrepôt trade more and more inter-related.

In the 1990s manufacturing will probably become more capital intensive, technology intensive and higher value added, with the simpler phases being relocated elsewhere. There is even the view, expressed by Sir Sze-yuen Chung, that 'Hong Kong does not need manufacturing industry now – except for textiles, because of the quotas'.

249

The importance of Hong Kong as a regional trade and finance centre in Asia and the Pacific is growing, and its entrepôt function *vis-à-vis* China will become more value-added, dealing in services as well as commodities. Some young business leaders are looking to a day when Hong Kong will export research software rather than industrial hardware, for example in the field of biotechnology, accepting contracts from outside.

What is left of manufacturing industry will face greater competition from high value-added competitors such as Taiwan and Korea, as well as lower-cost rivals in Southeast Asia, particularly Malaysia and Thailand. In financial and commercial services there will be challenges from Japan, Singapore and Australia. The new Pacific Basin configuration of business networks will grow in strength, with Hong Kong as one of its centres. Already one can detect, within the family of 'Anglo-Saxon' countries, that Hongkongers feel more at home with Australians and Americans than with Britons. The Stanford Research Institute in its 1989 report on Hong Kong identified a new complementarity with China and the Asia–Pacific region which would provide both challenges and opportunities for Hong Kong.

Basic manufacturing will continue to shift to South China, where more than twice as many workers are employed by Hong Kong companies than in the Hong Kong factories themselves, although this process was temporarily interrupted after Tiananmen Square. The trend is for Hong Kong to become a design, administrative and marketing centre for a new industrial system in Guangdong and its neighbouring provinces. China will make the goods but Hong Kong will add value to them at the 'front end', by sourcing, marketing, design, quality management and product development, and also at the 'back end' through warehousing, final quality control, forwarding, shipping and trade finance. Hong Kong may provide technical services for China's heavy industries.

That is the shape which Hong Kong's integration with South China is likely to take over the next decade. 'Our problem,' Sir David Akers-Jones suggested in August 1989, 'is likely to be not one of decline, but how to cope with the ever-increasing demands made on our economy and the supporting infrastructure and upon our workforce at all levels.' The lion will lie down with the lamb, but the lamb won't get much sleep. It all vindicates the motto of Sun Hung Kai, the securities firm which is so typical of the new Hong Kong: 'With our feet in Hong Kong, with our back against China, with our face towards the Asia–Pacific region, with our eyes open we scan the world.' It may sound like a joint-stretching yoga position, but that is precisely what Hong Kong will be doing.

All this could be jeopardised by the weaknesses which are only too apparent. There needs to be more industrial training, more university and polytechnic upgrading, a more flexible labour policy to allow perhaps temporary contract import when necessary, and a 'brain gain' campaign to bring experts in from outside. In entrepreneurial management and capital, Hong Kong already stands in the world class. But research and development, and industrial technology, lag behind. Economic leadership to deal with problems like the brain drain which will not find a solution in the marketplace, or at least not quickly enough, is also weak.

While individual professionals emigrate, companies are protecting their future by moving legal ownership and control of their holding companies to Bermuda or other Caribbean tax havens. Jardine started the ball rolling, but foreign-owned companies have grasped at this as a means of safeguarding the overseas assets of Hong Kong companies from the higher political risk expected to come with Chinese sovereignty in the eyes of the international financial community. Not every foreign company is worried by this, however, since there are some that already have branch offices in China itself, so that the change of sovereignty in Hong Kong will not make a big difference. This is the case with Mitsubishi, British Telecommunications and many others.

Xu Jiatun has often reassured foreign businessmen that China intends 'to look after their benefits and interests'. Simon Murray, Li Kashing's senior executive, declares quite forthrightly, 'I would rather have Mr Deng Xiaoping and all his policies than Arthur Scargill any day.' For once, Hongkongers and foreigners have a common interest in trying to attract more foreign companies. 'The more foreigners there are here,' said one local politician, 'the more difficult it will be after 1997 to break the joint agreement.'

The worst moment is likely to be around 1992. Most investors need five years to get their money back, so this could be the first year of serious investment nerves. It will immediately follow the first direct elections for Legco in 1991, which could see a frightening demonstration of Chinese capacity either to manipulate the polls or to bully those non-Communists who win them. On top of all that, some scanners of the distant economic horizon predict a world recession around that time.

No one has found the secret of predicting Chinese political developments. Biology suggests, however, that many if not most or all of the handful of Communist Party octogenarians, who intervened in 1988 to prevent Deng Xiaoping's liberal reforms getting out of hand and threatening the Communist Party's power, may not last until 1997. By then they will be nonogenarians, and if they have not allowed a greater degree of compromise with the younger generation hungry for more freedom, more participation, more economic progress, they could expose China to intense internal upheaval.

It is not that the conservatives are keeping the reformers out, because there are many reformist leaders still in place in government and party. The whole situation is a complicated compromise, and it would need a relatively small movement, a small loss of power or self-confidence or credibility on the part of the conservatives, for the pattern to shift again. Reform has become the mainstream of Chinese politics, though momentarily obstructed, and the only question is how long it will take to revert to it. From the patterns of Chinese political change before, it would seem a good guess that change in that direction will begin before 1997. Even if it were delayed, one would have to remember that the conservatives, too, were involved in the Sino-British agreement, and they are likely to find more need of Hong Kong in the later 1990s, because of the faltering Chinese economy, rather than less.

When the Union Jack comes down for the last time in 1997, there is one possible breathing space for companies still doubtful of their future under People's Republic autonomy, and that is in Macao. The Macao reversion to China will take place at the end of 1999, two and a half years later than Hong Kong. During that interim, businesses could move to Macao and observe China's handling of Hong Kong before having to decide whether to move away completely or come back (a similar role was played by Macao in 1941).

Could the system survive Chinese sovereignty? Could Hong Kong go on being what one of its bright young entrepreneurs calls 'the last place on earth where you have such a free market system'? Han Suyin admired the 'justice, fair dealing, conciliation and a sense of tolerance' which the colonial government had given to Hong Kong, enough to leave something of itself behind, 'something abiding and too precious to lose'. Can that be retained? Will Stanley Karnow's definition – 'an unbeatable combination of efficient and relatively honest (British) administration blended with bold and innovative Chinese enterprise' – hold? There are widespread fears, because of China's domestic economic record, about the ability of a Chinese government to supervise Hong Kong's capitalist economy, which, Denis Bray warned in 1985, could be 'destroyed by those that do not understand the underlying realities of life in Hong Kong'. Such fears are heightened by the general assumption that the Chinese would not opportunistically accept unbridled capitalism, but would manifest some ambition over the longer term to cleanse Hong Kong capitalism of its worst social consequences.

Some things must be conceded from the start. The Chinese way of handling Hong Kong will be more personalised, more vertical and less inter-departmental than the British, that is true. But that would have happened even with some form of local self-government by the Hong Kong Chinese themselves. It is also true that some Hong Kong leaders, both those who were already friendly with Beijing and those who believe that good relations with Beijing are now necessary if Hong Kong politics are to be effective, are succumbing to the many temptations and pressures which China is able to offer, from membership of congresses and committees which carry prestige in China, to credit from Chinese banks, business offers and even the assurance perhaps of places in the future political establishment of Hong Kong. The Hong Kong Chinese leaders find it difficult to know when to give face to

China and when to stand up to it on issues vital to Hong Kong. R.C. Lee was able to do that in the 1950s, and earned great respect from both sides for it, but since the Cultural Revolution no comparable figure has appeared. The big Hong Kong Chinese businessmen give an impression of opportunism, the worthies who drafted the Basic Law are mostly lacklustre, and no one has yet come out from the crowd. There is still time for that. But these tendencies are endemic to Hong Kong and do not represent a sudden new threat.

Some of those who fled from the Chinese Communists in the 1940s and 1950s say that 'they will wreck Hong Kong when they take over in 1997'. That is the prejudice of someone who has personally suffered and it surfaces almost every time the Chinese make a mistake. Newspapers in Hong Kong asked during the controversy over the nuclear power station just across the border, 'How can we feel safe when Daya Bay is operated by Chinese workers who could not even manage China's public toilets?' Christine Lo of the Hong Kong Observers questioned, 'How can we expect the Chinese Communists to provide stability and prosperity, when they have never had either?'

A short answer is that China does not have to provide stability or prosperity: that can be produced only by the Hongkongers themselves. What China is committed to doing is preventing the stability and prosperity from being spoiled or endangered, and it is perfectly legitimate to question its credentials for that role. However, if Hongkongers apply themselves with their usual vigour to making a success of their city after 1997, there is no reason why China should not be able to act to Hong Kong's minimal satisfaction as a guardian. Hong Kong has no armed forces and very little diplomatic clout. If a foreign country were to raid Hong Kong, or attack its ships or its representatives, Hong Kong would soon learn to be grateful for China's protection.

Might China introduce instability? That is the question. If the psychological climate is right on both the Hong Kong and China sides, Hong Kong could become an oasis of stability and prosperity in a country which consciously aims to imitate those qualities, cannot yet do so across the board, but is capable, meanwhile, of doing its bit to maintain that superior level of stability and prosperity in Hong Kong. It will not be automatic, but Hong Kong could engineer such a situation if it took the trouble to read the Beijing mind and devise an intelligent strategy accordingly. As Nellie Fong, the legislator and sister-in-law of Martin Lee, said in January 1990, long after Tiananmen Square, unification with China was for Hong Kong 'an opportunity not a threat'.

Some factors in Hong Kong's equation are not absolutely essential to its survival. They would include the traditions of refuge, asylum and neutrality and the role of being an apolitical regional headquarters. They must, alas, include the minority groups, notably the Indians, and would go on to embrace the general ethos of permissiveness which allows gambling, prostitution and crime to exist. These elements might disappear in 1997 or begin to be eroded: depending how strongly the local Hong Kong leadership felt about them, some might be preserved to some extent – to the extent of a half or two-thirds, perhaps, to express it in crude numerical terms.

Permissiveness and democracy go together, in the sense that they are the British-introduced features of Hong Kong which are taken to heart by only a small minority of Hong Kong Chinese. Those are the relatively Westernised and the relatively better educated, and they are precisely the ones most likely to emigrate before 1997. Those that remain behind are likely to follow the Chinese tradition of voluntarily tempering their own activities in order to avoid becoming conspicuous in the more ordered society of post-1997. By the same token, outspoken leaders like Martin Lee will most likely be replaced by the more traditional purveyors of conciliation and harmony, people who can bridge gaps with the new masters. Free speech and the quality of life will probably deteriorate, but slowly, eroding over decades rather than years – and, meanwhile, China itself is raising its level, despite such interruptions as we have seen in the past two years, so that Hongkongers should not have to drag themselves as far down as they might fear.

The Chinese leaders have taken a very strong position against permissiveness. 'The contamination of Hong Kong will be allowed to continue,' said Zhao Ziyang, then Prime Minister, in 1984, but not to spread into China itself. He cited for particular condemnation, 'murderers, terrorists, pornography and decadence'. China was building a cultural civilisation, he claimed, and would protect it. Deng told Hong Kong businessmen that the power of the triads would have to be cut back. Horseracing could continue, he added, but the dark side of capitalism, its 'overstaffed and overpaid bureaucratic apparatus', should be reformed. Social order in Singapore, he added for good measure, 'is better than that in Hong Kong'. Many Hongkongers agree, though they do not shout it from the penthouses. 'Hong Kong needs good steering,' said a US-educated Hong Kong Chinese technocrat, 'and more discipline.' He is no Communist, but he welcomes this aspect of Chinese sovereignty after 1997.

In forty years of government the Communists have not been able to eliminate these evils in their own backyard. They are unlikely to force the issue in Hong Kong, knowing that intervention in social matters will merge uncontrollably into intervention in economic matters. What is to be expected instead is that they will squeeze some undertakings from the Hong Kong Chinese leaders from time to time to deal with this social evil or that offending decadence, and then leave the local leaders to get the best result they can. Hong Kong society may be in for successive trade-offs whereby it throws one of its many decadent manifestations as a sacrificial offering in return for keeping across-the-board interference down to the lowest possible level.

The essential elements in Hong Kong's success may be summed up under eight headings. The first is Cantonese 'small enterprise', topped by

Shanghainese 'big enterprise' to become dynamic 'Hong Kong enterprise'. That will remain after 1997, though its successful tried practitioners may be partly replaced by new less experienced ones. The second is the overseas Chinese base, which Beijing wishes to continue for its own purposes and for which there is no rival elsewhere, although a few overseas Chinese may continue to feel so hostile to the People's Republic that they would prefer to do without Hong Kong. Thirdly, the presence of Western businessmen, professional men, administrators and lawyers, is important, but there is no reason for that to be reduced: Hong Kong may become a less attractive place for them to live in, but it will remain more attractive than anywhere else in China, and their salaries and profits will keep them there. After all, China is already the single largest reason for their being there. Fourthly, free trade is necessary, as China well understands and has made specific provision for continuing on a basis of disengagement from the People's Republic trade and membership of GATT.

Laissez-faire as an economic policy, with specific regulation where necessary or appropriate, is the fifth part of the formula. The Chinese understand that this is what primes the golden goose to keep a-laying, and though they would be uncomfortable trying to operate such a policy themselves, they are likely in the end to stand back and let the Hong Kong Chinese leaders pursue it. Of course, there are Beijing cadres so self-confident about their own system, so contemptuous of both Westerners and their 'lap-dogs' among the Hong Kong Chinese community, so unimaginative and bumptious that they might well step into Hong Kong and start giving orders having the effect of bringing its delicate economic machine to a grinding halt. But such cadres are now much rarer than they used to be. The bankruptcy of the radical leftist policies of earlier decades, coupled with the increasing awareness of the absolutely incontrovertible, copper-bottomed superiority of capitalism in producing large numbers of goods for large numbers of increasingly better off people, has made this type into something of a dinosaur. The open disaffection of the Chinese people with politics, their hardening demand for economic uplift, puts a premium on pragmatism.

During the 1980s, tens of thousands of senior cadres were exposed to training in every kind of skill and technology in Western centres. That process of education continues even now, after Tiananmen Square. The new breed of Communist is technocratic, specialised, sensitive and tolerant, though not yet in control at the top of the political pyramid. Chen Yun and his few fellow-survivors of the first generation Chinese Communists are able to put up a few sandbags against progress, but they cannot last long. Even today there are liberals and reformists in many positions of responsibility, from the highest to the lowest levels, and while they may argue with their colleagues over the timing of price reforms, or the extent of party disengagement from economic management, there is near-unanimity on the necessity of reforms.

255

They are not being rolled back. This makes it extremely unlikely that cadres would in future be sent to Hong Kong, or given responsibility for Hong Kong, who would act irresponsibly in intervening in the economy there.

It is remarkable that those entrusted by the Beijing leadership since the late 1970s to deal with Hong Kong affairs – Li Hou, Lu Ping, Xu Jiatun – are men eminently capable of learning, of understanding another system and of acting responsibly to preserve it in China's interests. They have all been under strain since Tiananmen Square, but it is hard to point to a single act, as distinct from talk, on their part, damaging to Hong Kong. Things can always go wrong, and a misguided ruler in Beijing could conceivably instruct a misguided cadre to follow a course of action regarding Hong Kong that would destroy its economy. But I would put that risk at very much less than 5 per cent, and even then the combination of Hong Kong lobbying, international pressure and reformist Chinese opinion might well combine to secure a change before the harm became irreparable. The apparent defection of Xu Jiatun to America in 1990, possibly in rejection of the Li Peng line in China, to be replaced by the tougher ex-Vice-Foreign Minister Zhou Nan, is a minor swing of the pendulum which does not undermine this analysis of probabilities.

Sixthly, those aspects of Hong Kong which make it attractive as a financial centre will be vital; China has no need to change them, no incentive to do so, and no apparent intention to. Seventhly, the economic link with Guangdong must be kept, and Guangdong and China need this as much as Hong Kong does. Eighthly, and finally, Hong Kong must have an adequate and competitive core of professional skills, and this is the only one of the eight factors which might baulk at the 1997 fence. On the basis of these eight factors, a professional punter would probably settle for a 75 per cent likelihood that these conditions for Hong Kong's economic viability continue after 1997. A cautious gambler might go for 70 per cent.

One cannot disregard the possibility that individual Chinese officials may spoil things or try to manipulate Hong Kong for their personal advantage. It should be remembered, however, how Xu Jiatun obtained very quick authority for the Bank of China to join the rescue operation for the Futures Exchange after the market collapse in 1987. The Chinese have repeatedly assured Hong Kong that they will not send cadres in to govern the place, and that has been clearly set out in the Basic Law and other documents. China's international reputation would lie in shreds if these promises were broken. There will be a complex sharing of power between mainland officials, on the one hand, who will stay at arm's length but seek, like the British, to ensure that the Hong Kong Chinese do what they should do and what the sovereign power wants them to do, and a group of Hong Kong Chinese leaders on the other hand, who may be expected quickly to learn how to square and even manipulate the Beijing representatives, just as they did the British.

It is significant that Beijing has so often exuded caution. It vetoed the suggested retrocession of Macao in 1967 because of its impact on Hong Kong; it continued cooperative policies on water and frontier-crossers in the 1960s, despite the urgings of its radical faction; and it recently vetoed the Bank of China's plan to use the Hong Kong Land Fund to finance an airport project instead of leaving it as a back-up for emergencies after 1997. China is more likely to honour than to dishonour the agreement over Hong Kong, because otherwise she would lose international reputation, economic advantage, progress in reunification with Taiwan and the contribution which a prosperous Hong Kong could make to future Chinese reform and development.

The Chinese are, however, likely to exert a strong leadership over Hong Kong: former Foreign Minister Ji Pengfei forecast that the relationship after 1997 would be 'one of leading and being led'. They are not mindlessly assuming that they can come in and change everything. But they would like to change some things. 'Unhealthy speculation will be stopped,' said Liao Chengzhi. Even Hong Kong's own capitalist R.C. Lee had declared in 1982 that speculation in property, shares and commodities 'may enrich a few individuals, (but) brings no real wealth into the community . . . Activities of a high speculative nature cannot be of benefit in a new "Hong Kong order".' The Chinese may be pardoned for aligning themselves with such a respectable Hong Kong Chinese voice.

On the other hand, when the new Hong Kong Stock Exchange opened, Ji Pengfei wrote a congratulatory message in his own calligraphy wishing it long life and prosperity, so some degree of speculation is envisaged. The present editor of the *Far Eastern Economic Review*, Philip Bowring, complained that the Bank of China was run by political cadres 'who do not understand that so-called speculation and free markets are inseparable. Clearly Hong Kong could not exist in its present form if these people had much to do with the running of it.' Xu Jiatun had a taste of the realities of Hong Kong life when he criticised the Tai Shing Developments Co. for saying that it was considering moving its legal headquarters to Bermuda. That clinched the matter for Tai Shing. It did move to Bermuda, commenting: 'If the movement of free capital was to be restricted today, Hong Kong would be a dead port tomorrow.'

One basic trouble is that Chinese officials have no experience of dealing with people used to freedom. Their attitude to the press alternates between false bonhomie and curt rebuff. 'I always feel frightened when I see you,' Deng Xiaoping confessed to Hong Kong journalists in Beijing. When a mammoth signed petition against the Daya Bay nuclear power station was presented to a senior Chinese official in Hong Kong, he walked away without a word. These cadres are visibly uncomfortable with freedom, democracy, openness or pluralism. And there are some Communists in China who believe that the Hong Kong middle class needs to be struggled against, in order to assert the power of the proletariat. It may sound old fashioned, but this is what some newspapers in Shanghai and Beijing said in 1982 in the context of a possible 'new class struggle' in China. That did not become the official line of the day, but it aroused so much anger and fear in Hong Kong that the Communist Chinese pressmen in Hong Kong felt it necessary to refute it as the 'pernicious influence of leftist ideas detrimental to the Chinese people'. This is not likely to become a mainstream theme in Chinese politics for a long time, if at all, but even if it exists at the back of the minds of some officials dealing with Hong Kong, it is unsettling.

Technically, Hong Kong and China are to remain separate socio-economic systems, but some Hongkongers believe there is no avoiding an absorption into China. 'Hong Kong will merge into China,' said Helmut Sohmen in 1988. 'The Special Administrative Region will become an integral part of China, not only in legal and territorial terms but in commercial and social terms as well.' Sohmen added that Hong Kong autonomy was another way of saying that China was maintaining, in commercial terminology, a different brand name. Hong Kong would become an operating division of a larger entity, and should not therefore insulate itself as a tiny autonomous city-state, but rather use its position to spearhead reform in China.

One has to use such distinctions as Westernised and non-Westernised Hong Kong Chinese in order to make some sense of the trends in Hong Kong society. In fact the gradations are numerous and minute, and one university sociologist puts it in a slightly different way. Hongkongers are distinct from mainland Guangdongers in the 'technical aspects of life such as education, washing dishes, going abroad', but they are all still Cantonese. Hongkongers, being more Westernised, have more achievements, and operate on more different levels in their lives, but they are still in the most important sense Cantonese Chinese. Even though Hong Kong is regarded as the most Westernised Chinese community, the vast majority of its population, only excepting a few high achievers who have entered into the Western world in a very committing way, would be able to assimilate into Guangdong society without excessive suffering or depression.

If Sohmen is right, then Hong Kong may indeed become an important influence on China. An article in *The New Leader* by William McCord in 1984 was entitled, 'The Tail that May Wag the Dog: China's Hong Kong Experiment'. The economic lessons for China to learn, while never admitting it was doing so, are clear. But Hong Kong's spell will be cast generally, not in restricted sectors only. Even before the Sino-British agreement of 1984, some 20,000 mainlanders had trained on the job in white collar positions in Hong Kong, and they and their successors will carry back to China a wide variety of impressions which will influence what they do in China afterwards. They may have been frustrated in not experiencing the full life of Hong Kong because of their lack of foreign exchange, and they may well put some of their Hong Kong memories into cold storage in order to be able to live again in a fundamentally anti-foreign conformist society, currently undergoing an illiberal phase. But some of it will filter through in one way or another.

Chinese teachers are extremely interested in Hong Kong's Chinese-language technical textbooks. Hong Kong's political system is bound to appeal to liberal intellectuals in China. One Hongkonger interested in housing told his hosts on a visit to Beijing: 'We build housing for workers better than you do, so why not try capitalism? Why not level up instead of level down?' One of the metaphors used for Hong Kong is that of a test tube. Whatever Hong Kong has been able to absorb from the West, surely China can, too. Or, as the Hong Kong Observers said in 1982, 'this Chinese territory can do a lot more than just earn China 40 per cent of its foreign exchange'. To go back to Sohmen's prediction, he forecast that the end result would be for Hong Kong to export its system across the border to speed up China's progress, and in the process come to act as the commercial and eventually even the political centre of South China. That would be taking over the role of Guangzhou and would require skilful management.

One thing is very clear, that China is going to have a considerable influence on Hong Kong after 1997, and vice versa. Can either hope to remain unscathed? By 1997 the mainland enterprises in Hong Kong will have had eighteen years of inside training in how to do business the Hong Kong way. With Hong Kong techniques spreading to China and Chinese capital coming to Hong Kong, Donald Anderson, the American Consul-General in Hong Kong, suggested in 1989 that a sort of gene-splitting was going on. The probable outcome, he suggested, would be 'a hybrid different from either China or Hong Kong as we now know them'.

Supposing it fails. Supposing Hong Kong heads for the empty skyscraper solution, with the last emigrant to leave turning out the lights of opportunity? The purveyors of gloom are legion, what with Simon Winchester's annual countdown programmes of despair and despondency on BBC television, and Alvin Rabushka, who was such an admirer of Cowperthwaite's *laissez-faire*, finding a 'fundamental and inherent incompatibility' between the Chinese and Hong Kong systems. Milton Friedman divines that Hong Kong 'is going to go down the drain', and a fellow American scholar sees Hong Kong turning into 'another proletarian slum' like Shanghai. But Hongkongers can at least see the humour of things, and they like to tell the story about Sir Run Run Shaw's blockbuster film about 1997, where for his last scene at the airport on 30 June 1997 he had to hire 6 million extras.

If Hong Kong does fail, it will have repercussions all over the world, because the big challenge of the twenty-first century will be the accommodation of the new China-centred 'yellow power' of East Asia in the Western-initiated and still Western-dominated world system. Hong Kong is the only showcase on Chinese soil for the Western democratic-capitalist system. If it shuts down we will be left to shout incomprehendingly at each other. In the long run, Hong Kong needs to be preserved for a far bigger stake than merely its 6 million people.

The shrewdest people in Hong Kong are those intellectuals who sense that if the transition can be navigated with only minimal loss, with China reassured that the place will not rebel or indulge in embarrassing non-performance, and everybody relaxing a little, Hong Kong could be destined for a remarkable reflowering on a much more durable and sound political base than it ever had under the British. They are of a mind with the businessmen and financiers, Chinese and foreign, who are waiting for the excitement of buying property and stocks at the bottom of the market sometime over the next seven years, knowing that they should be able to expect immense profit from that investment in the years after 1997. There are many Japanese and other foreign businessmen mulling this strategy, and not a few Chinese as well. Fortunes may be reversed by the good or poor investment decisions made over the coming seven years.

Prophecy is impossible when so many invariables are involved. In China, we cannot tell the timetable by which policies will return to a more rational and progressive mould. In Hong Kong, the 'brain drain' may or may not shatter the economy, so one has to deal with likelihoods and probabilities. If China wants to destroy Hong Kong, there is no force that can stop it. No doubt there were Chinese Communists in earlier days, and maybe there still are a few, who would like to see that bastion of Western capitalism and Chinese private enterprise destroyed, all the more for its being so successful. That breed of cadre is dying, but if there are enough of them left, and if they are given their day again, then Hong Kong could be destroyed. But the likelihood of that must be put very low indeed. Almost all the evidence points to the fact that there is a more businesslike, practical and non-ideological generation of Communists which is taking over, not smoothly, but in fits and starts, and their weight would almost certainly prevent a foolish gesture being made against Hong Kong – on which so much depends for China's future in terms of income, technical stimulus and world trade.

If, on the other hand, China does not intend to destroy Hong Kong, and that intention is reasonably efficiently carried out, then Hong Kong has problems only within itself and not from China. The real difficulty is the middle ground, where Beijing may not intend to harm Hong Kong, but may allow its emissaries or representatives to do damage to Hong Kong without being able or willing to control the cadres or countermand their policies. Again, the apprehension is justified, but the chances of such things happening without the individuals at fault being recalled, removed, dismissed or chastised do seem to be small.

The most plausible scenario is for a slightly depleted Hong Kong, shorn of its British administrative élite and an appreciable element of its local Chinese business, administrative and professional élite, limbering up for a twenty-first century battle of wits with whoever is currently in power in Beijing, and largely succeeding in carving out a considerable degree of autonomy to pursue the kind of goals and life it had before – only with some concessions to Chinese national pride and ideology, and some face-saving deals with individual emissaries or representatives and companies. Hong Kong has a great capacity for survival and for choosing the tactics of self-improvement.

Meanwhile bookings are mounting for rooms in the Peninsula and other leading hotels for the fateful night of Monday 30 June 1997, when Hong Kong will be restored to its rightful place as part of China. The rewarding socio-economic system which British administrators and Chinese business-men between them constructed over 150 years will hold its breath to see whether it can lodge fruitfully in that commodious terrain.

Acknowledgements

While gathering facts and sounding opinions for this book, I discussed Hong Kong with so many people that to list them all would be an imposition on the reader. Suffice it to say that I heartily thank all those friends and acquaintances, in or out of Hong Kong, working or retired, in government or business or professions, who spent so much time with me, and took so much trouble to answer my questions and pursue ideas and interpretations and generally help my quest.

To the friends who volunteered to read draft chapters, I am particularly grateful for helpful comments which improved the book: David Akers-Jones, Hugh Baker, H.J.C. Browne, William Dorward and Lau Siu-kai. Credit must also go to my assistant, Matthew Grenier, who struggled valiantly with difficult research problems in both Hong Kong and London, and I thank Frank Grenier for his artwork.

For a work like this there is need of help other than intellectual. On my visits to Hong Kong I benefited logistically from the goodwill of Lord Kadoorie and David Li, and I am most grateful to Standard Chartered Bank and its officers for their generous help towards the research and fieldwork for this book.

Finally, for their help on my visits to Hong Kong and research elsewhere I record my gratitude to T.K. Ann, Graham Barnes, Martin Barrow, Sir Robert Black, Michael Bond, W.C.L. Brown, Gordon Burrows, George Cardona, Alan Carter, Sir Jack Cater, Cha Chi Ming, Louis Cha, John Chan, Joseph Cheng, Paul Cheng, Hilton Cheong-leen, Horatio Cheung, Frank Ching, Nelson Chow, Amitabha Chowdhury, C.L. Chu, Sir S.Y. Chung, Richard Clift, Leon Comber, James Cotton, Sir John Cowperthwaite, L.W. Crissman, Derek Davies, Dong Ming, Baroness Dunn, Henry Fok, Sir David Ford, Gerry Forsgate, Victor Fung, L.F. Goodstadt, M.P. Gopalan, Sir Peter Graham, Lynn Grebstad, Sir Philip Haddon-Cave, Han Suyin, Hari Harilela, E.P. Ho, Elaine Ho, Stanley Ho, Ho Yan Ki, P.H.M. Jones, Sir Y.K. Kan, Li Kashing, Ke Zaishou, Henry Keswick, Christopher Koh, H.C. Kuan, Peter Kwon, Father Ladany, C.K. Law, Allen Lee, Dr Deanna Lee Rudgard, Joseph

Lee, Martin Lee, S.Y. Lee, Henry Lethbridge, Leung Chun-ying, Monita Leung, Wendy Leung, Joseph Li, Donald Liao, Lim Chong Yah, Dorothy Liu, Takshing Lo, Vincent Lo, Jimmy McGregor, John MacKenzie, Lord Maclehose, Richard Margolis, Michael Miles, Lawrence Mills, Peter Moss, Simon Murray, Margaret Ng, Ng Wing Bo, Peter Oates, Arthur Odake, John Pain, Lynn Pan, Sir Y.K. Pao, Ranjit Peiris, Herbert Pierson, William Purves, Qiao Zhonghuai, Yukio Sato, Elizabeth Sin, Alan H. Smith, Revd Carl Smith, Ralph Smith, Jack So, Helmut Sohmen, Sir William Stones, Kayser Sung, Sir John Swire, Maria Tam, David Tang, Robert Tang Wo, Stephen Tang, Brian Tisdall, Tong Zhiguang, Kenneth Topley, Marjory Topley, Daniel and Lois Dougan Tretiak, Donald Tsang, Dr Steve Tsang, Peter Tsao, Wang Guangying, Wang Gungwu, Steuart Webb-Johnson, Barry Wiggham, Michael Williams, Sir David Wilson, Dorothy Wong, John Wong, Wong Sie-lun, Tyrone Wong, Alex Wu, Gordon Wu, Sir Ti Liang Yang, Irene Yau, John Yaxley, James Yi, Adrian Zecha, Zhang Hueyao and Zhang Youyun.

Notes and Bibliography

Some of the material in this book derives from interviews with about 200 leading figures in Hong Kong, including some retired in Britain. Most of them took place in 1987–9, before and after Tiananmen Square, although I also dipped into my interview notes going further back, to the early 1950s. The persons range from four Hong Kong Governors and numerous business tycoons, to diplomats, academics, journalists, small shopkeepers, young professionals and students. Otherwise, the principal sources are the growing number of good books on various specialised aspects of Hong Kong, official and business reports, and the press – especially the *South China Morning Post* (referred to hereafter as *SCMP*), the *Far Eastern Economic Review (FEER)* and *Hong Kong Standard*. I owe much to the Hong Kong Collection at the Hong Kong University library, which is probably the richest single source of materials on Hong Kong, and also to the efficient and helpful library in the Hong Kong Government Office in London.

Very few readers want footnotes and so I have not included any. But I do undertake to supply documentation references to any readers who need them. The notes that follow give a few of the main sources for each chapter, and can also be used as suggestions for further reading.

Introduction

The following five books give good, sound, general histories or descriptions of Hong Kong: Austin Coates, *Prelude to Hong Kong*, Routledge, 1966; G.B. Endacott, *A History of Hong Kong*, Oxford 1964; Richard Hughes, *Hong Kong, Borrowed Place – Borrowed Time*, Deutsch, 1968; James Kirkup, *Hong Kong and Macau*, Dent, 1970; and G.R. Sawyer, *Hong Kong 1862–1919*, Hong Kong University Press, 1975.

1 The Cantonese Incumbents

See Hugh Baker, *More Ancestral Images*, South China Morning Post, 1979. pp. 101–4, 129; G.H. Choa, *The Life and Times of Sir Kai Ho Kai*, Chinese University Press, 1981; H.J. Lethbridge, *Hong Kong: Stability and Change*, Oxford, 1978; and Carl T. Smith, 'The Emergence of a Chinese Elite in Hong Kong', *Journal of the Hong Kong Branch of the Royal Asiatic Society*, 1971, p. 74.

2 The Shanghai Gatecrashers

See Liang Yen, *The House of the Golden Dragons*, Souvenir Press, 1961; and Wong Siu-lun, *Emigrant Entrepreneurs: Shanghai Industrialists in Hong Kong*, Oxford, 1988.

3 Asylum and Stairway

See 'Historical Traces of Sun Yat-Sen's Activities', in *Hong Kong, Macau and Overseas*, ed. Ng Lun Ngai-ha *et al.*, Chinese University, 1986; Han Suyin, *My House Has Two Doors*, Cape, 1980, pp. 11–44; Lo Hsiang-lin, *Hong Kong and Western Cultures*, East West Centre, 1963; Pan Ling, *Old Shanghai*, Heinemann, 1984 (for Du Yuesheng); and Albert H. Yee, *A People Misruled: Hong Kong and the Chinese Stepping Stone Syndrome*, API Press, 1989.

4 Capital of the Overseas Chinese

See *Changing Identities of the Southeast Asian Chinese since World War Two*, ed. J. Cushman and Wang Gungwu, Hong Kong University Press, 1988; and Mary F. Somers Heidhues, *Southeast Asia's Chinese Minorities*, Longman, 1974.

On Percy Chen, see Jane Ram's series in *Sunday Post Herald*, 13, 20 and 27 October, 1974; *SCMP*, 7 August 1983 and 21 February 1989.

On Wing On, see Simon Jensen 'The Wing On Group', *Hong Kong Tatler*, September 1977.

5 Hong Kong's Gathering Identity

See Michael Harris Bond, 'Intergroup Relations in Hong Kong', in *Ethnic Conflict*, ed. J. Boucher *et al.*, Sage Publications, 1987, p. 55; Michael H. Bond and Ambrose Y.C. King, 'Coping with the Threat of Westernisation in Hong Kong', *International Journal of Intercultural Relations*, 1985, p. 351; Leo Goodstadt, *The Times*, 8 May 1973; Lau Siu-kai and Kuan Shin-chi, *The Ethos of the Hong Kong Chinese*, Chinese University, 1988; Robert Lloyd Moore, *Modernisation and Westernisation in Hong Kong*, unpublished University of California thesis; Herbert D. Pierson, *Language Attitudes Towards Putonghua*, Chinese University, 1989; Marjory Topley, 'Is Confucius Dead?', *FEER*, 21 December 1967; T.L. Tsim, in *FEER*, 13 March 1981; and Li You, 'At the Luohu Bridge', *People's Literature*, no. 6, 1986 (*Ta Kung Pao*, 2 October 1986).

6   Colonial Chinese Politics

See Joseph H.S. Cheng, *Political Modernisation in Hong Kong*, unpublished paper for Chinese University, Department of Government, March 1989; Lau Siu-kai, *Utilitarianistic Familism: The Basis of Political Stability in Hong Kong*, Chinese University, Social Research Centre, March 1978; *Report of the Working Party on Local Administration*, Hong Kong Government, 1966; and Dr Steve Yui-shang Tsang, *Democracy Shelved: Great Britain, China and Attempts at Constitutional Reform in Hong Kong*, 1945–52, Oxford, 1989.

On corruption, see Derek Davies, *FEER*, 15 August 1963. On *feng shui*, see *International Herald Tribune*, 2 June 1987; on gambling see Hugh Baker in 'Ancestral Images Again', *South China Morning Post*, 1981, p. 33; on Guomindang, see *FEER* 8 October 1987; on superstition see Frena Bloomfield, *The Occult World of Hongkong*, Hong Kong Publishing, 1980; on Heung Yee Kok, see *SCMP* 6 May 1990.

7   Licence to Enjoy

See Maria Jaschok, *Concubines and Bondservants: The Social History of a Chinese Custom*, Oxford, 1989; *Hong Kong Standard*, 30 April 1989 (on 'Equus'); and *FEER*, 21 March 1985 (on homosexuality).

On horse racing, see Austin Coates, *China Races*, Oxford, 1984.

8   The Role of the Gwailos

See Stanley Jackson, *The Sassoons*, Heinemann, 1968; David M. Paton, '*R.O*'. *The Life and Times of Bishop Hall of Hong Kong*, Diocese of Hong Kong, 1985 (also Beverley Howells in *SCMP* 13 May 1990); and Else Tu, *An Autobiography*, Longman, 1988. On Kadoories, see *Financial Times*, 4 July 1977; and on Coates see *SCMP*, 14 November 1988.

9 Indian Sunset?

See K.N. Vaid, *The Overseas Indian Community in Hong Kong*, Hong Kong University Centre of Asian Studies, 1972; on Harilela see *Asia Magazine*, 19 May 1985; on Murjani, see *International Herald Tribune*, 17 November 1986; and on Zechas see *International Herald Tribune*, 29 November 1988.

10 Political Refugees

On Ho Chi Minh, see Dennis J. Duncanson, 'Ho Chi Minh in Hong Kong, 1931–32', *The China Quarterly*, 1974, p. 84; and also *SCMP*, 2 September 1989. On Robin Chan, see *SCMP*, 21 September 1989.

11 The People in Between

See Dr Alan Birch, *Interview with Bobbie Kotewall*, Hong Kong University History Department; Irene Chen, *Clara Ho Tung: A Hong Kong Lady*, Chinese University Press, 1976; G.H. Choa, *The Life and Times of Sir Kai Ho Kai*, Chinese University, 1981; Jean Gittins, *Eastern Windows – Western Skies*, South China Morning Post, 1969; and T.S. Lo, *A Family Album*, private pbl, no date.

On Hotungs, see *SCMP*, 25 June and 22 July 1989; and on Stanley Ho, see Clare Hollingworth in *Daily Telegraph*, 25 September 1982; and *Asia Magazine* 11 June 1989.

12 The Asia–Pacific Neutral

See Robert Sam Anson, 'The Pacific Press Wars', Manhattan Inc., November 1989; and E.F. Szczepanik, *The Embargo Effect on China's Trade with Hong Kong*, Oxford, 1958.

13 Playing the Oceans

On trade, see E.F. Szczepanik, *External Trade of Hong Kong*, Wolosh, 1961; and *Hong Kong's Trade with Mainland China*, Hong Kong University, 1961.

On Pao, see *Japan Times*, 8 September 1989; *The Times*, 3 May 1973; *FEER*, 17 January 1975 and 29 August 1982; and Lauriat in *FEER*, 16 February 1984.

On Tung, see *FEER*, 23 April 1982; *The Times*, 16 April 1982; and *The Listener*, 12 August 1982.

On Chao, see *SCMP*, 10 July 1989; and Simon Jensen, 'Wah Kwong Group', *Hong Kong Tatler*, February 1978.

On Cathay Pacific Airways, see Gavin Young, *Beyond Lion Rock: The Story of Cathay Pacific Airways*, Hutchinson, 1988. On the airport, see S. Glain in *International Herald Tribune*, 12 May 1990 and M. Westlake in *FEER*, 5 October 1989.

14   Five Billion Pairs of Trousers

See Edward K.Y. Chen, 'Multinationals from Hong Kong', in *The New Multinationals*, ed. Lall, Wiley, 1983; Jean-Francoise Blanc, *Suisse–Hong Kong, le defi horlager*, Nord-Sud, 1988; The Economist Intelligence Unit, *Industry in Hong Kong*, report for Federation of Hong Kong Industries, 1962; *Hong Kong's Manufacturing Industries, 1988*, Hong Kong Government, Industry Department, 1989; Y.C. Jao, 'Financing Hong Kong's Early Postwar Industrialisation', in *Eastern Banking*, ed. Frank H.H. King, p. 545; James Hsiung Lee, *A Half Century of Memories*, South China; and *Seminar on the Hong Kong Textile Industry*, ed. Yeuan Hughes, Hong Kong University, Extramural Department, 1973.

For textiles and garments, see *FEER*, 25 February 1988; for C.C. Lee, see *FEER*, 24 September 1959; and P.Y. Tang, see *FEER*, 10 September 1959; and for T.Y. Wong, see *FEER*, 22 October 1959.

15   A Bank in Search of a Role

See *Hong Kong's Financial Institutions and Markets*, ed. R.H. Scott *et al.*, Oxford, 1986.

For Hongkong Bank, see Maurice Collis, *Wayfoong: The Hong Kong and Shanghai Banking Corporation*, Faber, 1965; *FEER*, 22 December 1988; and S.G. Redding 'Organisational and Structural Change in the Hong Kong and Shanghai Banking Corporation', in *Eastern Banking*, ed. Frank H.H. King, p. 601.

16   A Little *Laissez-faire*

See Sir Robert Black, *Immigration and Social Planning in Hong Kong*, The China Society, London 1965; David Dodwell in *Financial Times*, 18 June 1987; Robin Hutcheon, 'State of the Arts', in *Hong Kong 1989*, Hong Kong Government, p. 6; W.P. Morgan, *Triad Societies in Hong Kong*, Hong Kong Government Press, 1960; Alvin Rabushka, *Hong Kong: A Study in Economic Freedom*, Chicago, 1979, and *Value for Money: The Hong Kong Budgetary*

Process, Stanford, 1976; and James Riedel, *The Industrialisation of Hong Kong*, Mar Tubingen, 1974.

In the sixteen years 1974–89 inclusive, Rolls-Royce sold 138 cars to Hong Kong, the peak being reached in 1983.

17   Hongs in New Hands

See Colin Crisswell, *The Taipans: Hong Kong's Merchant Princes*, Oxford, 1971; and Simon Jensen's articles in *Hong Kong Tatler*, 1977.

On Jardine, see *The Thistle and the Jade: 150 Years of Jardine Matheson*, ed. Maggie Keswick, Octopus 1982; *FEER*, 3 April 1981; and Christopher Wood in *FEER*, 15 March 1984.

On Swire, see Charles Drage, *Taikoo*, Constable, 1970; and *The Swire Group*, Hong Kong, 1987.

On Hutchinson and Li Kashing, see J. Bartholomew in *FEER*, 10 July 1981; 'From Refugee to Multibillionaire', *Macleans*, 17 August 1977; *FEER*, 4 August 1988; and 'Hutchinson Whampoa Ltd', *Sing Tao Business Magazine*, April 1988; and John Elliott in *Financial Times*, 27 Novembr 1989.

18   Britain Agrees to Hand Over

See David Bonavia, *Hong Kong 1997*, Columbus, 1984; John P. Burns, 'Immigration from China', *Asia Survey*, June 1987; Robert Cottrell, in *The Spectator*, 13 April 1988; Joe England, *Hong Kong: Britain's Responsibility*, Fabian Society, 1976; P.P. Harris, 'The Future of Hong Kong', *International Affairs*, January 1972; *Hong Kong: A Case to Answer*, Hong Kong Research Project, 1974; Y.K. Kan, in *SCMP*, March 1989; Ann Quon, In *SCMP*, 10 May 1987; R.C. Lee *The Importance of Hong Kong to China*, unpublished draft speech, June 1982; Andrew Kwok-Nang Li, 'Red Sun over Stanley', *FEER*, 20 July 1968; *The May Upheaval in Hong Kong* , Committee of Hong Kong Compatriots, 1967; *Civil Liberties in Hong Kong*, ed. R. Wacks, Oxford, 1988; and *The New Territories and its Future*, ed. A. Birch, Royal Asiatic Society, Hong Kong Branch, 1982.

On Walled City, see Simon Head in *FEER*, 20 February 1969.

19   After Tiananmen Square

See *The Basic Law of the Hong Kong SAR of the People's Republic of China*, Consultative Committee, April 1990; Joseph Y. S. Cheng, 'The Post-1997 Government in Hong Kong', *Asian Survey*, August 1989; Joseph Y. S. Cheng, 'The Democracy Movement in Hong Kong', *International Affairs*,

1989; David Glass, *China and Hong Kong, 1984–88: The Imperatives of One Country*, unpublished University of California thesis, 1988; *The Hong Kong Solution*, Beijing Review, 1985; Simon Ip, *The Times*, 11 July 1988; *Hong Kong and 1997: Strategies for the Future*, ed. Y.C. Jao *et al.*, University of Hong Kong, Centre of Asian Studies, 1987; Chalmers Johnson, 'The Mouse-Trapping of Hong Kong', *Issues and Studies*, August 1984, p. 26; Richard Margolis, *FEER*, 25 June 1987; C.K. Law, *China's Dampening Economic Adjustments: Can Hong Kong's 'China Plays' Avoid Being Dampened?*, BT Brokerage Research, 17 February 1989; William Purves (Chairman, Hongkong Bank), *Year of the Dragon*, address to Institute of International Bankers, New York, 4 May 1988.

On Wang Guangying, see *FEER*, 1 March 1984.

On Xu Jiatun, see *Ta Kung Pao*, 31 March, 7 and 16 April 1988.

On Gordon Wu, see *Hong Kong Business*, January 1990 and *Sunday Morning Post Magazine*, 31 December 1989.

20 Emigrating to the Colonies

See Martin Lee in *SCMP*, 12 and 13 April, 1989.

On UK see *Chinese Community in Britain*, House of Commons Home Affairs Committee, 1985, three volumes; and *SCMP*, 2 July 1989.

On Canada, see John Demont and Thomas Fennell, *Hong Kong Money: How Chinese Families and Fortunes are Changing Canada*, Toronto, 1989; Peter S. Li, *The Chinese in Canada*, Oxford, 1988; *SCMP*, 5 April 1989; and *Asian Wall Street Journal*, 29 December 1987.

21 Could the Tail Wag the Dog?

See Donald M. Anderson (US Consul General), *The Changing Nature of Hong Kong; The Evolving China–Hong Kong Relationship*, address to American Chamber, 13 April, 1989; John Andrews, 'Hong Kong: Weighing the Odds', *The Economist*, 3 June 1989; *Building Prosperity: A Five-part Economic Strategy for Hong Kong's Future*, Stanford Research Institute, September 1989; Paul Cheng, *Hong Kong Year 2000*, Rotary Club address, 28 February 1989; James Cotton, 'Hong Kong, Convergence or Divergence', *Journal of Northeast Asian Studies*, Winter 1987, p. 3; William McCord, 'The Tail That May Wag the Dog: China's Hong Kong Experiment', *The New Leader*, 6 August 1984; Andrew Scobell, 'Hong Kong's Influence on China: The Tail That Wags the Dog?', *Asian Survey*, June 1988, p. 599; and Dick Wilson, 'The Future of Hong Kong: Grounds for Cautious Optimism', *Royal Institute of International Affairs, 1990*.

Index

Index